W9-BUB-323

THE
EVERYTHING®
World War II Book
2nd Edition

Dear Reader,

Unfortunately, more and more World War II veterans are dying every day, and despite the millions of words already written about the devastating worldwide conflict in which they participated, many of these veterans are taking their war stories to their graves with them. These stories go untold for a number of reasons, a primary one of which is that they are too harrowing to relive. Additionally, as more and more time goes by and more and more wars take place, this particular war gets forgotten a little bit more, romanticized a little more, and discussed a little less. All of these events are unfortunate.

Many people know something about World War II but couldn't carry on an informed conversation about the subject. While we're not asking that you become an expert in the subject (although those people are fading as well), what we would like is that you take from this book a certain understanding of what the world was like before, during, and after this most brutal of all wars. This book can help guide you on that process, and it is our hope that you will continue your study or, at the very least, have a greater grasp of the subject and its place in the history of our planet.

David White

Daniel P. Murphy, Ph.D

The EVERYTHING® Series

Editorial

Publisher	Gary M. Krebs
Director of Product Development	Paula Munier
Managing Editor	Laura M. Daly
Executive Editor, Series Books	Brielle K. Matson
Associate Copy Chief	Sheila Zwiebel
Acquisitions Editor	Lisa Laing
Development Editor	Brett Palana-Shanahan
Production Editor	Casey Ebert

Production

Director of Manufacturing	Susan Beale
Production Project Manager	Michelle Roy Kelly
Prepress	Erick DaCosta
	Matt LeBlanc
Interior Layout	Heather Barrett
	Brewster Brownville
	Colleen Cunningham
	Jennifer Oliveira
Cover Design	Erin Alexander
	Stephanie Chrusz
	Frank Rivera

Visit the entire Everything® Series at *www.everything.com*

THE EVERYTHING®

WORLD WAR II BOOK

2nd Edition

From the rise of the Third Reich to V-J Day—
all the people, places, battles, and
key events you need to know

David White and Daniel P. Murphy, Ph.D.

Adams Media
Avon, Massachusetts

To my wife, who inspires my life and my work, and to my parents,
who started me on the road to appreciating history

Copyright © 2002, 2007, F+W Publications, Inc. All rights reserved.
This book, or parts thereof, may not be reproduced
in any form without permission from the publisher; exceptions
are made for brief excerpts used in published reviews.

An Everything® Series Book.
Everything® and everything.com® are registered trademarks of F+W Publications, Inc.

Published by Adams Media, an F+W Publications Company
57 Littlefield Street, Avon, MA 02322 U.S.A.
www.adamsmedia.com

ISBN-10: 1-59869-641-6
ISBN-13: 978-1-59869-641-7

Printed in the United States of America.

J   I   H   G   F   E   D   C   B   A

Library of Congress Cataloging-in-Publication Data
available from the publisher.

This publication is designed to provide accurate and authoritative information with regard to the subject matter covered. It is sold with the understanding that the publisher is not engaged in rendering legal, accounting, or other professional advice. If legal advice or other expert assistance is required, the services of a competent professional person should be sought.

—From a *Declaration of Principles* jointly adopted by a Committee of the American Bar Association and a Committee of Publishers and Associations

Many of the designations used by manufacturers and sellers to distinguish their products are claimed as trademarks. Where those designations appear in this book and Adams Media was aware of a trademark claim, the designations have been printed with initial capital letters.

This book is available at quantity discounts for bulk purchases.
For information, please call 1-800-289-0963.

Contents

Top Ten Things You Should Know about WWII

1. D-Day gets a lot of press, but it wasn't the most important battle in the war.

2. Pearl Harbor was certainly the instigation for the American involvement in WWII, but it's likely that Japan and the United States would have gone to war anyway.

3. The world might be a far different place today if Hitler had spent more time making speeches and less time directing troop traffic.

4. More than anything else, many historians believe, the weapon that turned the tide of battles more often than not was airpower.

5. The estimated American death toll for an invasion of mainland Japan was 1 million lives.

6. Winston Churchill, famous for being prime minister during the "Blitz," was already out of office a year after the war ended.

7. Weather played a vital role in nearly every important battle in the war.

8. Much has been said about the Holocaust. Much more needs to be said so that history doesn't continue to repeat this type of event.

9. What really made this war possible was the tremendous manufacturing capabilities of the major players involved, which thrived and made tremendous innovations while the majority of their "usual" workers were fighting on the front lines.

10. In a sense the war did not end in 1945 but was frozen in the new divisions of the moment, which continued in the Cold War.

Introduction

▶ LOOKING BACK from the vantage point of a new millennium, it's clear that no other event of the twentieth century was as momentous—or as horrendous—as World War II.

Many countries, such as Great Britain and the Soviet Union, were fighting for their very existence against the military might of a fanatical madman bent on global domination. But even those lands not directly involved in the fighting felt the war's influence. At the height of the conflict, no nation was left untouched.

Officially beginning in 1939 with Germany's invasion of Poland and ending six years later with most of Europe and much of the rest of the world in crumbling chaos, World War II proved to be, in terms of lives lost and cities destroyed, the most devastating conflict in human history. When the big guns ceased and the smoke cleared, freedom had proved victorious over dictatorial rule, but the world as we knew it would never be the same.

Much has been written and said about World War II since its official conclusion with Japan's formal surrender on September 2, 1945, yet the war, its goals, and the stories of the men and women who fought it grow dimmer with each passing year. Two generations have grown up in its shadow, with each becoming more distant and uninterested.

World War II defined an entire generation. For the United States, it was the last "good war," unmuddied by conflicting ideology or uncertain public opinion. The commitment to preserve everything all free countries hold dear can be traced back to those tumultuous six years.

It has been estimated that more than 22 million military personnel and civilians died over the course of World War II, and that another 34.4 million were wounded. Of that total, more than 408,000 deaths were those of American servicemen.

It is to them—and to all the military personnel throughout the world who fought so valiantly against tyranny and hate—that this book is dedicated.

Part One:
Setting the Stage

Chapter 1
Prelude to War

Germany's defeat in World War I was difficult for its people to accept. The nation had been one of Europe's strongest, proudest, and most impressive lands for centuries. But now, after four years of bloody fighting, it was literally helpless. How had this happened? Where had things gone wrong? In the eyes of the world, Germany had been justly humbled, but it was from these ashes that the German phoenix rose just a few years later in the form of a charismatic leader named Adolf Hitler.

Hitler's Rise to Power

Adolf Hitler, an ardent fan of composer Richard Wagner, the French writer Joseph Arthur de Gobineau, and the British-born writer Houston Stewart Chamberlain, all early proponents of Nordic supremacy and anti-Semitism, believed that Germany was preordained by God to be a world power. He also believed that the nation had become poisoned by what he considered "foreign elements" and inferior races (particularly the Jews), and that they were the reason for the nation's lowly position after World War I.

Hitler had been a soldier during World War I, volunteering for a Bavarian unit in the German army and serving through the entire conflict. It was during this period that Hitler's anti-Semitism grew into the demented brand of nationalism that eventually made him one of the most reviled leaders in world history.

After the war, Hitler joined the German Workers' Party, which he eventually led. He later changed the party's name to the National Socialist German Workers' Party, from which the word *Nazi* (German acronym for National Socialist) was derived, and borrowed the swastika as the group's defining symbol. Many of Hitler's followers were members of the Free Corps—supposed freedom fighters and foes of socialism who often took the law into their own hands, settling disputes with violence. By 1923, the organization boasted nearly 70,000 members.

Germany in Disarray

In the years after World War I, Germany fell deeper and deeper into chaos. By late 1923, its economy had bottomed out, making the German currency, the mark, virtually worthless. This is exactly the kind of environment in which dictators are born, and Hitler knew it. On November 8, he tried to incite a revolution against the Bavarian provincial government during a rally of monarchists and nationalists. Though his efforts resulted in nothing more than a small riot that was quickly put down by armed police, Hitler's Beer Hall Putsch became famous. He was sentenced to five years in prison but served only nine months.

Adolf Hitler's autobiography, *Mein Kampf* ("My Struggle"), was written while he was imprisoned at Landsberg am Lech for his failed Beer Hall Putsch of 1923. In the book, Hitler details his life and philosophy. Much of it is anti-Semitic, claiming that the Jews were responsible for all that was wrong in Germany.

When he was released, Hitler was more intent than ever on assuming power in Germany. The Germans needed help—they were barely surviving, their national pride in tatters. They needed an explanation, they needed self-assurance, they needed a common cause and a common scapegoat, and Hitler gave them what they asked for. He portrayed himself as the father figure that Germany so desperately needed. All the nation's problems, Hitler told his followers, resulted from unsavory influences and the poisoning of Germany's racial purity. As the years went on, Hitler's closest advisers and confidants came to include Hermann Goering, Heinrich Himmler, and Joseph Goebbels, all of whom would later help Hitler lead the nation into one of the most barbaric periods in human history.

FACT

Hitler's original title for *Mein Kampf* was "Four and a Half Years of Struggle Against Lies, Stupidity and Cowardice." It was his editor who suggested a title change.

In the 1932 election, Hitler made his first important step toward his goal of assuming power in Germany. Indeed, his timing couldn't have been better. The established coalition between socialists and middle-class parties in the Reichstag, the German parliament, had been all but destroyed by the Depression, opening the door for new leadership. In April, the Nazi Party won control of four state governments, and Hitler finished a distant second (with only 37 percent of the popular vote) after conservative president Paul von Hindenburg. Centrist chancellor Heinrich Brüning, who had grown increasingly unpopular as a result of the austerity measures he had imposed on the already suffering nation, resigned as a result of the election; his successor, Franz von Papen, called for Reichstag elections in July.

Nazis Consolidate Power

Spurred by Hitler's growing popularity, the election gave the Nazis 230 seats, making the party the largest and most influential in the Reichstag. The Nazi delegates, recognized by their brown uniforms, acted more like bullies than legislators, and debates with opposing delegates usually turned into brawls. Meanwhile, the nation's political conflict poured into the streets as Nazi storm troopers engaged Communist paramilitary fighters in almost nightly battles.

Hitler Rises to Power

Chancellor Papen hated the Nazis but needed their support to govern, so he reluctantly extended the hand of partisan friendship by offering Hitler the position of vice chancellor. But Hitler refused, demanding the chancellorship. A panicked Papen tried to bolster his own position by dissolving the Reichstag and calling for fresh elections again in November. The Nazi Party lost thirty-four seats but still retained its superior position.

Figure 1-1 A Sudeten woman weeps as she is forced to salute Hitler in 1938.

*Photo courtesy
of the National Archives (208-PP-10A-2)*

Papen tried briefly to convince Hindenburg to declare his own dictatorship in a desperate bid to keep Hitler from power, but both men quickly realized that such a move would be foolhardy because of the strength and number of Nazi storm troopers and because too many of the nation's military officers supported Hitler. Hindenburg dismissed Papen and replaced him with Defense Minister Kurt von Schleicher, who then offered the position of vice chancellor to the leader of the Nazi Party's left wing. However, the gesture only served to unite party members more strongly behind Hitler.

QUESTION?

What were the three reichs?

According to Hitler, the First Reich was the Holy Roman Empire, a group of Germanic tribes united by Charlemagne in the ninth century. The Second Reich was Germany unified under Otto von Bismarck and carved up after World War I. Hitler proclaimed the inauguration of the Third Reich, which he said would conquer all of Europe and last 1,000 years.

After failing to form a government with either the socialists or the conservative nationalists, Schleicher resigned as chancellor on January 23, 1933. Both he and Papen remained powerful members of the Reichstag and had convinced themselves that if they couldn't keep Hitler out, they could at least control him by surrounding him with more moderate cabinet ministers. After a frenzy of negotiations, Hitler became chancellor on January 30, 1933.

However, Hitler was not about to be appeased. He and his followers quickly set to work making him supreme and absolute ruler of the German republic by brutally eliminating all who might oppose him politically and making friends with the rich industrialists whose support Hitler desperately needed. When the long-ailing Hindenburg finally died on August 2, 1934, Hitler quickly abolished the office of president and with the cry "One race, one realm, one leader!" proclaimed himself *der Führer*—the Leader.

Fascism Takes Hold of Italy

Yet another match was held to the fuse that would ignite World War II with the rise of Italian fascist leader Benito Mussolini. A former newspaper editor and a gifted orator, Mussolini fanned the fires of political nationalism by convincing his beleaguered countrymen that Italy had emerged victorious from World War I. In truth, the sections of Austria that ended up under Italy's control had been given to it as part of several secret agreements and were not the result of military might. Nonetheless, the Italian people, swollen with national pride, took Mussolini's words to heart.

Mussolini also capitalized on the attempts by Communists to seize control of Italy after the war. With many people starving and the economy still in shambles, the Communists thought their timing was perfect for another "people's revolution" and instigated a number of strikes and shutdowns. Prime Minister Francesco Nitti, shaky and unsure of how to react, opened the door to a Communist takeover.

In March 1919, Mussolini and several other war veterans formed the Fasci di Combattimento, a right-wing, anti-Communist movement that quickly swept the country. Wearing signature black shirts, Mussolini's Fascist militia did all it could to strengthen national pride while dismantling labor and socialist groups—often with violence.

In 1922, Mussolini's followers stormed Rome, intimidating King Victor Emmanuel III into offering Mussolini the position of prime minister in what was supposed to be a coalition government. It was then that Mussolini adopted his famous title of *Il Duce*—the Leader.

Within four years, Mussolini turned the supposed coalition government into a dictatorship with himself at the helm. Thus, his rise to power was complete. Even though many personal freedoms were gradually withdrawn, including the right to strike, Mussolini managed to preserve some aspects of capitalism and expand social services. He also ended decades of conflict with the Vatican by signing the Lateran Pact of 1929, a compromise that recognized Rome as the capital of Italy but granted sovereignty to the Vatican.

Once Italy was in his grasp, Mussolini, like most dictators, began looking to expand his empire with an aggressive foreign policy. First to fall was Ethiopia, which Italy conquered in 1935 and 1936 despite protests from the League of Nations. Though condemned by the international community, the conquest was celebrated by the Italian people, and Mussolini's popularity skyrocketed. He soon decided to align Italy with Nazi Germany in what became known as the Axis.

Japanese Aggression

Ruled by an emperor but controlled by militarists, Japan—desperate for raw materials—was ready to continue the expansion it had started nearly forty-five years earlier with the acquisition of the island of Burile, the Bonin and Ryukyu Islands, and the Volcano group. In war with China in 1894 and 1895, Japan took Formosa (now Taiwan) and the Pescadores. Soon afterward, it seized Port Arthur and the southern half of the island of Sakhalin from Russia and took control of Korea, which it officially annexed in 1910. After World War I, Japan received mandates over the Marshall, Caroline, and Mariana Islands, which had formerly belonged to Germany.

Following the Naval Disarmament Conference of 1920, which weakened the American and British presence in the Pacific, Japan strengthened its powerful navy, fortified its mandates in violation of international treaty, and set its eyes on China while conditioning its people for the inevitability of war.

American Isolationism

The United States was condemned on many fronts for dragging its feet in entering World War I, but in truth the nation's isolationist policies were as old as the republic itself.

America's first political leaders encouraged commercial treaties and expansion of trade with other nations but discouraged political or military alliances because of their inherent dangers. One such view was expressed by George Washington, who in his 1796 farewell address advised the nation that he had helped to promote good relations with all the world's countries, particularly in regard to trade, but warned strongly against becoming involved in Europe's complicated and ever-changing political affairs.

The United States maintained an isolationist attitude for many years, preferring to expand into the sparsely populated land that spread from the

Atlantic to the Pacific rather than become involved in global politics. Such an attitude also helped protect the fledgling country from European domination—always a risk when dealing with older, more established nations.

With only a few exceptions, isolationism remained a steadfast policy throughout the nineteenth century and well into the twentieth. When hostilities finally broke out in Europe in 1914, the United States assumed a stance of neutrality, despite the fact that many of its most important economic allies were fighting for their lives.

The war raged for nearly three years before U.S. troops went to Europe in the spring of 1917, provoked by attacks on merchant ships by German submarines. American anger was aggravated by the discovery of what became known as the Zimmerman note—a secret message from German foreign minister Arthur Zimmerman to his ambassador in Mexico City, instructing him to offer Mexico financial aid in exchange for an invasion of the United States. Declaring that, "the world must be made safe for democracy," President Woodrow Wilson finally asked Congress for a declaration of war. The United States entered World War I four days later.

At the war's conclusion, America once again put up an isolationist wall. Even after just one year, the country had grown weary of fighting overseas and the Red Scare at home, and wanted nothing more to do with international politics. The men who served as president after World War I understood this sentiment and did all they could to keep the nation out of conflict. As President Warren G. Harding noted, the nation needed "not submergence in internationality but sustainment in triumphant nationality."

FACT

The League of Nations was established in 1920 in an effort to make sure another world war would never happen. Though the League was suggested by President Woodrow Wilson, the United States did not join. The U.S. Senate, angry over being left out of treaty negotiations by Wilson, and concerned about congressional war powers, refused to ratify the Treaty of Versailles, which governed the League's covenant.

Isolationism Following the First World War

President Calvin Coolidge, who assumed office after Harding's death in 1923, maintained his predecessor's position of international neutrality, preferring to concentrate on the growth and maintenance of his own country. The only issue that managed to penetrate the nation's staunch isolationism was the Kellogg-Briand Pact, which the United States signed along with sixty-one other countries, including Germany, Japan, and Italy. In so doing, the nations promised never to resort to war as an instrument of national policy. But as future events would show, the pact, merely a promise with nothing to back it up, ultimately proved to be worthless (as did the League of Nations, which, in the end, was unable to stop the Axis powers from taking the actions that led to world war).

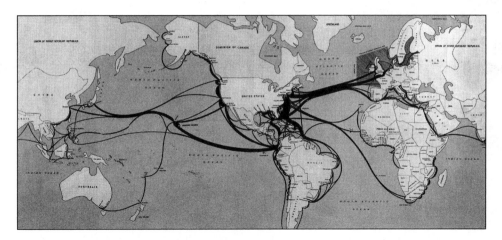

Map 1-1 U.S. foreign trade routes. The thickets of the trading veins extending from the United States will soon be cut off due to the war.

Map courtesy of the National Archives (Travel and Ship under the American Flag, Record Group 178, Maritime Commission)

Sadly, America's isolationist attitude served only to benefit those nations that made war a part of their expansionist policies. For example, when Japan finally decided to invade a nearly helpless China in 1931, President Herbert Hoover, a Quaker by faith, immediately ruled out military force to stop Japan's aggression. Instead, he expressed "moral condemnation" and told the world the United States would not recognize any international changes that conflicted with its Open Door policy or the Kellogg-Briand Pact. Faced with moral censure but little else, Japan's militarists continued their vicious assault against China, which included the invasion of Manchuria in 1931 and, a year later, a shocking bombing attack on Shanghai, one of China's most important trade centers, which killed thousands of civilians.

Similar problems soon occurred in Europe and Africa. In 1935, Italy invaded Ethiopia in Mussolini's quest for a contemporary Roman Empire. The League of Nations tried to quell the aggression with economic sanctions, but they did little good. Mussolini, like his counterparts in Japan, assumed that no one would try to stop his bully tactics, and he was right.

FACT

The Japanese pulled out of Shanghai in May 1932 following a truce brokered by the Western powers, most of which had important holdings in the area. However, the Japanese maintained control of Manchuria (which they renamed Manchukuo).

Germany also began stretching its militaristic wings in 1935, when, in direct violation of the Treaty of Versailles, it began to create its powerful air force, the Luftwaffe, and a new navy. The following year, German troops occupied the Rhineland, which had been designated a demilitarized zone. This, too, was in direct violation of the Treaty of Versailles. As with Italy and Japan, however, no one—least of all the United States, which continued to be bound by its isolationist attitudes—did anything to halt Germany's increasing aggression.

Chapter 2
Fanning the Flames

Shortly before German president Paul von Hindenburg died, Hitler secured the support of the military. Before joining him, the nation's generals called upon Hitler to curb the SA *(Sturmabteilung)*—Nazi storm troopers who had first intimidated their opposition and then demanded leadership of the military. Hitler, aware of his need for the military's support, was happy to comply. On June 29, 1934, Hitler used the pretext of a coup plot to purge his party of the most troublesome SA members. He organized the roundup and execution of SA chief Ernst Röhm and nearly 400 others. When the purge was over, the SA was left powerless and most of its duties went to the SS *(Schutz-staffel)*, the elite corps.

Germany Rearms

In January 1934, Hitler began his appease-and-attack campaign by signing a ten-year nonaggression pact with Poland, which boasted an army far larger than Germany's. This allowed Hitler to appear as a peacemaker while giving him time to secretly rearm his nation.

Later that year, Hitler visited Mussolini—one of his idols—for the first time, but the meeting didn't go well. Mussolini didn't particularly care for Hitler (he thought the German leader was mad and referred to him as a buffoon behind his back), and the two dictators parted without agreeing to anything significant. Soon after, Hitler angered Mussolini further with a failed attempt to place a puppet regime in Austria after the assassination by Viennese Nazis of Chancellor Engelbert Dollfuss, who was one of Mussolini's most valued allies. However, Hitler was able to publicly and successfully disavow his role in Dollfuss's killing—even though he was a primary instigator—and continued to court Mussolini as an ally. Two years later, the two men formed the Rome-Berlin Axis, which set the stage for war in Europe.

Hitler Takes Austria

With Mussolini now his ally, Hitler put into play his plan to annex Austria. In 1936, he had tried to placate Mussolini, who was then Austria's protector, by signing an agreement recognizing the nation's sovereignty. In return, Hitler had forced Austrian chancellor Kurt von Schuschnigg to declare his nation a German state and promise to share power with the national opposition. These provisions legitimized the Austrian Nazis who advocated reunification with Germany and laid the foundation for Hitler's takeover of the nation two years later.

The groundwork for the planned takeover began in February 1938 when Schuschnigg traveled to Berchtesgaden, Hitler's mountain retreat, to complain about a Nazi coup being planned against him. Hitler was far from sympathetic. With Schuschnigg on his turf, Hitler took the opportunity to browbeat him into signing a pledge to give moral, diplomatic, and press support to Germany; to stop prosecuting Nazi agitators; and to appoint a Nazi-affiliated lawyer named Artur Seyss-Inquart as interior minister. A frightened

Schuschnigg signed the demands. He quickly recovered after his return to Austria, however, and called for a plebiscite, or popular vote, to determine the people's wishes on Austrian independence. Then, Schuschnigg tried to exclude many Nazi sympathizers by limiting voting to those over the age of twenty-four.

Hitler became furious at Schuschnigg's attempts to prevent reunification. Hermann Goering, whom Hitler had ordered to handle the matter, demanded that the vote be postponed, and Schuschnigg agreed. Goering then demanded Schuschnigg's resignation, which he tendered. But when Goering demanded that Seyss-Inquart be made chancellor, Austrian president Wilhelm Milas refused. On March 12, Hitler ordered his troops into Austria. The occupation was met with little resistance because Schuschnigg urged the army to stand down. Despite his efforts to avert a military confrontation, Schuschnigg was arrested and spent seven years in prison.

Hitler followed his troops into Austria and was met with nearly nationwide adoration. As a result of Hitler's mesmerizing oratory, most Austrians had become convinced that reunification with Germany was the only way to reclaim their lost greatness. Unfortunately, it was also the end of any sort of democratic rule. With Hitler firmly in place as the nation's leader, anti-Nazi dissidents were brutally punished and Jews were sent into exile or to concentration camps.

FACT

Kristallnacht—the Night of Broken Glass—refers to the attacks on Jews in Germany and German-controlled territories on November 9, 1938. Over the course of the night, SA and SS units burned more than 200 synagogues, destroyed nearly 7,500 Jewish-owned businesses, and attacked any Jew they encountered. More than 200 Jews were killed, 600 were seriously injured, and approximately 30,000 were arrested.

These early years of German expansion also marked the beginnings of the "Final Solution," Hitler's plan to eliminate as many Jews as humanly possible on the theory that they were to blame for the country's ills. Kristallnacht was followed by a host of other terrible nights and days and weeks and years for Jewish and other "undesirables" in Germany and the countries absorbed by the Third Reich. The Jewish people, especially, were systematically, efficiently, and ruthlessly singled out, transported, and murdered in unimaginable ways. Deportations led to incarcerations led to forced labor led to mass killings. All of this was hidden behind a veneer of political expansion and military threat. The *lebensraum* that Hitler so publicly pined for—and got, in the Sudetenland and in Austria—didn't include space for Jews.

Despite the obvious force used by Germany to take over Austria, both the United States and Great Britain accepted Hitler's conquest. Italy also accepted the situation, sending congratulations to Hitler. "Tell Mussolini I will never forget him for this," Hitler told *Il Duce's* emissary. "Never, never, never, whatever happens."

The Nazis then ordered another carefully orchestrated plebiscite on the issue of reunification. More than 99 percent of Austrians approved the takeover.

The conquest of Austria—and other nations' unwillingness to confront him on it—gave Hitler the confidence he needed to pursue his dream of world domination, which he saw as Germany's divine right. On August 22, 1939, he made a speech to the German High Command in which he outlined his plan for the swift and brutal invasion of Poland, a nation he had lulled into complacency with a meaningless nonaggression pact.

Czechoslovakia Divided and Conquered

The stage for Hitler's invasion had been set earlier in the year with the dissection of Czechoslovakia. The previous year's Munich Conference, which was thought to have brought "peace in our time," had given parts of the country to Germany. Then Poland and Hungary received their shares as well. What remained of Czechoslovakia turned into a federation of three republics. Then, in March 1939, Slovakia seceded to become an independent state, though still under German domination.

The Czech Republic was the last prewar domino to fall before Hitler. President Emil Hacha tried desperately to appease Germany by enacting anti-Semitic and anti-Communist laws, but it didn't help. The Wehrmacht, Germany's armed forces, began gathering troops at the Czech border. On

March 14, the day Slovakia declared its independence, Hacha traveled to Berlin to beg for his nation's very existence. Hitler met with Hacha and his aides at 1:15 A.M., told them the invasion would begin at 6:00 A.M., and then stormed out of the room. German cabinet ministers Hermann Goering and Joachim von Ribbentrop told Hacha that Prague would be bombed to rubble if he didn't sign surrender documents immediately. Hacha, who suffered from a heart condition, passed out when he heard the demand but was revived by one of Hitler's doctors long enough to sign the document that effectively gave his country to the Nazis.

When he received the signed surrender, Hitler hugged Goering and Ribbentrop, shouting, "Children! This is the greatest day of my life!" That evening, he rode with his troops into Prague. Hacha remained in power as a puppet president of the new German protectorate of Bohemia and Moravia.

France and Great Britain knew of Hitler's intentions long before his troops crossed the Czech border but hoped they could placate the mad dictator and avoid a confrontation. At a conference in Munich in September 1938, British Prime Minister Neville Chamberlain and French Premier Edouard Daladier met with Hitler to work out a peace deal. Chamberlain and Daladier agreed to let Germany take the Sudetenland, a German-speaking part of Czechoslovakia. Hitler promised to leave the rest of Czechoslovakia and the rest of Europe alone, and Chamberlain and Daladier wrote out a pledge of friendship among the nations, which Hitler signed with absolutely no intent of honoring.

Shortly after annexing Czechoslovakia, Hitler demanded the return of the former German port of Memel, which was then part of Lithuania. His demand met with little resistance.

World war became a near certainty on March 31, 1939, when Great Britain and France, embarrassed by Hitler's successful manipulation of their mutual promises, guaranteed aid and assistance to Poland and Romania if Hitler acted against them. To Hitler, England and France— once two of the most powerful nations in the world—were mere gnats buzzing about his head and offered little to fear.

Hitler's remarkable success at snatching nearby countries without rebuke emboldened Mussolini, who was eager to extend his new Roman Empire. Mobilizing his army, he quickly conquered nearby Albania. Shortly after Italy conquered Albania, U.S. President Franklin D. Roosevelt sent a cable to Mussolini and Hitler asking the dictators to promise that they would rein in their armies for at least twenty-five years. As might be expected, both men saw the cable as a sign of weakness.

Mussolini didn't like Hitler, but he admired the fact that Hitler was able to take Czechoslovakia without firing a single shot. In 1939, the two countries signed an alliance that came to be known as the Pact of Steel. Although most people didn't know it at the time, the alliance would soon pit the two daring dictators against the rest of the world.

Figure 2-1 Hitler and Mussolini in Munich, circa June 1940.

Photo courtesy of the National Archives (242-EB-7-38)

Hitler Pushes East

Hitler's next move—the bold invasion of Poland—was the final stroke that ignited World War II. In the days following his speech to the German High Command, there was much diplomatic discussion as Hitler tried to overcome British opposition to his plans. Chamberlain had announced that if Poland's sovereignty were threatened, the British would "feel themselves bound at once to lend the Polish government all support at their power."

CHAPTER 2: FANNING THE FLAMES

Mussolini was also bothered by Germany's planned aggression, and he strongly encouraged Hitler to continue negotiating with Poland rather than invade it. But Hitler refused to listen, and on August 31 he ordered his troops across the border. At the same time, he ordered that all terminally ill patients in German hospitals be euthanized to make room for the anticipated wounded.

Polish leaders had long believed that if Germany did attack, the Soviet Union would respond swiftly with troops. After all, Germany and the Soviet Union had been at odds ever since taking opposite sides in the Spanish Civil War. However, Hitler had cleverly eliminated any Soviet threat by signing a nonaggression pact with Stalin on August 23, 1939. As history would show, this pact was as meaningless to Hitler as the one he had signed with Poland.

Figure 2-2 Soviet commissar Vyacheslav Molotov signing the nonaggression pact between Germany and the Soviet Union.

Photo courtesy of the National Archives (242-JRPE-44)

To give Hitler an excuse for his invasion, SS chief Heinrich Himmler concocted the story that Polish soldiers had attacked a German radio station in the border town of Gliwice. An unnamed prisoner was taken from a German concentration camp, placed in a Polish uniform, and shot by the Gestapo (the secret state police) outside the radio station. It was all Hitler needed to put his plan into motion.

Poland Is Brought to Its Knees

Germany invaded Poland on September 1, 1939, with a brutally fast attack known as a *blitzkrieg* (a combination of two German words meaning "lightning war") in which the enemy is hit with ruthless speed and efficiency with multiple methods of attack in an effort to destroy it before an effective defense can be mounted. This was in extreme contrast to the trench warfare of World War I, in which enemy armies dug in at fixed positions and then slugged it out.

The blitzkrieg against Poland was devastating. Even though Poland had a larger army, sudden air attacks destroyed much of its air force while it was still on the ground; then another wave of bombers took out the nation's roads and railways, assembly points, and munitions dumps and factories. German planes also attacked numerous civilian centers, causing extraordinary panic.

Figure 2-3 German troops parading through Warsaw, September 1939.

Photo courtesy of the National Archives (200-SFF-52)

German dive-bombers then attacked marching troops without mercy in an attempt to decimate enemy forces and demoralize anyone who was left. Civilian refugees were strafed with machine gun fire as they fled the approaching troops, causing still more chaos on Poland's already crowded roads and hindering Polish troops. Within a matter of hours, Hitler's troops brought Poland to its knees.

While the Luftwaffe rained bombs on Polish soldiers and civilians alike, wave after wave of motorized infantry, light tanks, and motor-drawn artillery poured into the country, followed by heavy tanks, doing as much damage as possible as they plunged deep into Poland. Once a region had been softened up with air attacks and artillery, it was occupied by German foot soldiers supported by artillery, who mopped up whatever resistance remained. More than 2 million German civilians living in Poland aided the German army by giving precise information on Polish troop movements.

Hitler's invasion of Poland had two goals: to regain territory lost after World War I and to impose German rule over the rest of the country. To this end, he almost immediately began a campaign to eradicate both enemies of Nazism and those he considered inferior, particularly Poland's large Jewish population. Numerous atrocities were committed in the weeks following the German invasion, including massacres of hundreds of unarmed military personnel and civilians, destruction of entire villages, and incarceration or murder of anyone who voiced any type of opposition against the new leadership. Hitler's army was a merciless iron hand held at the throat of the Polish people and its government, and it tightened its grip with each passing day.

FACT

Hitler's blitzkrieg succeeded beyond his wildest hopes. The Polish government was forced into exile, and of the nation's 1 million soldiers, 700,000 were taken prisoner and another 80,000 fled the country. Germany's expeditionary force of 1.5 million soldiers suffered minimally—just 45,000 dead, wounded, or missing.

Sixteen days after Germany invaded Poland, the Soviet Union sent troops into eastern Poland, supposedly to assist the Ukrainians and Belorussians who lived there. In reality, this action was part of a secret agreement between Germany and the Soviet Union to divide Poland among them, and it dealt the deathblow to Poland's struggle. On September 28—the day after a heavily battered Warsaw finally fell—Germany and the Soviet Union signed a pact that divided Poland in two, with the eastern half going to the Soviet Union and the western half going to Germany. Hitler also conceded the Baltic States and Finland to the Soviet sphere of influence.

The Role of Finland

Finland's role in World War II can appear a little confusing as a result of its ongoing conflict with the Soviet Union. The nation was freed from Russian rule following the Bolshevik Revolution, but the relationship between the two nations remained tense. In early 1939, as Finland and Sweden were negotiating the fortification of some islands they shared in the Gulf of Bothnia, the Soviet Union began harassing Finland. In August, the secret pact between Germany and the Soviet Union placed Finland and the Baltic nations under the USSR's sphere of influence, and the Soviets began planning the conquest of Finland, Estonia, Latvia, and Lithuania. Relations between Finland and the Soviet Union continued to deteriorate, and on November 30, 1939, after claiming that Finnish soldiers had fired on Soviet troops, the Red Army attacked—only to be beaten back. The Soviets regrouped and attacked again early in 1940. Finland fought valiantly but faced overwhelming odds, so it reopened negotiations with the USSR and, in return for peace, lost the Karelian Isthmus and other territory along the border.

Late in 1940, Finland—technically neutral in the war but still anti-Soviet—allowed German troops to pass through from Soviet territory for the German occupation of Norway. When Germany attacked the Soviet Union in June 1941, Finland joined in. As a result, the nation was considered an Axis power by the United Kingdom, which declared war on Finland on December 6, 1941.

Great Britain and France declared war on Germany two days after Hitler invaded Poland. Those declarations of war included a blockage of German ports, which was initially very successful at denying Germany needed raw materials, especially food. Hitler asked the two nations to rescind their declarations and promised to leave the surrounding nations alone. This time, Great Britain and France refused to budge. The standoff would continue until Hitler's attack on Denmark and Norway in April 1940.

Hitler Takes Denmark and Norway

As the smoke cleared over a vanquished Poland, an uneasy calm settled on Europe. Great Britain and France were both engaged in a sea war with Germany (an ongoing conflict that became known as the Battle of the Atlantic), but there was no war on land—at least for a while.

Hitler next turned Germany's military might against Norway and Denmark. The reason was simple: Germany needed to safeguard important iron ore shipments arriving mostly from neutral Sweden and to give its navy a safe passage through Norwegian coastal waters into the North Atlantic. Taking the Scandinavian peninsula would also provide Germany with much-needed food and other goods that were in short supply as a result of the British-French blockade of German ports.

The invasion of Norway and Denmark was placed in the hands of the German navy. Naval forces were to land along the Norwegian coast on April 9, 1940, while airborne units were dropped on Norway and Denmark to capture essential airfields.

Norway, which tried to remain neutral during Hitler's grab for land, learned of the planned invasion a day before it was to occur when Norwegians in Kristiansund picked up 122 survivors from a German transport that had been torpedoed by a Polish submarine. The captured Germans admitted that they were part of a planned invasion force, but, incredibly, the Norwegian cabinet did nothing to set up defenses.

Others, however, were doing what they could to halt Germany's aggression. Great Britain defied international law by laying mines in Norwegian waters to slow the iron ore trade between Germany and Norway. It was initially believed that when Germany invaded Denmark and Norway on April 9, it was in response to this British mining of Norwegian waters. However, the attack had been planned for two months.

Once again, the blitzkrieg offense proved devastatingly effective. It took Germany just four hours to invade and conquer Denmark. German troops marched across the Danish border early on the morning of April 9, overwhelming the surprised Danes into surrendering. At the same time, German troops emerged from cargo ships in Norwegian ports, and aircraft dropped German paratroopers onto Norwegian airfields. Simultaneously, German destroyers, protected by thick fog, moved up Norway's main fjords to unload additional troops and provide artillery support to the assault.

Caught somewhat by surprise, the Norwegians fought with all they had, assisted by British troops and planes, but the German army was far too powerful. Despite their heroic efforts, the Norwegian soldiers never really had a chance.

The accompanying sea battle, however, went a little differently. The first German losses were at the hands of Norwegian defenders at Oslo Fjord, who opened fire from coastal defense batteries at close range. On the first morning of the sea war, the heavy cruiser *Blücher* was sunk with the loss of several hundred troops and civilians who were to act as occupation officials. Two other coastal defense ships managed to damage another German cruiser, and gunners at Oslo Fjord took out a German torpedo boat.

FACT

Germany's use of paratroopers during the 1940 blitzkrieg invasion of Norway was the first ever in war. The largest mass drop of the war was Operation Varsity on March 24, 1945. In that remarkable effort, 1,285 transports and 2,290 gliders were used to lift more than 9,300 U.S. paratroopers and 4,976 British troops across the Rhine. Bombers followed, dropping supplies.

British destroyer guns and British naval aircraft flying from the Orkney Islands also managed to inflict heavy damage on the invading German forces, sinking a light cruiser and ten destroyers. The battleships *Scharnhorst* and *Gneisenau* were also damaged during the battle, which continued into June. British and French naval losses included the sinking of several destroyers and the aircraft carrier *Glorious*.

By late May, the British and French troops had established strong positions near Narvik (Norway), but the military collapse the Allies were facing in northern France and the Low Countries forced them to abandon the Norwegian campaign. During the first week of June, the Allies were able to evacuate 27,000 people with almost no losses, as well as King Haakon and the officials who would quickly establish Norway's government in exile.

It took two months, but Norway and Denmark now belonged to Hitler. However, the conquest had a downside for Germany. More than 300,000 troops had to be stationed in Norway, which kept them far from battle, and their presence did little to quell seething anti-German resistance.

The Fall of France

The German blitzkrieg into Norway and Denmark foreshadowed what lay ahead for France, which had joined forces with Great Britain to try to halt Hitler's conquest of Europe. Internally, France was going through a political shift. Communist organizations were dissolved, and a vote of no-confidence resulted in new leadership as Daladier stepped down to become minister for the war and Paul Reynaud was selected to be premier.

Things happened quickly in Europe from May to July of 1940. Germany simultaneously invaded the Netherlands, Belgium, and Luxembourg, taking the three countries with remarkable swiftness. French and British troops tried to halt the German invasion but found themselves overwhelmed and forced to retreat. On May 13, German troops established a bridgehead at Sedan, the gateway to France; the nation, which had been invaded by Germany during World War I, again found itself fighting for its existence.

Breaking through the French border defenses took just two days. German forces outflanked the famed Maginot line—a defensive perimeter of forts along the French-German border—and raced through the Ardennes.

Almost immediately, France found itself an occupied country. British prime minister Winston Churchill learned of France's fate when he received a telephone call from Premier Reynaud who, speaking in English, said simply: "We have been defeated."

On June 10, the French government fled Paris, first to Tours and then, on June 14, to Bordeaux. Two days later, Reynaud resigned as premier and his successor, Marshal Henri Philippe Pétain, surrendered the French army. Germany and France signed an armistice on June 22, and two days later, General Charles de Gaulle, who had fled to Great Britain before the German army had invaded, was recognized by the British government as the leader of the Free French.

As the war drew to a close, French Resistance leaders executed an estimated 10,000 French collaborators. Thousands more were sent to jail.

France Carved Up

Germany claimed the Alsace-Lorraine area of France, long a point of contention in previous wars, as a territory and occupied northern and western France as a conquered land, putting it under the military governor of Belgium. The remainder of France was left unoccupied and was administered, along with all French colonies, by a collaborationist government that became known as Vichy France because its capital was the city of Vichy, approximately 200 miles southeast of Paris.

Intent on punishing France for its role in humiliating Germany with the provisions of the Treaty of Versailles as well as for transgressions in previous wars, Germany fined France an estimated $120 million and assessed occupation costs of nearly $2 billion a year. In addition, the Bank of France was forced to extend huge credits to Germany. These figures were as staggering as those imposed on Germany by France and its allies at the end of World War I.

Worst of all, however, according to many, was the plunder of France's priceless artwork. A total of 140 railcars of looted art—including irreplaceable works by many of the world's great masters—were taken from France to Germany. Hitler, himself a failed painter, coveted great works of art and thought that his nation, which he considered to be the strongest on the planet, had a right to inherit the legacy of such masterpieces.

The German invaders found life in France much to their liking, at least for the first few years. The best wines were reserved for high-ranking German officials, as were specially designated seats on all public transportation. Many Germans also enjoyed the company of French women who found it easier to join their nation's conquerors than to resist them. (After the liberation of France, many such women, loathed by their countrymen, were forced to parade through town with their heads shaved as a sign that they had been Nazi sympathizers.)

A strong French underground resistance sprang up almost overnight, but the price for its activities was high: 100 French hostages killed for every German. Nonetheless, the underground succeeded in hindering the Nazi war effort through sabotage and guerrilla warfare.

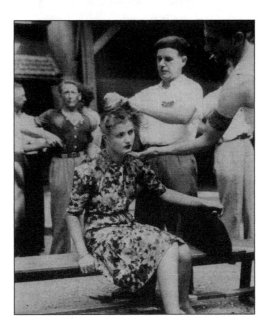

Figure 2-4 A French woman who had collaborated with the Germans during the occupation has her head shaved.

Photo courtesy of the National Archives (111-SC-193785)

Operation Dynamo

The war could have ended for the Allies with the fall of France, if not for the astounding evacuation of nearly 300,000 troops from the French port of Dunkirk.

The German advance, which had been lightning-swift, trapped nearly 200,000 Britons and 140,000 French and Belgians in the coastal city near Belgium. To save them, the British Admiralty rounded up virtually every sea-worthy vessel available—from warships to tiny pleasure craft. On May 26, the first vessels sailed across the English Channel, protected by Royal Air Force planes, and the waiting soldiers crowded the beaches and piers to greet them.

The evacuation, code-named Operation Dynamo, lasted ten frightening days. British and French destroyers raced to the port, took on as many soldiers as they could, then, with guns firing almost constantly, raced back to Dover, England. Smaller boats carried troops to ships located outside the ruined Dunkirk harbor. Hitler, who certainly had enough troops and tanks in the country to prevent such a thing, had misread the situation and halted his advance too soon to prevent this massive relocation of troops. Instead the Luftwaffe was sent to do what damage it could.

The horrors and hazards of the evacuation—the largest of its kind in history—were tremendous. German planes rained a constant barrage of bombs on both land and sea, terrorizing those still waiting for rescue. The Royal Air Force (RAF) engaged the Germans at every opportunity, downing 159 enemy planes (which was significant but not too threatening, since the Luftwaffe possessed many more planes and the capacity to manufacture a great many more). Making things worse was the knowledge that every hour brought the invading German army closer and closer. Three days into the evacuation, the nearby port of Calais fell to the Nazis, and the following day Belgium surrendered. The situation might have ended far worse if Hitler had not twice suspended his drive toward Dunkirk to concentrate on other objectives.

When the rescue was over, only 2,000 had died. Those who made it to the Dover shore were greeted with cheers and soon left to continue the fight against Germany.

Figure 2-5 British prisoners at Dunkirk.

Photo courtesy of the National Archives (242-EB-7-35)

In the United States, there was a sense of shock as France fell to the Nazis, leaving an ill-prepared Great Britain to fight alone. While the United States remained neutral regarding affairs in Europe, Congress decided to prepare for the worst by enacting the first peacetime conscription in American history and greatly increasing the military budget. However, the public, while sympathetic toward Great Britain's plight, was not eager to engage Germany, and most Americans maintained that isolationism was still the best policy.

Mussolini Joins the Fray

Benito Mussolini watched with awe as Hitler's troops stormed across Europe. He desperately wanted to join in, fearful that there would be little left to conquer once Hitler was finished, but several factors prevented him from acting immediately. Foremost, his people weren't in the mood for war and conquest, preferring to enjoy a more pacifistic lifestyle. Moreover, his army was ill-prepared to enter a major war. Mussolini was also angered by Hitler's pact with Stalin and his vicious treatment of Poland, which had taken even Mussolini by surprise and made him think twice about joining forces with such a tyrannical leader. In the back of Mussolini's mind was the thought of what would happen if Germany lost the war.

However, Mussolini's grand ego and Hitler's strong urging eventually overcame any doubts Mussolini may have had about bringing his nation into what was obviously gearing up to be a full-blown world war. In March 1940, the two dictators met at the Brenner Pass on the Austrian-Italian border to formalize their alliance. During the meeting, Mussolini promised to commit his troops the moment Germany's attack on France appeared successful.

Italy Declares War, Begins Blunder

That moment came sooner than expected. On June 10, as France fell to the Nazis, Benito Mussolini declared war on Great Britain and France with the statement: "This is the struggle of the peoples who are poor and eager to work against the greedy who hold a ruthless monopoly of all the wealth and gold of the earth."

Though personally doubtful of his own army's chances of success, Mussolini had boasted to Hitler of Italy's military might. Appointing himself the new commander of Italian armed forces, Mussolini ordered his troops to attack France from across the Alps. The results were far less than Mussolini—or Hitler—had expected. Italy's first assault on southern France resulted in the acquisition of very little territory, as Italian troops were pushed back by the smaller but better prepared French forces.

The other battles in which Italy engaged were equally unimpressive. An August invasion of British Somaliland by 40,000 Italian troops succeeded only because the Italians outnumbered the British four to one. And even then, Italy lost 2,000 men to Britain's 260, and the engagement took a full two weeks. In September, 80,000 Italian soldiers marched from Libya into Egypt, heading for the Suez Canal. They faced just 30,000 British troops—and were driven back, losing much of eastern Libya in the process.

In October, without consulting Hitler, Mussolini sent 155,000 troops into Greece from Albania. And once again, the Italian army failed to win. Worse, a third of Albania fell into Greek possession, while the British landed on the strategically important island of Crete.

Mussolini was supposed to be waging a parallel war in the Mediterranean while the Germans took control of northern Europe, but such was not the case. There were no devastating Italian blitzkriegs, just a mishmash of battles fought by poorly trained and ill-prepared Italian troops who wished they were anywhere but on the frontlines of a war. As a result, Hitler came to view Mussolini more as a hindrance than an ally and spent much time cleaning up Mussolini's messes.

The Axis Expands

In November 1940, Hitler brought Romania and Hungary into the Axis alliance, primarily because he needed to cross them to get to Greece and, later, the Soviet Union. Bulgaria joined in March 1941. Yugoslavia, however, refused to follow, so Hitler ordered an invasion, which began on April 6, 1941.

FACT

The invasion of Yugoslavia was a tough conquest, with German military officials having to pull together an army of nine divisions from Germany and France in less than ten days.

On April 10, German forces began attacks on Belgrade from the northwest, north, and southeast. The city fell three days later, quickly followed by the surrender of the Yugoslav army. Like many other conquered countries, however, Yugoslavia proved more difficult to hold than it had been to take. Guerrilla fighters would continue to harass the Nazi invaders over the course of the war.

Next, Hitler went after Greece, which was better prepared to fight than Yugoslavia had been. Its fighting force of 430,000 men was fully mobilized and battle-tested, but things went poorly from the start. The Greeks' efforts to defend the Metaxas line northeast of Salonika proved to be a disaster, and German troops forced the surrender of the line and nearly half the Greek army on April 9. Almost two weeks later, the Greek First Army was attempting to pull out of Albania but became trapped at the Metsovon Pass and was forced to surrender.

The German drive accelerated after that, with the Nazis taking the Isthmus of Corinth by April 27 and the Peloponnesus by April 30, forcing

British defenders into an evacuation that cost nearly 12,000 men. In addition, a week-long airborne assault in late May brought Crete under German control.

As all this was going on, German general Erwin Rommel had launched a very successful counteroffensive against the British in Libya, pushing them from the country with the exception of an isolated garrison at Tobruk. North Africa was quickly falling into German hands.

Japan Extends Its Military Might

The Japanese leadership watched the events in Europe closely in 1939 and 1940 and found in Germany's rapid victories the encouragement it needed to expand its control into Southeast Asia. The expansion was necessary to meet Japan's desperate need for natural resources such as petroleum and rubber to help carry on its military efforts against China and elsewhere.

Its reliance on supplies from other countries was a major problem for Japan. As a result of a commercial treaty signed in 1911, a high percentage of Japan's resources came from the United States, including oil (66 percent), aviation fuel (100 percent), metal scrap (90 percent), and copper (91 percent). But in July 1939, President Roosevelt, angered by Japan's growing militarism, threatened to terminate the treaty and sever this essential source of supplies. Realizing that it could no longer rely on the United States for resources, Japan began to hungrily eye its neighbors.

The descent into war in the Pacific began to accelerate. When France, Belgium, Luxembourg, and the Netherlands finally fell to the Germans, the government of Prime Minister Fumimaro Konoe announced Japan's plan to create a self-sufficient economic and political coalition under Japanese leadership to be known as the Greater East Asia Co-Prosperity Sphere, which would dramatically change the balance of power in the Pacific because the defeated European nations had ruled much of southeastern Asia as colonies.

Then, in September 1940, the Konoe cabinet joined the Axis by signing the Tripartite Pact. In so doing, Japan received permission from Germany to occupy French Indochina, which had been a source of supplies for China. In Indochina, Japan would be able to establish bases it could use to conquer nearby regions rich in the natural resources it so desperately needed. Of special interest to the Japanese were the Pacific colonial territories of the Netherlands and Great Britain, particularly the oil-rich Dutch East Indies.

Meanwhile, relations between Japan and the United States continued to worsen. After a series of shakeups, the Japanese cabinet hardened its expansionist policies. The message was clear: Japan needed land and resources and was more than willing to take them by force. On April 13, 1941, Japan and the Soviet Union signed a neutrality pact that greatly benefited both countries. The Soviet Union agreed to respect the borders of the puppet state of Manchukuo, and Japan pledged to do the same in Mongolia. The pact gave Japan important protection on its Soviet flank and opened the door for war against the United States and the European colonial powers.

Japanese militarists wasted little time. In July 1941, after removing the remaining moderates, the military-dominated Japanese cabinet ordered an invasion of the rest of Indochina and demanded more conscripts. U.S. President Roosevelt responded to Japan's increasingly warlike attitude by freezing all Japanese assets in the United States and cutting off oil exports to Japan. Prime Minister Fumimaro Konoe struggled for a diplomatic solution, but the armed forces favored a more militant policy and urged at a conference in October that the nation prepare itself for war.

Konoe resigned as prime minister and was replaced by General Hideki Tojo, Japan's minister of war. Tojo, a career military man, drew a line in the sand when he demanded that the United States cease sending aid to China, accept the Japanese conquest of Indochina, resume normal trade relations, and not reinforce American bases in the Far East.

Negotiations between Japan, represented by Ambassador Kichisaburo Nomura, and the United States, represented by Secretary of State Cordell Hull, quickly hit an impasse. On November 26, the United States again demanded that Japan withdraw from China and Indochina if negotiations were to continue, but Japan wasn't about to give back what it had already taken. Considering Hull's demand an ultimatum and thus seeing no need for further talks, Tojo ordered to sea a Japanese task force that had been assembled secretly off the island of Etorofu. Its target: the U.S. naval base at Pearl Harbor.

Chapter 3
The United States Enters the War

The morning of December 7, 1941, could not have been more beautiful at Pearl Harbor, on the Hawaiian island of Oahu. Eight American battleships sat moored on Ford Island along what had become known as Battleship Row. Nearby were five cruisers and twenty-six destroyers and at sea were seven other cruisers and the three carriers. Onshore, two army radar operators saw their screens indicate approaching aircraft. They notified an officer, who dismissed their concerns with the explanation that it was probably a flight of American B-17s arriving from California. But the officer was horribly wrong. It would prove to be a costly mistake.

The Attack on Pearl Harbor

Military intelligence in Washington, D.C., had intercepted a series of memoranda from Tokyo indicating that the Japanese were planning some kind of aggressive action. The messages were delivered to President Roosevelt that evening, but he took no action. He believed that war with Japan was imminent but that the Japanese would never attack American soil, preferring instead to push farther into Asia.

On the morning of December 7, what was thought to be the last of the fourteen communiqués from Tokyo was intercepted and decoded. It noted that Japan was breaking off all negotiations with the United States. The message was delivered to President Roosevelt at 10:00 A.M. EST, but again, he saw no cause for immediate concern. Then another message was intercepted, this one instructing Ambassador Saburo Kurusu to present the Japanese reply at exactly 1:00 P.M. EST, or 7:30 A.M. Pearl Harbor time. If everything went as planned, that would be the exact moment Japanese bombers would be over Pearl Harbor.

An astute naval officer immediately understood the significance of Japan's timing and arranged to have General George Marshall, who had been enjoying a horseback ride along the Potomac, brought to the War Department for consultation. Marshall also understood the significance of the final Japanese memorandum, but his message of warning to Pearl Harbor could not be delivered immediately because the department was not in radio contact with Honolulu. Instead, the message went by commercial wire and radio and was not received until 7:33 A.M. Pearl Harbor time. The bicycle messenger sent to deliver the warning was furiously pedaling to Fort Shafter when, at 7:55 A.M., destruction came raining down from the sky.

All Hell Breaks Loose

The first wave of Japanese bombers and attack planes consisted of forty torpedo bombers (known as Kates), fifty-one Val dive-bombers, and approximately forty-nine high-level bombers escorted by forty-three Zero fighters. The torpedo bombers came in low to drop their destructive torpedoes while the Vals dropped bombs and armor-piercing shells on the docked ships below. At the same time, the Zeroes dropped bombs on American planes in the airfields, a move designed to thwart saboteurs; no thought had been given to an enemy air attack.

The massive ships along Battleship Row never stood a chance. The first to go down was the *Oklahoma*, its hull ripped open by three torpedoes, and the deathblow delivered by two more. Panicked sailors screamed for their lives as the ship exploded and began to sink. The crew of the *Maryland*, which was moored next to the *Oklahoma*, used the smoke and burning wreckage of their sister ship as protection while they fought the surprise attackers with everything they could find. Astoundingly, the *Maryland* survived the two bombs that struck it.

Figure 3-1 The USS *Shaw* exploding during the attack on Pearl Harbor.

Photo courtesy of the National Archives (80-G-16871)

While Japanese planes screamed overhead and bombs exploded all around, the sailors on the ships along Battleship Row used axes and hammers to open the locked boxes containing the ammunition they needed to fight back. With the first explosions ringing over the island, sailors on shore leave raced back to their ships, even swimming when necessary.

The other moored battleships, unable to maneuver, also proved easy targets for the attacking Japanese planes. The *West Virginia* went down after being hit with two bombs and several torpedoes; its hulk provided protection for the *Tennessee*, which escaped most of the torpedoes aimed at it but was set afire by flaming debris from the *Arizona* moored behind it. The *Arizona* was hit so hard by the Japanese that it sank in minutes, taking more than 1,100 crewmen with it, including Rear Admiral Isaac C. Kidd, commander of Battleship Division One, and the ship's commanding officer, Captain Franklin Van Valkenburgh. The *California*, which was moored alone, exploded in a fireball that reached 500 feet into the sky when a bomb struck its arsenal.

The only battleship to attempt to get out to sea was the *Nevada*, which was also moored alone. Its frantic crew engaged in a grueling battle with Japanese planes before finally being forced aground. The crew of the *Pennsylvania*, which was in dry dock at the time, fought valiantly, blanketing the air with so much antiaircraft fire that the ship took only one bomb hit.

The Japanese had sent two waves of attack planes against Pearl Harbor (a third wave was waiting and ready but was not called into action), intent on inflicting as much damage as possible in the hope of permanently crippling the American military presence in the Pacific. By midmorning, as the last Japanese planes headed back to Admiral Chuichi Nagumo's carrier fleet, four U.S. battleships had been sunk and four had been severely damaged. In addition, three light cruisers, three destroyers, and four smaller vessels were also destroyed or severely damaged. All but three of the sunken ships were raised and returned to action. The military decided to leave the *Arizona* where it went down and later turned the site into a solemn memorial to the military personnel and civilians who died during the assault.

Land Targets

The nearby airfields also suffered tremendous damage. Dozens of planes, parked wingtip to wingtip, made an easy and vulnerable target for Japanese bombers. In the end, only a handful of American fighters managed to make it into the air to engage the enemy attackers.

At Hickam and other area airfields, 188 aircraft—75 percent of the island's military air fleet—had been destroyed before they could take to the air. Luckily, the fleet's three aircraft carriers—the primary target of the Japanese attack—were out to sea on maneuvers and escaped harm. Human casualties were also high: 2,403 servicemen and civilians killed and another 1,104 wounded. Most of the casualties were aboard the destroyed ships, though a direct hit on the mess hall at Hickam Field killed 35.

FACT

American forces did manage to inflict some damage on the attacking Japanese, downing twenty-seven planes and killing sixty-four airmen and seamen. In addition, the Japanese lost five two-man midget submarines, which had been deployed to penetrate the harbor minutes before the attack.

A Well-Planned Attack

The attack on Pearl Harbor was anything but a last-minute decision by the Japanese military. In truth, the assault was more than a year in the planning, and was under way even as the Japanese government went through the motions of negotiating with the United States regarding Japan's ongoing aggression in the Pacific.

The mastermind behind the attack on Pearl Harbor was Admiral Isoroku Yamamoto, commander in chief of the Japanese Combined Fleet. Yamamoto began planning the attack in November 1940, just two months after signing the Tripartite Pact, which brought Japan into the Axis with Germany and Italy.

It is commonly believed that Yamamoto had two sources of inspiration for the attack on Pearl Harbor. The first was a 1925 book titled *The Great Pacific War* by Hector Bywater, a British naval expert. Bywater's book realistically describes a war between the United States and Japan that begins with the destruction of the Pacific Fleet and a Japanese invasion of the Philippines and Guam. The second source was the November 1940 RAF strike at Taranto, Italy, in which torpedoes heavily damaged two Italian battleships. The event impressed Yamamoto because it was the first practical attack by aircraft on battleships.

In January 1941, Yamamoto instructed Rear Admiral Takijiro Onishi, a renowned naval aviator, to prepare a preliminary study on the feasibility of an attack on the U.S. naval base at Pearl Harbor. The plan was completed in April and called for Japan to make a surprise air and submarine attack on Pearl Harbor. The site was selected because it was both a major U.S. military installation and close enough for Japanese forces to approach with little risk of detection.

Commander Mitsuo Fuchida, director of the air attack, spent the next several months developing the tactics and equipment necessary to fly to Hawaii and take out the ships along Battleship Row. In November, after the Japanese government approved the attack, it became known as the "Hawaiian Operation."

On November 30, the Japanese cabinet set December 7 as the date Japan would declare war on the United States. On December 1, Yamamoto's flagship in Japan's Inland Sea sent out a prearranged coded message—"Climb Mount Niitaka"—which was the signal to attack Pearl Harbor on Sunday, December 7.

FACT

The first U.S. prisoner of war was Ensign Kazua Sakamaki, the sole surviving crewman of the five Japanese midget subs destroyed by American forces during the attack on Pearl Harbor.

Victory Breeds Confidence

Pearl Harbor was not the only target of the Japanese on that fateful day. Simultaneously, Japanese planes attacked the British in Malaya and Hong Kong and American military bases in the Philippines, Guam, Midway, and Wake Island. The barrage caught everyone by surprise, and there was little time to mount a defense. Within twenty-four hours, a huge expanse of the Pacific belonged to Japan.

Yamamoto and Tojo both believed the war was over at that point, confident that the United States and Great Britain had been weakened to the point where they could not and would not fight back. Hitler, too, believed that the United States would not pursue war, telling his aides, "Now it is impossible for us to lose the war. We now have an ally who has not been vanquished in 3,000 years."

Figure 3-2
Roosevelt signing the Declaration of War against Japan the day after the bombing of Pearl Harbor.

Photo courtesy of the National Archives (79-AR82)

Lulled by America's earlier neutral stance and now believing the nation to be weak and essentially defenseless, Hitler declared war on the United States on December 11, 1941. Italy followed suit shortly after. But rather than rolling over as anticipated, the United States reacted almost immediately with its own declarations of war against Germany and Italy, while Great Britain declared war on Japan.

Pearl Harbor Investigations

The Japanese attack on Pearl Harbor sparked a flurry of questions, the most obvious being "How could it have happened?" Despite a worldwide intelligence and surveillance network and a meticulously trained home guard, the United States could not prevent Japan from sneaking up and delivering a devastating blow. In the years following the attack, eight major investigations would attempt to answer the question of how it had happened.

The first investigation was a closed-door board of inquiry ordered by President Roosevelt eleven days after the attack. The Roberts Commission, named after its chairman, Supreme Court Justice Owen Roberts, concluded its investigation January 23, 1942, by laying the blame on Admiral Husband Kimmel, commander in chief of the U.S. Pacific Fleet, and Lieutenant General Walter C. Short, commanding officer of the U.S. Army's Hawaiian Department. In its official report, the Roberts Commission declared that the two men had failed to exhibit the qualities of high command. Kimmel and Short had been relieved of duty by the time the commission concluded its investigation, and both men soon retired.

Six more closed-door investigations were conducted by the U.S. Army or Navy over the next few years, their results cloaked in secrecy because of concerns over military security. It wasn't until after the war that the public would learn exactly what had happened on December 7, 1941.

Congressional Investigations

November 15, 1945, saw the beginning of a joint congressional investigation into the disaster. It lasted six months and produced more than 15,000 pages of testimony. Both the majority and minority reports issued at the end of the investigation placed the primary blame on Kimmel and Short, noting that the two men had failed to heed warnings from Washington of a potential enemy attack and that they had failed to properly alert their forces. The committee concluded that while Kimmel and Short had made "errors in judgment," they were not guilty of "dereliction of duty."

FACT

Conspiracy theorists continue to have a field day with Pearl Harbor. One idea has President Roosevelt moving the Pacific Fleet from California to Hawaii to lure the Japanese into attacking the United States and thus opening the door to war, which the nation needed to break out of the Depression. However, facts suggest that this was not the case. The fleet was moved at the urging of the State Department because it believed that having the Fleet in Hawaii would deter Japanese aggression—not tempt them to attack.

The congressional committee's report was not the end of the debate. Many questions remained, but the documents that might answer them would not be declassified for many years.

Why Warnings from Washington Were Not Heeded

As for war warnings from Washington, they were received and acted on, but ineffectively. Kimmel received a dispatch from the Navy Department warning of anticipated aggression by Japan, and Short received a similar warning from the War Department. Kimmel decided not to raise the alert status of the navy forces he commanded because he didn't want to frighten Pearl Harbor's civilian population. He did, however, send two aircraft carriers with escorts to deliver planes to Wake Island and Midway, an action that accidentally helped save the valued ships when the Japanese finally attacked.

Short, who was in charge of Pearl Harbor's defenses, reacted to the warnings from Washington by bolstering precautions against sabotage, considered the main threat because of the island's large Japanese American population. To that end, he followed military policy and ordered all the warplanes parked wingtip to wingtip so they would be easier to guard. Sadly, the plan only made them a more convenient target for Japanese bombers.

Kimmel and Short were also hobbled in their defense by the fact that they were denied access to intelligence reports based on the decoding of Japan's communiqués to its diplomats in the United States. Had they known what the intelligence community knew—but failed to share—they might have reacted differently.

The American Response

The Japanese believed that by striking first, they could effectively disable the American military presence in the Pacific and thus prevent any formidable intervention as Japan continued its conquest of smaller nations in the pursuit of land and resources. However, rather than destroying the U.S. military and demoralizing the nation as planned, the attack only strengthened the country's resolve. Previously, a neutral and politically divided United States might have been content to let Japan continue its warlike ways as long as it didn't touch American interests or harm American citizens. But with a single blow, Japan managed to unleash the fury of the entire nation.

FDR's Radio Address

On December 8, 1941, President Franklin Roosevelt made the following address, asking Congress to declare war on Japan. Its opening line remains one of the most famous quotes regarding the attack on Pearl Harbor:

Figure 3-3 President Franklin D. Roosevelt addresses the nation following the attack on Pearl Harbor.

Photo courtesy of the Franklin D. Roosevelt Presidential Library and Museum (ARC 196055)

Yesterday, December 7, 1941—a date which will live in infamy—the United States of America was suddenly and deliberately attacked by naval and air forces of the empire of Japan.

The United States was at peace with that nation and, at the solicitation of Japan, was still in conversation with its government and its emperor looking toward the maintenance of peace in the Pacific. Indeed, one hour after Japanese air squadrons had commenced bombing in Oahu, the Japanese ambassador to the United States and his colleague delivered to the secretary of state a formal reply to a recent American message. While this reply stated that it seemed useless to continue the existing diplomatic negotiations, it contained no threat or hint of war or armed attack. It will be recorded that the distance of Hawaii from Japan makes it obvious that the attack was deliberately planned many days or even weeks ago. During the intervening time, the Japanese government has deliberately sought to deceive the United States by false statements and expressions of hope for continued peace. . . .

As commander in chief of the Army and Navy, I have directed that all measures be taken for our defense.

Always will we remember the character of the onslaught against us. No matter how long it may take to overcome this premeditated invasion, the American people in their righteous might will win through to absolute victory. I believe I interpret the will of the Congress and of the people when I assert that we will not only defend ourselves to the uttermost but will make certain that this form of treachery shall never endanger us again.

Hostilities exist. There is no blinking at the fact that our people, our territory, and our interests are in grave danger. With confidence in our armed forces—with the unbounded determination of our people—we will gain the inevitable triumph, so help us God. I ask that the Congress declare that since the unprovoked and dastardly attack by Japan on Sunday, December 7, 1941, a state of war has existed between the United States and the Japanese Empire.

A Nation Reeling

On December 8, Congress declared war on Japan by a nearly unanimous vote. Within a day of the declaration of war, long lines formed at every draft board as men clamored to join the service. Most isolationists suddenly changed their beliefs, fully aware that the United States could no longer sit out a war that was threatening to engulf the world. Most people hoped the conflict would be short but knew in their hearts that it would take everything at the nation's disposal to eliminate fascism's threat to the world. As men lined up to enlist in the service, women replaced them in the workplace, giving birth to role models like Rosie the Riveter.

The automotive industry became the primary arms maker in the war. An estimated 35 percent of the nation's ordnance was produced in or around Detroit. General Motors Corporation became the nation's largest producer of war materials by developing specialties for its divisions. The company's Cadillac plant, for example, produced tanks and howitzer carriers, while its Chevrolet plant manufactured gears for aircraft engines and axles for army vehicles. The Chrysler Corporation, Packard, and other large manufacturers also did their share of war production, turning out machinery and weapons at an astounding rate. At Ford's huge River Rouge plant, the largest industrial facility in the world, raw materials arrived by ship, and finished jeeps and trucks moved out from the same docks.

On the afternoon of the attack, First Lady Eleanor Roosevelt addressed the nation by radio. "For months now," she said, "the knowledge that something of this kind might happen has been hanging over our heads. . . . That is all over now, and there is no more uncertainty. We know now what we have to face, and we know we are ready to face it. Whatever is asked of us, I am sure we can accomplish it; we are the free and unconquerable people of the United States of America."

Hawaii under Martial Law

Immediately after the attack on Pearl Harbor, Hawaii was deemed a war zone, meaning it was a potential target of invasion and a possible refuge for enemy agents. On the day of the attack, the territorial governor suspended the writ of habeas corpus—the constitutional protection against being imprisoned or detained without judicial approval—and signed a declaration of martial law prepared by the army. General Short, the army commander on Oahu, declared himself military governor. He was relieved of command December 17, but martial law—the most severe since the Civil War—continued until October 24, 1944.

Martial law during wartime was allowed in Hawaii under the same act of Congress that had made the island chain a U.S. territory. As a result of the declaration, the military ordered a strictly enforced nighttime blackout. Anyone caught with a lit cigarette, pipe, or cigar during the blackout was subject to arrest, as was anyone else if the light of their radio dial or kitchen stove burner could be seen through the house windows. The army also instituted a 6:00 P.M. to 6:00 A.M. curfew for anyone not on official business and drew up intelligence reports on 450,000 Hawaiians.

FACT

In 1946, the U.S. Supreme Court, after hearing appeals from Hawaiian residents arrested during the war, declared that the writ of habeas corpus should not have been suspended and that declaration of martial law did not automatically allow the military to take over civilian courts, even during wartime.

Fearful of another enemy attack at any time, officials confiscated more than 300,000 acres of land for military use and enacted severe censorship. All outgoing mail was read by military censors, and letters that could not be edited with black ink or scissors were returned to the sender to be rewritten. Long-distance telephone calls were required to be in English so that military personnel could listen in.

Fearing that Japanese invaders might try to disrupt U.S. currency, the military ordered all Hawaiians to turn in all U.S. paper money, which was burned and replaced with bills with HAWAII overprinted on them. In addition, Hawaiians were forbidden to make bank withdrawals of more than $200 in cash per month or to carry more than $200 in cash. To keep track of civilians, the military issued identification cards to everyone over the age of six; anyone caught without a card was subject to arrest.

The military also oversaw the Hawaiian legal system, with military courts trying thousands of cases, most of them having nothing to do with wartime security. People accused of a crime went before a military judge who heard the charges—typically without the presence of a lawyer—and then passed sentence, which could be revoked only by a pardon from the military governor.

Many people fought the sustained martial law. In 1944, a federal judge ruled that military governing of Hawaii was no longer valid, but the military ignored the ruling and President Roosevelt had to step in. In October 1944, he announced the suspension of martial law and the restoration of habeas corpus.

The American Internment Camps

Following America's entry into the war, thousands of Japanese Americans, German Americans, and Italian Americans were rounded up and placed in internment camps, ostensibly to ensure that they did nothing to help the Axis.

Figure 3-4
Young Japanese girl on her way to an American internment camp.

Photo courtesy of the National Archives (210-G-2A-6)

The fear of traitorous acts by Japanese aliens and Japanese Americans was not a new concept. As early as the 1930s, as Japan began to flex its military might in the Pacific, the military expressed concern about such a possibility. The fear was particularly strong in Hawaii, where military intelligence officers created secret lists of potential espionage suspects among the territory's sizable population of Japanese descent.

Hatred toward Japanese aliens and Americans of Japanese ancestry ignited immediately after the attack on Pearl Harbor. Suspicion ran especially deep in Hawaii, where everyone with Asian features was instantly viewed as the enemy. Newspapers fueled this hysteria with headlines such as "Caps on Japanese Tomato Plants Point to Air Base." As a result, every Japanese fraternal and business organization was suspected of anti-American activity.

Not all Japanese Americans went willingly to relocation centers. Gordon Hirabayashi fought his internment all the way to the U.S. Supreme Court with the claim that the army had violated his rights as an American. However, the court ruled that the threat of invasion and sabotage gave the military the right to restrict the constitutional rights of Japanese Americans.

Panic Sweeps the Nation

A similar panic quickly swept the mainland, and on February 19, 1942, President Roosevelt issued an executive order identifying specific military areas in the United States that were immediately off limits to Japanese, German, and Italian aliens and Japanese Americans.

On March 18, the War Relocation Authority was established as part of the Office of Emergency Management. Its goal, according to a report to President Roosevelt, was to "take all people of Japanese descent into custody, surround them with troops, prevent them from buying land, and return them to their former homes at the close of the war."

An estimated 120,000 men, women, and children of Japanese descent were rounded up on the West Coast and taken to ten relocation centers in isolated areas of several states, including Arizona, Arkansas, California, Colorado, Idaho, New Mexico, Utah, and Wyoming. Nearly two-thirds of those forced from their homes were American citizens, and more than one-fourth were children under fifteen. The internees were divided into three groups: *Nisei* (those who had been born in the United States of immigrant Japanese parents and therefore were United States citizens), *Issei* (Japanese immigrants), and *Kibei* (*Nisei* who had been educated primarily in Japan).

Life in an internment camp was hard and demeaning. Internees ate in mess halls, used communal bathrooms, and lived in tarpaper barracks with a twenty-by-twenty-five-foot room allowed for each family. Razors, scissors, and radios were banned. Barbed wire surrounded the camps, and armed soldiers patrolled them. Children went to schools operated by the War

Relocation Authority and were routinely indoctrinated with "patriotic" assignments such as writing essays on why they were proud to be Americans.

The camps were, for the most part, quiet and peaceful. The only serious problems occurred at the Tule Lake Relocation Center at the California-Oregon border. In June 1943, Tule Lake was designated a "segregation center" for Japanese Americans who had proclaimed their loyalty to Japan or whom the Department of Justice considered disloyal to the United States. Frequent strikes and demonstrations at the Tule Lake center forced the army to tighten control.

Approximately 2,000 people of German and Italian ancestry were placed in American relocation camps in addition to the 120,000 people of Japanese ancestry.

Japanese American Reactions, Results

Japanese Americans were prevented from entering the service until 1943. When the ban was finally lifted, 9,500 Japanese Americans in Hawaii volunteered for military duty, and 2,700 were accepted. In total, more than 17,000 Japanese Americans fought for the United States in World War II, many of them distinguishing themselves with remarkable bravery. The 442nd Regimental Combat Team, whose soldiers were born in America of Japanese ancestry, fought in the Italian campaign and became the most decorated military unit in U.S. history. By the end of the war, members of the unit had received 4,667 medals, awards, and citations, including a Medal of Honor, 52 Distinguished Service Crosses, and 560 Silver Stars. (See Appendix D for more about medals.)

In 1990—forty-five years after the end of the war—the United States government finally apologized to the 60,000 survivors of internment camps and their heirs. Each received $20,000 in reparations.

Part Two:
The Major Battles

Chapter 4
Europe

Although Hitler may have eased his way into his position of aggressor, once war was declared, things exploded into absolute mayhem. After the German blitzkrieg took most of continental Europe, the country turned its eye on the territory just a few miles off the coast of France—Great Britain.

4

The Battle of the Atlantic

The battle for control of the Atlantic was one of the most important struggles of the war. Without the arms and supplies that came across the ocean from the United States, Great Britain was sure to lose. Winston Churchill was well aware of this, noting in 1940 that a minimum of twenty supply ships (approximately 120,000 tons of weapons and supplies) had to arrive in Great Britain each day if the country was to survive the German onslaught.

The Atlantic later became crucial to the United States as well, because its forces had to cross the ocean to bring the war to Germany and halt Hitler's aggression. As a result, the Battle of the Atlantic was one of the longest and most complicated of the war, costing thousands of lives on both sides and a tremendous amount of equipment and materials.

At the onset of hostilities, Germany made the Atlantic a top priority, with the navy and the Luftwaffe working together to make passage across the ocean as hazardous as possible. The German strategy was known as "tonnage warfare" and was based on the assumption that if 750,000 tons of British shipping could be sunk every month, Great Britain would be forced to surrender within a year.

Submarine Warfare Ensues

At the start of the European war in 1939, the German navy had just fifty-seven U-boats (submarines) available, twenty-six of them large enough to safely patrol the Atlantic. The average of twenty-three U-boats covering the Atlantic and the North Sea by September were able to inflict little damage because of recurrent torpedo problems and a lack of air reconnaissance needed to pinpoint potential targets. But the situation quickly grew more hazardous for Allied ships as these problems were fixed.

The first attack of the Atlantic campaign occurred on September 3, 1939, when the German submarine *U-30* torpedoed the British liner *Athenia*, which carried more than 1,100 passengers. A total of 120 lives were lost, including 28 Americans. Had the country not been so firmly entrenched in isolationism at the time, the attack might have provoked the United States into war.

Shortly after, the British carrier *Courageous* was sunk by *U-29*, killing 519 men. When the carrier *Ark Royal* almost suffered a similar fate, the Royal

Navy realized that using carriers and its few available destroyers to hunt Nazi subs was simply too ineffective and dangerous. The solution was to send merchant ships in convoys on the theory that there was safety in numbers. Nonetheless, German subs sank forty-one merchant ships by the end of the first month of the war.

Germany relied on both its submarine fleet and the Luftwaffe to help gain control of the Atlantic, but the Luftwaffe ceased to be a major factor in the sea war after June 1941 because it was needed more on the eastern front.

The situation got progressively worse, though the number of ships sunk declined briefly as the first fleet of subs returned to German naval bases to take on fresh supplies and restock their torpedoes.

In October 1939, the Royal Navy experienced a devastating blow when *U-47* torpedoed and sank the battleship *Royal Oak* within the British base at Scapa Flow in the Orkney Islands off Scotland. The crew barely had time to react to the attack, and the ship sank quickly with her admiral and 785 crewmen.

Germany's Position Improves

The Battle of the Atlantic escalated with the fall of France, as Germany used the shores of the newly conquered country to launch submarine attacks in Atlantic shipping lanes. The French coast provided much easier access to waters frequently used by Allied convoys, and U-boat attacks increased accordingly.

Germany dramatically increased U-boat production as the war progressed, and soon Karl Dönitz, the German admiral in charge of the U-boat fleet, was able to again employ the "wolf pack" tactic he had used with great success in 1939. In the first use of the wolf pack strategy, four U-boats simultaneously attacked a convoy sailing from Gibraltar to England. Three merchant ships went down, and the convoy was forced to scatter. Dönitz realized immediately that the strategy could be very effective, though he did not have enough subs then to put it into full-scale use.

Though America was not officially at war with Germany during the early days of the Atlantic battle, its warships had frequent encounters with German submarines as the American ships assisted British convoys. On September 4, 1941, after Hitler declared the waters off Iceland a danger to Allied and neutral shipping, the U.S. destroyer *Greer*, sailing alone, made contact with and started following a German submarine off Reykjavik. The U-boat fired a couple of warning torpedoes at the *Greer*, which responded with depth charges. Neither ship was damaged in the incident.

A month later, the destroyer *Kearny* was struck by a U-boat torpedo while supporting a British convoy. The explosion killed eleven seamen and injured another twenty-four, but the ship was able to hobble to Iceland unassisted. Two weeks later, a U-boat sank the destroyer *Reuben James* off Ireland, killing all but 45 of the ship's 160-man crew.

FACT

The Battle of the Atlantic raged throughout the entire war, with the Allies the ultimate victors. However, the cost of that victory was tremendous. According to American military records, U-boats sank more than 3,500 merchant ships. Of that total, 2,452 ships were sunk in the Atlantic. U-boats also sank 175 naval warships serving as armed auxiliaries.

Heavy Losses

When the United States and Germany officially declared war on each other, American merchant ships were no longer protected by neutrality and became more frequent targets of German U-boats, particularly off the eastern United States and in the Caribbean. Allied antisubmarine efforts were extremely ineffective during the first months of the war. The first American victory over a U-boat didn't occur until March 1, 1942, when a navy ship sank the *U-656*.

The Battle of the Atlantic slowly escalated, with the Germans inflicting heavy casualties on Allied ships trying to bring much-needed supplies to

England. Just in June 1942, the Allies lost more than 170 ships to German submarines, most of them in the western Atlantic.

The mass production of U-boats continued, and by March 1943 an estimated 400 German submarines were in service, more than 200 of them suitable for ocean patrol. The result was an almost constant harassment of Allied shipping and several major battles between U-boats and convoy defense ships. Many of these battles took a terrible toll on Allied naval defenses. During the first week of March, Convoys SC 121 and HX 229 both lost thirteen ships, HX 228 lost four, and SC 122 lost nine. By the end of the month, German submarines had managed to sink a stunning eighty-two ships in the North Atlantic and another thirty-eight in other waters. The loss of so many supply ships wreaked havoc in England, threatening its very survival. It also prevented the Allies from mounting any kind of major cross-Channel offensive into occupied France.

Technological Advances

Just when all seemed lost, science came to the rescue. Allied ships began using a number of new antisubmarine technologies with remarkable success. The most effective was radar, allowing ships to detect subs in the area and mount a quick defense or, if undetected, launch an attack. In addition, advances in code-breaking technology enabled the Allies to monitor U-boat activity more effectively.

The Battle of the Atlantic ultimately went to the Allies, but the cost on both sides was high in terms of ships, equipment, and lives lost. For Great Britain, the victory at sea was painfully close. Noted Winston Churchill: "The only thing that ever really frightened me was the U-boat peril. I was even more anxious about this battle than I had been about the glorious air fight called the Battle of Britain."

Within just a few months, the tide began to turn in the Battle of the Atlantic. Thanks to the new technology and additional support, the number of Allied ships lost decreased while the number of German submarines sunk skyrocketed. In May 1943, Convoy SC 130 was attacked by more than thirty U-boats over the course of its voyage, but it managed to sink five of them without losing a single ship. After that, Admiral Dönitz pulled his U-boat fleet out of the North Atlantic convoy routes, though he was certain that Germany would be able to counter the new technology with advances of its own in time.

One German countermeasure was the introduction of specially designed torpedoes that homed in on the sound of a ship's propeller, allowing more effective attack from a distance. However, these were soon countered with devices known as Foxers, which acted as decoys and drew enemy torpedoes away from ships.

Figure 4-1 Poster by Ben Shahn.

Photo courtesy of the National Archives (44-PA-246)

This give-and-take continued throughout the Battle of the Atlantic, with one side gaining a slight advantage only to be countered by a new strategy or new technology. For example, when Allied forces started using radar-equipped aircraft to spot surface-cruising U-boats leaving French ports at night, Dönitz had his submarines fitted with antiaircraft guns and ordered them to travel on the surface during the day (when they could spot and shoot down enemy reconnaissance and attack planes). The Allies countered by attacking the submarines with larger, more destructive weapons. Dönitz eventually had his submarines outfitted with snorkels that allowed them to remain relatively submerged almost indefinitely. Dönitz also instituted a plan in which U-boats were provisioned and refueled at sea via special supply subs, though the Allies learned of the plan from broken German codes and quickly went after the supply ships.

The Battle of Britain

Great Britain, lying just a few miles off the coast of France, was extremely vulnerable to German attack, particularly from the air. Hitler was well aware of this and used it to his advantage in the two-month bombing campaign that came to be known as the Battle of Britain. (As a matter of note, though most military historians view October 31 as the formal end of the Battle of Britain, Germany continued its air assault against London through May 1941.)

Technically, Britain's involvement in the war began in 1939 when British leaders realized that Hitler could neither be calmed nor contained. His blitzkrieg invasions of Poland and France confirmed that nothing less than European domination was his ultimate goal—and it quickly became obvious that Great Britain was high on his list.

FACT

American aid to the embattled British started in December 1939 with the founding of the Bundles for Britain campaign, which sent food, clothing, and medical supplies to the British people. The program was started by Natalie Wales Latham and other upperclass New Yorkers, and it quickly spread throughout the United States. Winston Churchill's wife was eventually named honorary sponsor of the charitable program.

Great Britain enacted its first ever peacetime draft in July 1939, requiring all able-bodied twenty-year-old men to sign up for what was supposed to be six months of military training. However, the draftees quickly found themselves involved in an all-out war, and it would be six years before those who survived the conflict could return to civilian life.

A nationwide blackout was imposed across Great Britain on September 1, 1939, the day Hitler invaded Poland. An evacuation of the major cities was also ordered in anticipation of an air attack that failed to materialize. The United Kingdom declared war on Germany two days later, and again, Germany failed to respond with the anticipated air assault.

Britain Braces for the Worst

When war was declared, morale in Great Britain was extremely poor, thanks to a government uneasy over the idea of taking on Hitler. However, morale increased dramatically after Hitler's drive across Luxembourg toward France on May 10, 1940, and the creation that day of a coalition government under Winston Churchill. On May 22, legislation known as the Emergency Powers Act was passed requiring all British citizens to place "themselves, their services, and their property" at the disposal of the government for the conflict that was sure to come.

FACT

On September 24, 1940, British bomber attacks on Berlin forced Joseph Goebbels, the Nazi Party's propaganda chief, to finish his dinner with the Spanish foreign minister and other dignitaries in the air raid shelter of the Adlon Hotel.

Plans for the rapid evacuation of children from obvious target areas and the creation of civil defense measures had been taken care of in 1939, so in 1940 the government concentrated all its efforts on strengthening and maintaining military preparedness. Over the course of the war, virtually everyone in Britain would be called on to serve the nation in one capacity or another.

Operation Sea Lion

Hitler had hoped that Great Britain would be willing to engage in peace talks after the fall of France; but the British government and military were by then well aware that Hitler's word meant nothing, and they refused to negotiate. Hitler's only recourse was a full-scale invasion of the nation, which lay just twenty miles away across the English Channel. The code name for the German invasion was Operation Sea Lion.

Great Britain's greatest defense against a German attack was the Royal Air Force (RAF). Although fewer in number than the Luftwaffe, it was nonetheless skilled, prepared, and ready to take on whatever Hitler sent its way. Germany was also briefly hobbled by the fact that the Luftwaffe was tired and in need of rearming after the earlier invasions. Stores of bombs, fuel, and other supplies needed to be set up in France if the Luftwaffe was to engage in an extended air attack. This gave Great Britain time to bolster its defenses.

While the main German air force readied itself, exploratory flights flew over England and German bombers attacked British ships offshore and laid mines in coastal waters. Great Britain responded quickly, and from July 10 to August 10, 1940, the mighty Luftwaffe lost 227 aircraft to Great Britain's 96. In many cases, RAF pilots whose planes were shot down in battle were able to parachute to safety in Britain, an option unavailable to their German adversaries.

During this period, Great Britain was able to increase the number of fighters at its disposal and, even better, discovered the secret of the German bomber navigation system, which was based on electronic beams sent from the European continent over the bombers' designated targets.

Starting August 13, 1940, code-named Eagle Day by the German military, the Luftwaffe was given six weeks to remove the threat of the RAF from the skies and soften up British ground defenses before Operation Sea Lion was put into action.

FACT

During the Battle of Britain, hundreds of Britons were assigned to patrol the countryside on bicycle to watch for and fight German paratroopers.

As the battle began, the RAF was able to launch slightly more than 900 Spitfire and Hurricane fighters, in addition to 84 older aircraft. Facing them was a German air force of more than 2,800 fighters and bombers divided into three air fleets: Luftflotte 2 in Belgium, the Netherlands, and northern France; Luftflotte 3 in northwestern France; and Luftflotte 5 in Norway and Denmark. Reichsmarschall Hermann Goering was placed in command of the aerial attack by Hitler, who trusted his close friend and confidant to get the job done quickly.

FACT

Once Great Britain declared war on Germany, its people knew that bombing attacks were inevitable. The Blitz, as the sustained nighttime bombing of London and other cities came to be called, began in earnest September 7, 1940, over London. The bombing continued for fifty-seven consecutive days, with subsequent attacks occurring until May 1941. London was devastated by the attacks, but Great Britain prevailed.

Things Go Badly for Germany

Germany's assault got off to a bad start. Waves of German bombers and escort fighters took off on the morning of August 13, unaware that a last-minute report of bad weather had caused Goering to delay the raids until that afternoon. Recall messages were quickly sent, but not all of the escort fighters received them. The RAF, warned by radar, was ready and waiting as the bombers approached, and shot down a considerable number.

At the end of the day, German losses totaled forty-six aircraft, with many more heavily damaged. The RAF lost thirteen fighters in the air and forty-seven planes on the ground, though only one was a fighter plane. Worse for Great Britain, the Luftwaffe had succeeded in destroying one of the radar stations on the Isle of Wight and damaging five others. The loss of the radar stations was a serious blow to the British air defense because the RAF needed them to know when and where German planes were approaching.

The German High Command was unaware of how desperately the British relied on their radar defense or how badly the bombers had damaged it. In fact, on August 15, Goering told the three air fleet commanders: "It is doubtful whether there is any point in continuing the attacks on radar sites, in view of the fact that not one of those attacked has so far been put out of operation."

The RAF Holds Its Ground

The Battle of Britain continued, with German bombers darkening the country's skies almost every day. The first—and last—major daylight attack, by Luftflotte 5 from Norway and Denmark, occurred August 15 when the approaching air fleet was set upon by RAF Hurricanes and Spitfires over Scotland. The Luftwaffe High Command was taken by surprise, having assumed that Great Britain would be too busy defending its western coast to effectively defend Scotland. Eight German bombers and seven fighters were destroyed in the battle, and many German bombers were forced to drop their loads in the water well before their intended targets. None of the RAF fighters was lost.

Germany quickly discovered that many tactics that had worked against Poland and France were ineffective against Great Britain. For example, the Stuka dive-bombers that had inflicted so much damage on an unprepared Poland were easy targets for RAF fighters. Of the eighty-five Stukas thrown at Britain on August 17, a total of twenty-six were shot down and another fourteen were severely damaged. As a result, Goering withdrew the planes from the Battle of Britain two days later.

Despite its successes, the RAF Fighter Command found it difficult to keep up with the German air assault. From August 24 to September 6, an average of 1,000 German bombers and fighters flew over Great Britain each day. The RAF took out a great number of German aircraft and lost far fewer, but the defense was pushing the planes and their pilots to the breaking point. Exhausted pilots fell asleep as soon as their planes hit the tarmac, requiring ground crews to turn off the engines. Pilots napped while their planes were refueled and rearmed. Programs to produce new pilots were hampered by the lack of experienced instructors because all skilled pilots were in the air aiding in the defense of the nation.

The situation became increasingly dire as the battle raged on. British government and military officials knew the Fighter Command couldn't go on much longer. The defense system and the men who maintained it were on the verge of exhaustion. If the daily German raids didn't subside, there would be too few pilots and aircraft to mount an effective defense, and Germany would be free to launch a land invasion.

Germany was having problems of its own. Frustration was setting in as the sustained air attack seemed ineffective against Great Britain. On August 24, Goering decided to try a new strategy: attacking the RAF's sector control stations, which received information provided by radar, plotted the incoming raids, and sent fighters where they were most desperately needed. These stations, manned primarily by members of the RAF Women's Auxiliary Air Force, suddenly became the target of sustained air strikes.

The two-week battle took a huge toll on both sides. The RAF lost 277 fighters defending the target stations, and the Luftwaffe lost 378 aircraft. Of the 1,000-man RAF Fighter Command pilot pool, nearly a quarter were killed or wounded during this stage of the conflict.

FACT

On the night of November 14, 1940, in retaliation for the November 8 RAF bombing of Munich, a flight of nearly 450 German bombers dropped 150,000 incendiary bombs, 503 tons of high explosives, and 130 parachute mines on the city of Coventry, killing 550 people, injuring more than 1,000, and destroying or damaging 50,749 homes.

The Assault on London

The German assault against the sector stations slowly succeeded in impeding the British air defense and almost certainly would have led to a British defeat had the attacks continued. But Goering decided on yet another change in strategy and halted the campaign against the sector stations. His new target: London itself.

The assault on London began on the afternoon of September 7. Explosive and incendiary bombs fell throughout the night, setting much of the city ablaze and sending its residents, most of them civilians, fleeing for whatever safety they could find.

That first day was just a taste of what would come. For fifty-seven consecutive nights, German bombers flew over London. The attack took a heavy toll on the city and its residents but provided some relief to battered radar sector stations and the RAF Fighter Command.

The RAF still had its hands full. Dogfights and interception runs occurred on an almost daily basis. On September 7, the RAF lost forty-one Spitfires and Hurricanes, plus a high-speed bomber known as a Blenheim. The Germans lost sixty-three aircraft in that one-day battle. Many of the air battles were fought at night, with powerful spotlights illuminating approaching German bombers.

Figure 4-2
American bomber over Marienberg, Germany, 1943.

Photo courtesy of the National Archives (208-YE-7)

As the Luftwaffe bombed Great Britain, RAF bombers were doing the same to Germany, with almost daily attacks on Berlin. The targets were munitions factories, gasworks, and railway yards—anything that assisted the German war effort. The bombings, which brought the conflict home for the first time to many Germans, had a serious effect on civilian and military morale.

Germany's air assault on Great Britain continued day and night through October, inflicting heavy damage but never achieving an outright victory. The RAF and the British people proved themselves far tougher than the German High Command had anticipated, and on September 17, Hitler was forced to postpone Operation Sea Lion indefinitely. Great Britain remained a German target for the rest of the war, but Germany was never able to initiate a land invasion.

FACT

Over the course of the Battle of Britain, Great Britain lost 915 fighters in the air and many other aircraft on the ground. The Luftwaffe suffered far more, losing 1,733 aircraft to British fighters and antiaircraft fire.

On August 20, 1940, Winston Churchill acknowledged before the House of Commons the tremendous sacrifices made by RAF pilots, their support crews, and the thousands of others who worked and died to protect their homeland from invasion. As he noted, "Never in the field of human conflict was so much owed by so many to so few."

Germany's Soviet Campaign

The decision to invade the Soviet Union was, in large part, economic. Germany needed the Soviet Union's agricultural resources, manufacturing capability, and oil fields for its own people and intended to enslave the Soviet people for German industry. Although ideology fired a huge part of the recruiting and strengthening of the German armed forces and it was understood by many that the Soviet Union and its Communism would eventually become a target, the invasion, from a military point of view, was more about resources than about government and way of life.

The invasion was originally scheduled to begin on May 15, 1941, in an effort to make as much progress as possible before the harsh Russian winter hit. Many German commanders believed the Soviet Union wouldn't put up much of a fight and that the invasion would take ten weeks at the most. However, Hitler was forced to postpone it until June 22 because Germany had to help Mussolini take Greece and intervene in Yugoslavia when negotiations between that nation and the Soviet Union threatened the southern flank of German operations.

Early Warnings

Thanks to both Soviet and British intelligence, Hitler's plans were known well in advance. But Stalin refused to let his military commanders prepare for a German invasion in the belief that a lack of Soviet provocation would placate Hitler and prevent or at least delay an assault. Stalin's unwillingness to prepare cost his country greatly.

Hitler didn't even try to be subtle as he massed his army at the western borders with the Soviet Union. At 3:00 A.M. on June 22, German troops invaded across a front extending from the Arctic Sea to the Black Sea—a line some 1,500 miles long. As with earlier invasions, the Luftwaffe flew ahead of the ground forces, bombing strategic Soviet airfields and engaging Soviet fighters in combat. More than 400 Soviet planes were shot out of the sky, and twice that number were lost on the ground. Only about 35 German planes were lost during the first day's fighting.

Figure 4-3 A German soldier tosses a grenade during the German invasion of the Soviet Union.

Photo courtesy of the National Archives (242-GAP-286B-4)

The invading force made excellent use of its artillery, softening up the opposing army as it proceeded forward. Interestingly, most of the 7,200 pieces were drawn by horses rather than trucks because they could handle the rocky terrain better and didn't need gasoline. In total, the invasion included 3,350 German tanks, 600,000 other motor vehicles, and 625,000 horses. The Luftwaffe air fleet consisted of 2,770 bombers.

Germans Plow Onward

Germany quickly gained air superiority, and the invaders often found themselves aided by a supportive populace, most notably in the Baltic republics and the Ukraine. (However, atrocities committed by the Germans against the local populations quickly turned Soviet sympathizers against them, resulting in ongoing guerrilla warfare.) Soviet defensive lines were quickly annihilated by the German blitzkrieg, and Minsk fell on June 28, followed by Smolensk on July 10, and Kiev on September 27.

FACT

Germany divided its invasion force into three groups. Army Group North, coming in from Finland and Poland, was assigned the Baltic republics and Leningrad. Army Group Center from East Prussia and Poland was to invade Minsk and Smolensk and then push toward Moscow. And Army Group South, coming in from Czechoslovakia, was to take Ukraine and then move toward the Caucasus. Over 3 million German soldiers took part in the invasion, the largest army ever assembled for a single operation.

One of the longest battles occurred at Leningrad, the Soviet Union's second largest city. Hitler initially wanted to give the city to Finland, which at the time was fighting on Germany's side. But Finland wanted only the border it had before the 1939 Soviet invasion and refused to push farther. Ultimately, Hitler decided to level Leningrad, which he insisted on calling by its former name of St. Petersburg. In a September 29 communiqué to his generals, Hitler said: "The Führer has decided to have St. Petersburg wiped off the face of the earth. The further existence of this large city is of no interest

. . . for the problem of the survival of the population and of supplying it with food is one which cannot and should not be solved by us."

FACT

Russian composer Dmitry Shostakovich wrote his Seventh Symphony during the siege of Leningrad, where he worked as an air raid warden. Shostakovich was later evacuated to perform the work in Moscow.

Leningrad Surrounded

German forces surrounded nearly all of Leningrad in August 1941 and immediately severed its rail link with Moscow. When an assault on the city failed, German forces laid siege, bombarding the city of 3 million with artillery and aircraft. Food quickly grew scarce, and people starved by the thousands. The only supplies came from Novaya Ladoga across Lake Ladoga, a sixteen-hour voyage by barge. Supplies arrived at the port city of Osinovets and were transported by rail to Leningrad. The barges were easy targets for German bombers (twenty-four were sunk during the first two months of the siege), and the food that arrived could feed only a small percentage of those who needed it. Soviet naval forces used the route to evacuate nearly half a million refugees, though thousands stayed behind to defend the former Russian capital.

During the siege of Leningrad, supplies for the starving city were brought through the winter by truck from Novaya Ladoga across frozen Lake Ladoga. German bombers, fissures in the ice, and blizzards were constant dangers. More than 1,000 vehicles were lost crossing the lake, but the supply line never closed.

Soviet soldiers in Leningrad fought the Nazis with all they had, desperate to break the siege and turn their defense into an offense. However, they were unable to breach the German lines and open supply routes until January 1943. By then, hundreds of thousands of people had died of starvation or from the constant German bombardment.

The Battle of Moscow

Equally important was the battle of Moscow, code-named Operation Typhoon, which began October 2, 1941. The Germans made great strides during the early days of the battle, taking 650,000 prisoners, and by mid-October were just 60 miles from the city. But again, the delay of the initial invasion hampered German progress.

The night of October 6, 1941, snow began to fall. It melted the next morning, turning the roads into muddy bogs that slowed the German military advance as heavy equipment sank axle-deep in muck. Moscow, once so close, now seemed a long way off. German commanders asked Berlin for winter clothing, just in case the invasion took longer than originally believed.

The weather wasn't the only thing that adversely affected the German invasion of Moscow. On October 10, Marshal S. K. Timoshenko was relieved as commander of the western strategic sector by Marshal Georgi Zhukov. The Germans saw little importance in this move, but Zhukov was a skilled strategist who had organized the defense of Leningrad. He had arrived to save Moscow.

Zhukov based his defensive strategy on the one factor the German invaders had not counted on: the Soviet Union's muddy, almost impassible roads, and the impending Russian winter. The first sign of winter came on November 6 when temperatures fell below freezing and stayed there. The Germans, initially pleased with the cold temperature because it would freeze the mud, soon found themselves at its mercy because of a lack of cold-weather clothing, portable heaters, and winterizing machinery lubricants.

Still, the Germans attempted to press on toward Moscow. On November 30, combat engineers came within 10 miles of the city, though the main combat force was 50 miles behind them. The Germans were attacked by Soviet tanks and cavalry, which were able to traverse the frozen roads quite well. On December 4, the Germans realized that they simply could not compete with the vicious Russian winter and initiated a pullback from Moscow. It was the Russian cold that had also halted Napoleon's invasion of Russia in 1812.

Hitler, against the advice of his military advisers, ordered the army to make one last push into Moscow. His goal was the destruction of the Kremlin as proof to the Soviet people that Communism was dead. The attack was launched on December 7 amid a growing snowstorm and winter darkness. A handful of infantry managed to make it to the outskirts of the city but were driven back by Soviet soldiers assisted by workers armed with hammers, clubs, and whatever else they could find. By the time Hitler authorized a pullback, the temperatures had dropped to twenty-eight degrees below zero. Moscow was saved.

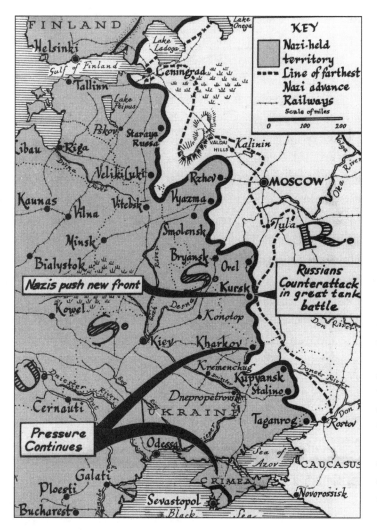

Map 4-1 German attack and Russian counter-attack at Kursk, the site of the greatest tank battle in history.

Map courtesy of the National Archives (U.S.S.R., RG 160, Vol. 1, No. 11)

Other German-Soviet Fronts

Germany's Soviet offensive continued on a number of other fronts, with the Germans winning strategic victories the next summer in Ukraine, at Sevastopol in the Crimea, and elsewhere.

By November 1942, German forces were on the verge of taking Stalingrad, one of the nation's largest industrial cities and the gateway to the Soviet oil fields. General Friedrich Paulus, commander of the Sixth Army, was given the job of bringing the city under German control, a task that proved more difficult than anticipated.

Paulus and his army started the attack August 21 and quickly fought their way to the city's outskirts, where they faced extremely heavy fighting. Paulus laid siege to Stalingrad on September 12. Throughout the long siege, the Germans used bombers and artillery to destroy as much of the city as possible, but the defending Soviets under General Vasily Chuikov refused to give up. Eventually, the Germans were reduced to fighting building to building in an attempt to rout the entrenched Soviet soldiers.

Then General Zhukov implemented a counterattack that started with a Soviet assault within the city on November 19 while additional Soviet forces surrounded the German army at Kalach. When the Soviet pincers closed, the Sixth Army and much of the Fourth Panzer Army were trapped. General Paulus probably could have broken out early in the counterattack but was ordered by Hitler to defend his position at Stalingrad based on assurances that the Luftwaffe would be able to deliver plenty of supplies and reinforcements to the trapped army of nearly 284,000 men.

It quickly became apparent that Goering had dramatically overstated the Luftwaffe's capabilities. In fact, it was physically impossible for the German air force to deliver sufficient supplies to the trapped forces; on its best days, it was able to drop just eighty tons of food and equipment—far less than what was needed.

Paulus's men fought with all they had, but the Soviet squeeze grew tighter by the day and the German force was quickly decimated by the cold and the lack of food and supplies. Wounded soldiers had their rations slashed or eliminated so available food could be used to feed those able to fight. On January 22, Paulus sent a radio message to Hitler: "Rations exhausted. Over 12,000 unattended wounded in pocket. What orders should I give to troops who have no more ammunition and are subjected to mass attacks supported by heavy artillery?"

Hitler's response: "Surrender is out of the question. The troops will defend themselves to the last."

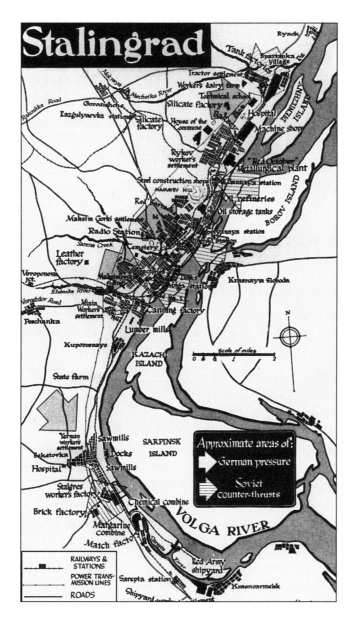

Map 4-2 German and Soviet offensives in Stalingrad.

Map courtesy of the National Archives (Stalingrad, RG 160, Vol. 1, No. 27)

German Army Suffers Heavy Losses

The Germans continued to fight, but the battle was all but over as Russian forces closed in. Paulus, who was promoted to field marshal by Hitler on January 30, surrendered his headquarters on January 31, becoming the first German field marshal to do so. Sporadic fighting by German troops continued around Stalingrad until February 2, 1943.

The Battle of Stalingrad took a tremendous toll on the German military machine, as did the entire Soviet offensive. More than 140,000 German soldiers lost their lives at Stalingrad, with another 91,000 taken prisoner. Germany also lost a huge number of planes and other equipment—material it could ill afford to lose at that point in the war.

Having spent so much time defending itself against Germany, the Soviet Union was now poised to launch a major offensive.

The Italian Campaign

The two-year Italian campaign resulted from a May 1943 meeting in which Winston Churchill and Franklin Roosevelt discussed the most effective way to get Italy out of the war and at the same time provoke the Germans into battle there so their forces in France would be weakened before the Normandy invasion, which had been scheduled for May 1944.

It was also hoped that a victory in Italy would hurt the morale of the other Axis nations and give the Allies air bases in Italy to accelerate the air war against German-held territories.

The Taking of Sicily

The first goal of the Italian campaign was the conquest of Sicily, the largest island in the Mediterranean Sea, which was made possible by the Allies' victories in North Africa (discussed in Chapter 5). General Dwight Eisenhower, who had commanded the Allied invasion of North Africa, was made Supreme Allied Commander in charge of the Sicily invasion.

The invasion took thirty-eight days and started with an amphibious landing on July 10, 1943. The Seventh Army under General George S. Patton landed in the Gulf of Tela, and the British Eighth Army under General

Bernard Montgomery landed south of Syracuse. Even though Axis forces in Sicily totaled more than 400,000, the Allied landings, which were accompanied by air and naval support, met very little resistance.

The airborne phase of the Sicily invasion was a disaster for the Allies. American and British paratroopers dropped on the eve of the invasion suffered heavy losses as a result of harsh winds, friendly fire from Allied antiaircraft fire, and poorly trained troop transport pilots. In all, American paratroopers suffered 27 percent casualties and British paratroopers 23 percent.

FACT

German Tiger tanks attacked a unit near the beachhead, but the U.S. destroyer *Cowie* made short work of them with its powerful five-inch guns. It was the first destroyer versus tank "battle" in military history.

The land invasion fared better. Patton's army cut through Axis defenses on its way to Palermo on the island's northern coast, though Montgomery's forces, after taking Syracuse, were slowed at Catania by difficult terrain and stronger-than-anticipated opposition by German forces. Montgomery's objective was Messina, the coastal town that would be the launching point for the invasion of the Italian mainland. He reached it on August 17, nearly a month after Patton reached Palermo. Because of the delay, Axis forces were able to withdraw across the Strait of Messina.

Mussolini Deposed, Bailed Out by Hitler

Shortly after the Allied invasion of Sicily, Fascist leaders in Italy called a conference with Mussolini, who was instructed to appear before the Fascist Grand Council. Mussolini tried desperately to salvage his political career with blustery oratory but was deposed by a council vote of nineteen to eight, with one abstention. Mussolini was quickly arrested and, on order of King Victor Emmanuel III, replaced by Marshal Pietro Badoglio, chief of the Italian General Staff. However, Mussolini still wasn't out of the picture. While under arrest, he was rescued in a daring raid by German commandos and set up by Hitler as head of a puppet state in northern Italy known as the Italian Social Republic.

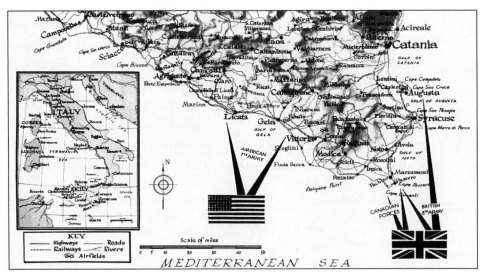

Map 4-3 The invasion of Sicily by U.S., Canadian, and British forces on July 9 and 10, 1943.

Map courtesy of the National Archives (Invasion of Sicily, RG 160, Vol. 2, No. 13)

Secret Surrender?

The capture of Sicily sent shockwaves through Italy, and Italian military and government officials soon engaged the Allies in secret surrender negotiations in Lisbon, Portugal. Brigadier General Walter Bedell Smith, Eisenhower's chief of staff, represented the United States, and Major General Kenneth Strong represented Great Britain. The men carried with them special "short terms" documents for Italy's surrender, while the U.S. State Department and the British Foreign Office drafted the "long terms" agreement stipulating the Allied war aim of unconditional surrender. The surrender documents were signed on September 3, 1943, and Italy was taken out of the war.

While the surrender was in the works, the Allies prepared for the invasion of Italy. On September 3, the British Eighth Army crossed the Strait of Messina and landed on the Calabrian coast. Italian resistance was minimal.

General Mark Clark's Fifth Army landed at Salerno on September 9. At the same time, British forces landed at Taranto, moving swiftly to take Bari and Brindisi. Fearing German reprisals, Marshal Pietro Badoglio, the new head of the Italian government, and King Victor Emmanuel III fled Rome and established a provisional capital in Brindisi.

Clark's Fifth Army met an extremely strong German defense and was nearly driven back to the sea. However, the day was saved when Allied forces in the air, at sea, and on the ground successfully secured the beachhead. Within a few days, nearly 190,000 troops, 100,000 tons of supplies, and 30,000 vehicles arrived for the scheduled push up the Italian peninsula.

While troops and equipment were being amassed in Salerno, British forces pressed northward, pushing the Germans into retreat. Capri and other islands in the Bay of Naples surrendered as the Allied invasion continued, and on October 1, the Fifth Army marched into Naples, where the harbor, badly damaged in the fighting, was quickly put back into commission.

The Gustav Line

The Germans had been working frantically to create a series of strong defensive lines across Italy from coast to coast, and the Allies ran into the first of them—the Gustav line—in early November. Suddenly, the easy capture of Italy became extremely difficult. Stalled by the rocky terrain, winter weather, and well-entrenched German defenses, the Allies tried a different strategy: an amphibious landing at Anzio to harass the German flank while additional forces pressed the Gustav line.

The landing at Anzio was met with a blistering response by the Germans, who pinned down Allied troops with vicious artillery fire. Meanwhile, General Field Marshal Albrecht Kesselring, a skilled battle strategist, thwarted the Allied offensive plan calling for Clark to break through the Gustav line by crossing the Garigliano and Rapido rivers and moving up the Liri Valley to Rome. At the same time, French and British forces were supposed to feint momentarily, then strike at the center of the German line.

Once the German defense at Anzio was destroyed, Clark's army headed east, then turned to take Rome. Clark's army liberated Rome on June 4, 1944. The entire campaign had taken 275 days and cost the Fifth Army nearly 125,000 men, including more than 20,300 dead.

The plan was intended to throw Kesselring off balance as he tried to determine which threat to address first, thus allowing both the Anzio and river-crossing operations to move forward. But Kesselring anticipated the plan and set up formidable defenses. As a result, Clark's crossing at the Rapido was a total disaster, resulting in high casualties.

Fighting continued at Anzio, in the Liri Valley, and around Monte Cassino, which was a Gustav line stronghold, for months. In May 1944, an offensive finally pierced the German defensive line. Combined Allied forces were able to break through at Anzio, and French troops pushed through the supposedly impassable mountains. After a hard-fought battle and the loss of many men, members of the Polish Corps planted the Polish flag on Monte Cassino. Allied forces from around the world had joined hands to help break the German defense.

Italy Falls

Despite a series of setbacks in Italy, the Germans weren't ready to call it quits. Retreating north from Rome after tremendous Allied gains, German forces made a stand at Florence, only to be knocked back on August 4, 1944, by advance units from a South African armored division. From there, the Germans dug in at the Gothic line, which stretched from above Leghorn to the Adriatic Sea. An Allied offensive led by the U.S. and British armies started on September 10 and quickly sent the Germans into another retreat.

By then, the German army was being attacked on two additional fronts: across northern France after the Normandy invasion and in southern France, which Allied forces had stormed on August 15.

German forces continued to fight through the fall and winter of 1944, establishing a number of defensive positions in Northern Italy. In April 1945, the Eighth Army pressed through west of Ravenna and the Fifth Army fought its way up the Po Valley, often engaging the enemy in brutal hand-to-hand fighting.

On April 17, 1945, *Il Duce* was kidnapped by Italian guerrillas and was executed the next day, along with his lover and a handful of political supporters. All remaining German troops in Italy surrendered to the Allies on April 28, bringing the war in Italy to an end.

The Normandy Invasion

Few battles of World War II are as enduring in the American public consciousness as the Allied invasion of Normandy on June 6, 1944, an event known to most people as D-Day. This assault—the largest amphibious landing in military history—was of paramount importance to the Allies. If successful, it would mean the liberation of France, which had been held under Germany's iron fist for four years, and the Allies' best chance to push Hitler's weakened army all the way back to Berlin. If it failed, it would give Germany at least one more year to bolster its flagging military force, drive off the Soviet offensive on the eastern front, and perfect a number of secret weapons, including V1 and V2 rockets, more powerful intercontinental ballistic missiles, and transcontinental aircraft.

Figure 4-4 U.S. Marines on Peleliu Island, September 14, 1944.

Photo courtesy of the National Archives (127-N-97628)

When and where to invade German-occupied France was not a spur-of-the-moment decision. Indeed, plans for the invasion had been discussed by the Americans and the British since early 1942, but strategic weaknesses and military infighting forced several postponements in favor of a Mediterranean strategy. At the Quebec Conference in August 1943, the British agreed to name an American as the commander of the D-Day invasion, and in December, Eisenhower was named Supreme Allied Commander. His first move was to direct British General Bernard Montgomery to prepare detailed invasion plans and act as commander of the invasion ground forces.

When the Normandy invasion was being planned, military leaders wanted to train the men using live ammunition. Finding enough space to do this in England proved difficult. The problem was solved with the acquisition of twenty-five square miles in south Devon, in a coastal area known as Slapton Sands. All 3,000 residents of the area were evacuated.

Time, Place Chosen

In March 1943, the Allies had decided to invade in Normandy. The region was right because it was within fighter cover of British airfields and, perhaps more important, was considered a less likely site than Calais. It was important that the Germans remain confused about the actual invasion site, so elaborate plans were enacted to make them think Calais was the true target, including the creation of the fictional First U.S. Army Group and the placement of a fleet of unseaworthy landing craft in British ports across from Calais. Adding credence to the hoax was the appointment of General George Patton, one of the most successful and recognizable leaders of the war, as commander of the First U.S. Army Group. The ruse worked: Germany, certain that the high-profile Patton would be in charge of the invasion, kept its Fifteenth Army in the Calais area in the belief that it was to be the real invasion site.

The assembled invasion force consisted of more than 1.5 million troops: 620,500 men of the ground forces in twenty-one divisions plus support troops. The invasion fleet had more than 4,400 ships and landing craft to carry 154,000 troops (50,000 of them were the assault forces who would first storm the beaches) and 1,500 tanks. Accompanying the fleet were 11,000 fighters, bombers, transport planes, and gliders. On the other side were an estimated sixty German divisions. It was a formidable defense, and many in the German High Command thought it was invincible.

The date of the Normandy invasion was based on a number of factors, including the tides (which would have to be low when the invasion force struck), the weather (minimal winds to reduce choppy seas), and the light (moonlight was important on the eve of the invasion, and enough early morning sunlight was needed at the moment the assault was to begin). Based on these and other factors, the best time to invade was determined to be from early May to early June. June 5 was the set date, but bad weather forced Eisenhower to postpone the event twenty-four hours. It was a crucial decision: If the Germans were to discover at the last minute what was happening, the additional day would give them time to bolster coastal defenses at the invasion point. The weather report for June 6 wasn't perfect, but Eisenhower was set against postponing the invasion again.

Air Preparations

The assault troops leading the invasion—Operation Overlord—were scheduled to land at 6:30 A.M. on June 6. A few hours after midnight, one British and two American pathfinder airborne divisions were dropped by transport aircraft into the French countryside behind German lines. On landing, the men were to mark out drop zones for paratrooper battalions that were to secure the flanks of the Allied amphibious lodgment area and hold the bridges, railroad lines, roads, and airfields needed for the Allies' planned inland advance.

Only one American soldier was executed for desertion during World War II, a private named Eddie Slovik, who was assigned to G Company, 109th Infantry Regiment, 28th Infantry Division. He was tried and convicted of desertion on November 11, 1944, and later executed by firing squad on January 31, 1945.

An hour later, soldiers of the American 101st Airborne Division and 82nd Airborne Division jumped out over the Cotentin Peninsula to secure the exits from the westernmost American beach. As the same time, paratroopers of the British 6th Airborne Division dropped on the eastern flank to capture the crossings over the River Orne and the Canal de Caen. The extremely valuable "Pegasus Bridge" over the canal and the Orne had previously been captured by a special force from the 6th Airborne Division, which had come in with the pathfinders via glider.

It was feared that the airborne divisions would experience heavy casualties as they landed behind enemy lines. But the drop went remarkably well, though some of the American parachute battalions became disoriented dropping at night over unfamiliar territory and ended up widely scattered. As a result, all future Allied airborne operations were conducted during the day.

A little under two hours after the paratroopers hit their targets, nearly 2,000 Allied heavy and medium bombers began preliminary bombing of the German defenses along the invasion area. Fifteen minutes before the landing craft carrying troops reached the beaches, there was a second attack by 1,000 American heavy bombers on the German main line of resistance. At 6:30, supported by one last attack by rocket-firing assault craft, the first American troops began to land.

The Amphibious Assault

American forces landed on two western beaches code-named Utah and Omaha. British and Canadian troops landed farther east on beaches nicknamed Gold, Juno, and Sword. General Montgomery was overall commander of the ground forces, with Lieutenant General Omar Bradley commanding the American First Army during the landing and General Miles Dempsey leading the British Second Army.

Despite the heavy bombardment from air and sea, the Germans remained well entrenched in many areas and fired on the Allied invaders the moment they hit the beach. Germans at Omaha Beach were relatively unscathed by the Allied shelling, and American casualties there were especially high—nearly 2,000 compared with only 210 on Utah Beach.

The landing at Omaha got off to a poor start when two amphibious landing craft sank after striking mines. The bad weather resulted in higher tides, and submerged obstacles were more of a threat than had been anticipated. Many of the landing craft were swamped by high waves as they approached the shore or were lost to obstacles or enemy fire. The soldiers, some of them ill from the pitching of the tiny amphibious landing craft, were easy targets as they exited the craft, many of them shot dead before they were out of the water. German machine guns mowed down the wet soldiers by the dozens. Enemy fire kept the landing forces pinned down on Omaha Beach until finally giving ground in the early afternoon.

The bombing had accomplished its job better a little more to the east, where British and Canadian troops met far less resistance and suffered far fewer casualties. The British Third Division defeated a counterattack by a Panzer tank battalion northwest of Caen.

The German Defense

The Germans' initial reaction to the Allied landing was one of confusion and poor coordination, primarily the result of their top-heavy command system. Field Marshal Erwin Rommel, overall commander of German troops in the area, wasn't even at the scene when the invasion started; he had returned home to Germany for his wife's birthday party, leaving his chief of staff to oversee Army Group B. General Friedrich Dollman, commander of the Seventh Army, was also away from headquarters, attending a practice war game in Rennes, while Obergruppenführer "Sepp" Dietrich, commander of the I SS Panzer Corps, was in Brussels.

All the commanders rushed back immediately after being notified of the invasion. During the early hours of D-Day, before the first Allied ground troops had reached the shore, Field Marshal Gerd von Rundstedt responded to reports of the invasion by ordering both of Dietrich's divisions to move toward the Normandy beaches, then sought confirmation for the order from the High Command. It took Hitler several hours to respond, though the delay probably had little effect on the course of the battle because any movement at all resulted in sizable losses by Allied air attacks. One Panzer division lost five tanks, eighty-four armored vehicles, and 130 other vehicles during the ninety-mile trek from Lisieux to Caen.

The Germans put up as strong a defense as they could under the circumstances. Rommel continued his strategy of holding the Allies to their initial landing area by a static defense that yielded as little ground as possible. Such a defense helped reduce the effect of Allied air power and left open the possibility of an armored counterattack onto the beaches.

However, Rommel's choices became limited after a June 11 directive from Hitler forbidding any withdrawal.

QUESTION?

How many people died in Normandy?
Approximately 15,000 Allied soldiers were killed or wounded during the first day. German losses were approximately the same. According to a report by Field Marshal Erwin Rommel, an instrumental part of the German defense command, his casualties for that month were 28 generals, 354 commanders, and approximately 250,000 men.

Indeed, Hitler became his commanders' worst enemy by wresting control from them and attempting to direct the German defense from his command post at Rastenburg some 600 miles away. On June 16, he issued a directive adding an additional Panzer division to the two already being sent to reinforce the Normandy defense and begin a counteroffensive, and ordered all troops to hold their present positions. Rommel and Rundstedt, however, knew from the previous week and a half that any divisions sent to Normandy would arrive late and with insufficient supplies and that they would likely be eliminated by Allied firepower.

Allied Forces Gain Control

Allied forces were hampered by the nature of the land in Normandy, an area covered with farmland and high hedgerows that looked like a checkerboard from the air. This greatly restricted visibility. In addition, coordination of firepower was made difficult by the fact that forward observers often had little idea where they were. In fact, one Royal Artillery observer solved the problem by calling in a strike on what he believed to be his own position, then noting where the shells actually fell.

By dusk on June 7, the Allied forces had become well entrenched, and the chances of a German counteroffensive strong enough to push them back to the water were reduced to almost zero. The Allied forces had linked up to create a formidable front, and the push through France was set to begin very shortly.

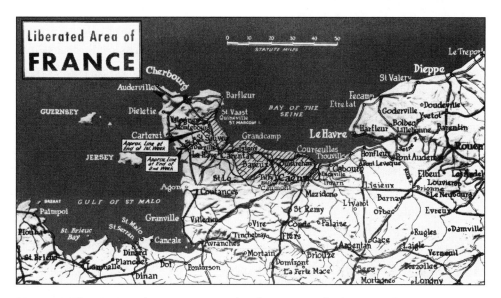

Map 4-4 The Normandy coast two weeks after D-Day. The horizontal stripes indicate the areas liberated by the Allies.

Map courtesy of the National Archives (RG 160, Vol. 3, No. 10F)

By the end of the first day of the invasion, nearly 150,000 Allied troops, vehicles, and support equipment had been unloaded on the beaches of Normandy. Within a week, the invasion force would number nearly 500,000, and by late July, the number would skyrocket to nearly 2 million troops and a quarter of a million vehicles. The Allies had succeeded in capturing the French coast and were poised to liberate the country and push on toward Berlin.

After Normandy

Plenty of obstacles remained in the path of the advancing Allied armies, however. In a series of offensives aimed at crossing the Rhine River and entering into the German command center, the Allies conducted risky maneuvers and determined advances, with sometimes mixed results. British general Montgomery was instrumental in launching Operation Market Garden, a daring series of airborne and land-based operations designed to secure strategic locations along the Rhine, including a handful of important bridges. The eight-day offensive achieved some temporary gains, but resulted in the destruction of the British First Airborne.

Meanwhile, Allied soldiers were advancing along Germany's stolid Siegfried line, probing for weaknesses and overall pressing their advantage. The Belgian port of Antwerp was liberated on September 4. The German city of Aachen, a tremendously important city to Hitler because of its connections to Charlemagne and the First Reich, was taken after a furious battle that claimed more than 10,000 lives in total.

Allied forces eventually overwhelmed many positions along the Rhine River, further encircling German forces. Some of the heaviest fighting took place in the Ardennes Forest, site of one of the war's fiercest counterattacks.

The Battle of the Bulge

The Battle of the Bulge in December 1944 was the last German offensive of the war. Named after a bulge in the Allied line created by an unexpected German offensive, it was a vicious battle and extremely costly in terms of U.S. casualties. The battle was the largest fought on the western front and the largest ever fought by the U.S. Army. More than 600,000 American soldiers took part; nearly 20,000 were killed, another 20,000 were captured, and an estimated 40,000 were wounded.

The battle began on December 16, when fourteen German infantry divisions, backed by five Panzer divisions, broke through an Allied line stretching between Monschau, Germany, and Echternach, Luxembourg. The troops and equipment had been secretly concentrated in the Eifel region and included captured U.S. tanks and vehicles, which the Germans rightly assumed would confuse the American defenders.

On the day of the attack, the region was blanketed in thick fog, which effectively hid the German invaders until the very last minute. The fog also prevented Allied planes from bombing the German columns that filled the roads leading west.

Eisenhower immediately ordered reinforcements to the breakthrough point and started looking for signs of more dramatic German movement based on intelligence reports of twenty-four German divisions in the Ardennes. The size of the German assault baffled everyone, because it was commonly believed that Germany lacked both manpower and equipment.

FACT

The sad fact of the German attack, historians would later learn, was that the majority of the soldiers were teenage boys, many of them younger than sixteen. Lacking experienced fighting men, the German High Command had conscripted anyone strong enough to hold a gun.

The American Defensive

The use of American military equipment and English-speaking German soldiers wearing American uniforms and dog tags was conceived by Otto Skorzeny, a German officer who specialized in commando operations. As anticipated, the plan threw U.S. soldiers into a panic—suddenly, no one in an American uniform could be trusted.

American units, many of them facing much stronger German forces, fought the enemy with everything at their disposal. In one battle, Americans—outnumbered five to one—managed to turn the Germans southward. Slowly, hour by hour, the initial 50-mile bulge began to shrink.

The Fight for Bastogne

But the German offensive was far from over. One of its primary objectives was the Belgian town of Bastogne, which both the Germans and the Allies saw as an extremely important junction; whoever controlled it held access to France. Eisenhower ordered the U.S. 101st Airborne Division to Bastogne and the 82nd Airborne Division to Saint-Vith on the northern end of the bulge.

German forces surrounded and laid siege to Bastogne shortly after the U.S. airborne troops reached the town. Eisenhower had a gut feeling that the German offensive was beginning to weaken and wanted a counterattack that focused on Bastogne. He called General Patton, whose Third Army was along the Moselle River, readied for a long-planned attack, and asked how long it would take him to move his force of 250,000 men and their equipment to the beleaguered town. "Forty-eight hours," Patton said confidently. What he didn't reveal to Eisenhower was that he had already worked out the plans for the difficult maneuver and was simply awaiting orders to put it into effect.

In Bastogne, Brigadier General Anthony McAuliffe, acting commander of the 101st, was ordered to surrender by the commanders of the German army that surrounded the town. McAuliffe's now legendary response: "Nuts!" When the Germans asked the American officer who delivered the reply what it meant, he told them, "It means, go to hell!"

Allies on the Verge of Victory

Reinforcements eventually arrived, in the form of British and American troops. The Battle of the Bulge ended with the German withdrawal after January 7, 1945.

FACT

The Battle of the Bulge resulted in more than 30,000 Germans killed, 40,000 wounded, and 30,000 taken prisoner. The Third Reich, reduced to using children to fight its battles, was on the brink of collapse.

After the repulse of the Bulge, Allied forces drove on toward Berlin. Crossings of the Rhine were a bit easier after the German defeat in the Ardennes, although the German soldiers' defense of their homeland was fierce. The U.S. First and Ninth Armies encircled the strategic Ruhr area, while British forces crossed the Elbe River and moved northeast, toward Hamburg, Denmark, and the Baltic Sea. The American encirclement resulted in the surrender by German Field Marshal Walther Model of more than 300,000 troops. With these POWs secure, the American armies moved east, meeting up with Soviet troops on April 26.

The Soviet Offensive

The Battle of Stalingrad was a major turning point in the war in Europe. The German defeat proved that Hitler's army was not unstoppable. It also proved that Hitler was a flawed military leader. His adamant refusal to let his commanders retreat when strategically wise cost him hundreds of thousands of able soldiers and untold amounts of weaponry and other equipment.

Another important factor in Germany's inability to conquer the Soviet Union was the tactical skill of the Soviet military leaders, particularly Generals Chuikov and Zhukov. Though often outnumbered, they knew how to make the best use of everything available to them, including the weather and ground conditions. They were also adept at maintaining the fighting spirit of the men who served under them.

The Soviet offensive began just as the German offensive was ending. In July 1943, as German and Soviet tank battalions duked it out in the Soviet city of Kursk, the Red Army began its offensive. The first attack occurred at the German-held town of Orel on July 12. By August 6, the Soviets had retaken the town and destroyed 1,500 German tanks in the process. On August 3, General Zhukov launched an offensive against the German line at Kharkov, south of Kursk. Three weeks later, the city was again under Soviet control, with Germany losing another 1,500 tanks. Smolensk was recaptured on September 25 and Kiev on November 6. Within just a few months, most of Germany's victories in the Soviet Union had been reversed.

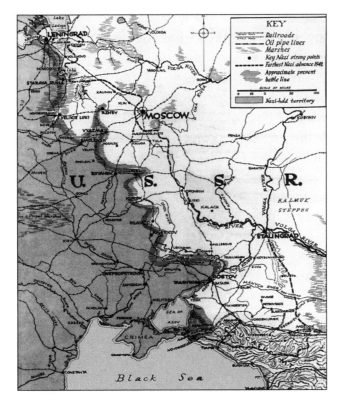

Map 4-5 The Soviet counteroffensive against Germany just after the Soviets took back Kursk on February 8, 1943. This was the turning point of the Russian campaign.

Map courtesy of the National Archives (U.S.S.R., RG 160, Vol. 1, No. 43)

In January 1944, the Red Army succeeded in establishing a rail line into Leningrad, a move that would help break the lengthy siege and push back the German line. In the south, Soviet forces pushed to remove the Germans from the Ukraine with a major offensive in February. And a third offensive along the coast of the Black Sea allowed the Soviets to retake Odessa and Sevastopol in May. The German army, once so close to a victory over the Soviets, was now on the run.

In June 1943, Soviet troops broke through the German-Finnish defensive line and managed to push the invaders back to the Finnish border. The Soviets were quick to take advantage of their military successes, driving into Estonia and Latvia toward Poland, and southwest into Hungary and Romania. On August 31, 1944, Bucharest came under Soviet control.

Red Army Reaches Poland

The push into Poland brought the Red Army to within striking distance of Warsaw, but Soviet military leaders stopped short of the city to resupply and let their exhausted troops rest a bit. The halt was also a political move—Stalin wanted the 60,000 Polish freedom fighters in the city to be crushed by the Germans to facilitate creation of a Communist government in Poland when the war was finally over.

The Red Army was a liberating force within its own borders but a conquering army elsewhere. The Soviets were intent on punishing all who had aided the Nazi force that wreaked so much havoc on their homeland. When they entered East Prussia, Soviet military officials ordered all males between the ages of ten and seventy to be rounded up. Those identified as Nazi officials were executed on the spot. The rest were used to remove mines and tank traps, then shipped off to the Soviet Union to be used as slave labor. Thousands of others in the region were subjected to beatings, rape, and other atrocities.

Indeed, as the Soviet force pushed farther into German territory, its anger seemed to grow. Soviet soldiers stole everything that could be carried away, including furniture, plumbing, and even electrical wiring. Livestock was especially prized, with animals that weren't eaten by the troops shipped through Poland back to the Soviet Union.

Hitler's directives did little to protect his country. Cities became fortresses to be defended by whatever means necessary, with very little regard for the civilian population. In many cases, Hitler and his commanders gave cities no warning of advancing Soviet troops so that the residents could flee. Millions died on the streets and roads of Germany as victims of Soviet artillery and air raids.

By April 1945, the Red Army was poised to take Berlin. On April 16, more than 20,000 Soviet guns positioned along the Oder River opened fire on German troops. The Oder was the last river before Berlin.

The Fall of Berlin

The Soviet army amassed a huge force on three fronts. To the north was the Second Belorussian Front commanded by Marshal K. K. Rokossovsky, in the center was the First Belorussian Front commanded by Vasily Zhukov, and to the south was the First Ukrainian Front under Marshal I. S. Konev. On April 1, the lineup changed slightly when the First Belorussian Front was given to General V. D. Sokolovsky in order to let Zhukov take command of the overall assault on the German capital. The Eighth Guards Army was selected to lead the attack.

Map 4-6 German advances over a one-year (thirteen-month) period, from June 22, 1941, to July 17, 1942.

Map courtesy of the National Archives (The Russian Front, RG 160, Vol. 1, No. 13)

The Soviet military machine facing Berlin was overwhelming. The three fronts totaled 193 divisions, more than 2.5 million soldiers (both men and women), 6,250 tanks, more than 41,000 mortars and other artillery, more than 3,000 multiple rocket launchers, and 7,500 bombers and fighters.

Berlin's defense was far less than what Hitler would have had his countrymen believe. Facing the Soviets were approximately eighty-five divisions totaling around 1 million soldiers, many of them exhausted, starving, and horribly ill prepared for the battle in which they were about to engage. The Germans also had about 10,000 mortars and other artillery pieces, 1,500 tanks, and a few hundred aircraft.

The Red Army quickly crossed the Oder River and on April 18 broke through the German defensive line 20 miles east of Berlin. Hitler decided to stay in the city, confident that his presence would help rally his troops to victory. Just to be safe, however, he ordered several German ministries to move out of the capital.

The Soviets bombed Berlin without mercy, advancing closer every day. By April 24, Soviet artillery had encircled Berlin, and troops moved in for what they expected to be vicious hand-to-hand combat with the German defenders. On April 25, as Soviet troops began their final assault on Berlin, troops from the U.S. First Army and the Soviet Fifth Guards Tank Army met up at Torgau on the Elbe River.

On April 30, Adolf Hitler committed suicide. After disposing of his body, his surviving generals sought out Soviet military leaders to discuss the surrender of Berlin, which became official on May 2.

Chapter 5

North Africa

The three-year North Africa–Middle East Campaign (1940–1943) was the Allied effort to prevent Italy and Germany from taking control of that very strategic part of the world. Axis control of the region would pose a tremendous threat to a great many Allied nations. The campaign began with Great Britain taking on Italy and then Germany, when Hitler decided to come to Mussolini's aid. Field Marshal Erwin Rommel—the North African theater's fabled "Desert Fox"— would quickly prove himself one of the Allies' greatest adversaries.

Egypt

Great Britain began the first phase of the North African campaign shortly after Italy declared war on June 10, 1940. General Archibald Wavell, commander in chief of British forces in the Middle East, felt it necessary to prove to Mussolini that the Allies were not about to let any Axis aggression go unchecked. Wavell sent a couple of armored vehicles from British-controlled Egypt to the Italian colony of Cyrenaica in Libya. After smashing through the barbed wire fence erected by the Italians, the British force paraded around two Italian forts, then crossed the border back into Egypt. The action was the beginning of a fight that would go on almost to the end of the war.

FACT

Mussolini showed little concern for the British presence in Egypt. His forces in the region greatly outnumbered those of the British, and he believed that the British posed little threat to what he saw as the start of the new Roman Empire.

On August 4, Mussolini ordered his forces to invade British Somaliland, southeast of Egypt. The British, greatly outnumbered, quickly withdrew from the territory, and on August 17 the Italian forces took the colony's capital, Berbera. The move had dire potential consequences for the British; if the United States, still neutral at the time, were to declare the Red Sea unsafe because of the Italian presence, it could cut off an important British supply line.

While Great Britain bolstered its forces and tried to formulate a military response to the Italian invasion of Somaliland, Mussolini, having learned from Hitler that an invasion of England was imminent, encouraged Marshal d'Armata Rodolfo Graziani, commander in chief of Italian forces in North Africa, to press Italy's advantage by invading Egypt. When Germany was forced to cancel Operation Sea Lion—the invasion of England—Graziani was reluctant to move, but he finally did so at Mussolini's urging on September 13. Five divisions crossed the border and, despite British resistance, successfully advanced about sixty-five miles to the coastal town of Sidi Marrani, where a strong defensive perimeter had been established.

Wavell was not about to let the Italians take Egypt, and on December 9, a British Western Desert Force of 30,000 attacked the Italian stronghold, taking the Italians by surprise and capturing 20,000 prisoners. Flushed with an easy victory, Lieutenant General Richard O'Connor, commander of the British force, decided to press on into Libya. He very quickly took the border town of Bardia, then proceeded forward, capturing nearly every town his force encountered. In just ten weeks, O'Connor's army, which was greatly outnumbered in the region, crossed 500 miles, captured the province of Cyrenaica, and took an amazing 130,000 prisoners.

O'Connor felt unstoppable and was eager to advance on the Libyan capital of Tripoli, but Wavell said no. His orders were to supply fresh troops to Greece, so he cut the Libyan force in the hope that the smaller army would still be able to control Cyrenaica.

Germany Enters the African War

The decision not to take Tripoli had serious consequences for the British. On February 12, 1941, General Erwin Rommel, newly appointed commander of Germany's Afrika Korps, arrived in Tripoli to help Italy get back what the British had taken. Though officially under an Italian general, Rommel, a savvy military strategist and gamesman, pretty much ran the show on his own. In March, after amassing a strong German-Italian force fortified with tanks and heavy artillery, Rommel headed to Cyrenaica. The small British force there was quickly overwhelmed by the German war machine, and by April Rommel had succeeded in retaking everything except Tobruk, where the British had set up a strong defense. Over the course of the campaign, Rommel managed to capture General O'Connor and two other generals who were sent to Italy as prisoners of war, but O'Connor escaped in December 1943.

By the end of his offensive, Rommel had crossed the border into Egypt, where he took Halfaya Pass. Having initially bypassed Tobruk, he returned to lay siege to the fortified port city. Wavell tried to break the German hold on Tobruk with two assaults, code-named Brevity and Battleax, but succeeded only in losing nearly half his armor to Rommel. The defeat was a serious problem for Winston Churchill, who had gone against his military advisers by taking tanks and fighter aircraft from Great Britain and giving them to Wavell. Churchill had no recourse but to replace Wavell with General Claude Auchinleck, who in November 1941 mounted another offensive against the Germans. His goal was twofold: Cover a breakout from Tobruk and recover the territory taken by Rommel.

The battle lasted until mid-December, when Auchinleck's army successfully lifted the siege of Tobruk and pushed Rommel all the way back to El Agheila. Both sides experienced heavy casualties, but the victory went to Auchinleck, who lost less of his military strength than did Rommel.

However, the German defeat did not mean the end of the war in North Africa. If anything, it only served to accelerate the action. Rommel's supply lines were far shorter than Auchinleck's, and his army was soon reinforced, resupplied, and rearmed. The situation might have been quite different had the RAF not been preoccupied supporting British forces in Malta.

On January 21, 1942, Rommel struck again against the British, this time with overwhelming force. He recaptured Benghazi (and the British arsenal stored there) and pressed to within 35 miles of the British stronghold at Tobruk. Startled by Rommel's strength, the British withdrew to the Gazala line, a series of defensive structures linked by minefields that ran from El Gazala on the coast to Bir Hacheim, approximately 40 miles southwest of Tobruk.

Rommel and Auchinleck paused to regroup and amass supplies. Auchinleck also used the time to reinforce the center of the Gazala line. On May 26, Rommel finally made his move, maneuvering swiftly around the southern end of the Gazala line in the hope of taking Bir Hacheim and then eliminating the defensive boxes one at a time. But things suddenly turned sour for Rommel, who found himself trapped between British bunkers and facing almost certain annihilation.

It was then that Rommel demonstrated his true skill as a military leader. Through sheer drive, he rallied his army to overrun Bir Hacheim, smash a series of British defensive boxes, then make a mad run for a large British supply dump east of Tobruk. Four days later, Rommel's Afrika Korps swarmed Tobruk, capturing the town and its huge cache of supplies—enough to supply 30,000 men for three months. The only thing denied Rommel was the British gasoline supply, which was set ablaze before the Germans could get to it.

Having lost Tobruk, the British regrouped and formed another defensive line at Mersa Matruh deep inside Egypt. Behind that was a last-ditch defense at El Alamein, which protected Alexandria. If that fell, so would Egypt.

Rommel, his reputation taking on almost legendary proportions, took Mersa Matruh at the end of June, then set his eyes on the El Alamein line, which stretched for 35 miles and was protected at the flanks by a series of natural obstacles that made access extremely difficult. The sea lay to the north of the line, and to the south was the Qattara Depression, nearly 7,000 square miles of terrain so harsh that it was virtually unpassable.

FACT

Hitler was extremely pleased with Rommel's performance and rewarded him with a promotion to field marshal. Unimpressed, Rommel reportedly responded by saying, "It would be better if [Hitler] sent me another division."

Adding to Rommel's woes were dwindling supplies, constant harassment by the RAF, and the fact that his men were exhausted after weeks in the desert. As a result, when Rommel's forces finally reached the El Alamein line on July 1, they lacked the strength and resources to smash through.

Great Britain Reorganizes

Churchill, reacting to the fall of Tobruk, flew to Egypt to review the situation, then replaced Auchinleck with General William Gott. But Gott was killed while flying to take command, so Churchill transferred General Bernard Montgomery and sent him to command the British forces in Egypt. Montgomery, a by-the-book military man, immediately set about strengthening the Eighth Army. He replaced officers he considered lacking in leadership, increased troop training, and arranged for closer air support.

Montgomery correctly assumed that Rommel would attempt to break through at the south end of the line in August, and made sure his Eighth Army was prepared. Rommel attacked on August 31 at exactly the spot Montgomery had anticipated and was quickly repelled by blistering fire. Unable to proceed, Rommel was forced to withdraw.

While Rommel was trying to break the El Alamein line, RAF bombers were doing all they could to destroy the German tanker convoy that was bringing the Desert Fox the fuel he needed to continue. Meanwhile,

Montgomery enjoyed a plentiful resupply effort from the United States. At Churchill's request, President Roosevelt had authorized the loan of Sherman tanks and artillery to assist Montgomery's defense.

Two months after Rommel's ineffective drive against the El Alamein line, Montgomery began a remarkably strong offensive campaign designed to force the German-Italian forces into a retreat. The Eighth Army quickly decimated four German divisions and eight Italian divisions and captured nearly 30,000 prisoners. Montgomery then turned his attention to the fleeing Rommel. On November 20, 1942, Benghazi fell, and three days later Rommel was back where he started, in El Agheila. The Eighth Army chased Rommel through Libya, taking Tripoli on January 13, 1943, and eventually made its way to French North Africa, where it hooked up with other Allied troops in April.

The Northwest Africa Campaign

Northwest Africa was a strategic goal for both the Allies and the Axis since the fall of France in 1940. Germany's conquest left the French-held territories in North Africa open to occupation, while the British were eager to keep Germany away from French North Africa and its military installations. The British were fearful that Germany and Italy, already in Northeast Africa, would bring reinforcements through Italy.

FACT

The campaign offered both political and military benefits. On the home front, Roosevelt believed that military action in Northwest Africa would stimulate morale among Americans while putting U.S. forces into action. It was also a way to placate Stalin, who had been calling for a second front against Germany. At the same time, an invasion of the region would provide a staging ground for action against Italy while putting pressure on Rommel, who was wreaking havoc in the east.

Roosevelt and Churchill first discussed a joint military campaign in French North Africa at the Atlantic Conference in August 1941, when both men acknowledged that U.S. involvement in the war was just a matter of time. During other meetings in December 1941 and January 1942, the two leaders discussed the idea in greater detail, confident that action in Northwest Africa would help put additional pressure on Hitler.

The campaign was slow to start, however, because of international political problems. For example, the United States had established diplomatic ties with the Vichy government in France, but the British refused because they viewed it as a German puppet government. Relations between Great Britain and Free France, led by Charles de Gaulle, had also taken a bruising. The Royal Navy had attacked French warships to keep them from coming under German control—an act that also enraged the Vichy French. As a result, Great Britain could not contemplate acting alone in French North Africa; diplomacy dictated that others also take part.

Figure 5-1 From a Coast Guard-manned sea-horse landing craft, American troops leap forward to storm a North African beach during final amphibious maneuvers.

Photo courtesy of the National Archives (James D. Rose, Jr., ca 1944, 26-G-2326)

The situation changed dramatically in June 1942 when Rommel's Afrika Korps made substantial gains in Libya and left the Eighth Army in temporary disarray. Churchill met with Roosevelt on June 17 to discuss the issue and agreed on a plan to land in North Africa. The plan was code-named Torch.

The U.S. Joint Chiefs of Staff were uncomfortable with the plan, preferring a larger, more forceful landing in Europe. But they were overruled by Roosevelt, who felt that Operation Torch was a necessary endeavor. Plans for the operation were made during the summer of 1942, as the Soviets continued their push for a second front. Churchill finally told Stalin about Operation Torch in August after Stalin insinuated that the Soviet Union was doing all the fighting against Hitler while the British stood idly by.

The North African Assault

The North African assault—the first joint endeavor between Great Britain and the United States—was put under the overall military command of Lieutenant General Dwight Eisenhower, who was a relative unknown at the time. Royal Navy Admiral Andrew Browne Cunningham was placed in command of all naval forces, and RAF Air Chief Marshal Arthur Tedder was put in charge of all air operations.

On October 21, 1942, Major General Mark Clark, one of Eisenhower's deputies, sailed from Gibraltar for a top secret meeting with Robert Murphy, the U.S. consul general in French North Africa, and Vichy representatives in North Africa. Clark's goal: a promise of assistance from the French or, lacking that, at least a promise that they would not interfere with an Allied landing in North Africa. After two days of talks, Clark received a promise of cooperation. In return, the French were promised a month's notice of the pending invasion—though, in fact, U.S. warships were already on their way and were expected to reach North Africa in about two weeks.

The goal of the invasion, which began November 8, was to push German and Italian forces out of North Africa by linking the invasion force with Montgomery's Eighth Army, which in October had broken through Rommel's lines at El Alamein and forced Rommel to retreat westward across Libya. Unfortunately, the Allies' plan hit a snag when their push eastward was slowed to a crawl by a lack of air support and rains that turned the roads into unpassable bogs. The Germans reacted immediately by pouring supplies and troops into Tunisia from Sicily by sea and air, capturing airfields in Tunis and Bizerte.

The airfield at Bone had been taken by British airborne troops by November 12, but Allied forces—many of them inexperienced recruits—moved too slowly to take advantage of the Axis rout in Egypt. The situation greatly angered Eisenhower, who fumed at the missed opportunities.

Allied troops on their way to Tunis, hampered by poor weather and dwindling supplies, were stopped by a smaller German force. By the beginning of the new year, the Axis had created a strong defense in Tunis with combined German-Italian forces numbering more than 100,000.

Churchill and Roosevelt were concluding their Casablanca summit in mid-January just as Montgomery and his Eighth Army was pushing westward after Rommel. Montgomery took Tripoli on January 23 and was eager and ready to drive the Axis out of North Africa.

Rommel Combines His Forces

However, the situation proved more difficult than originally thought. Rommel managed to connect his fabled Afrika Korps with a German Panzer division on the Tunisian front and then launched an offensive against Allied forces to the east. Rommel hoped his new combined army would be able to break through the Allied line and enable him to establish a new supply route at Bone.

The German force was formidable, and the antitank guns were almost invincible. American troops took heavy casualties, including the loss of forty tanks in a single battle. On February 14, the Germans broke out of the Faid area with a double thrust maneuver that effectively split the Allied lines and pushed American troops back to the Kasserine Pass, a two-mile gap in the Dorsal mountains of western Tunisia. It was there that American troops met Rommel's army on February 19. The fighting was heavy, but the U.S. forces were able to hold off the Germans. Rommel received armored reinforcements that night, and the following day—with Rommel in the lead—the Germans attacked again. The Americans fought valiantly, but they were overwhelmed and forced to withdraw. More than 1,000 U.S. soldiers died in the battle, and hundreds were taken prisoner.

From the Kasserine Pass, Rommel advanced toward Tala, 20 miles north, and Tébessa, near Algeria. It was there that Rommel would meet his match. American forces pushed the Germans back at Tébessa, then were joined by Allied forces that sent the Germans into retreat while attacking them from the air. Rommel's troops retreated through the pass and almost certainly could have been taken, but Allied ground forces missed the opportunity by hesitating to pursue them.

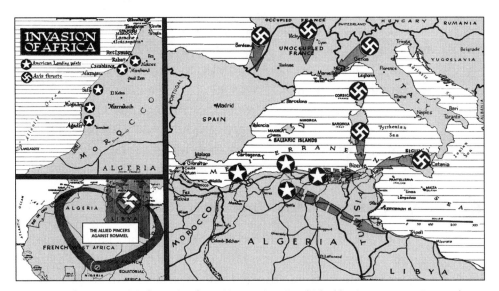

Map 5-1 The invasion of North Africa (Operation Torch) led by Lieutenant General Dwight D. Eisenhower.

Map courtesy of the National Archives (RG 160, Vol. 1, No. 30)

Allied Forces Work Together

The combined Axis forces faced the Eighth Army at the Mareth line, a 22-mile length of fortifications built by the French that ran from the sea to the Matmata Hills. While both sides prepared, General Harold Alexander, commander in chief of the British Middle East Forces, was named deputy commander for ground forces in an important command reorganization. Under Alexander were the British Eighth Army, U.S. Army troops, and forces of the Free French—a combined total of more than half a million men.

For nearly a month, from February 26 to March 20, the Axis forces were gradually weakened through a series of battles that took a heavy toll on their troops and equipment. Once the Axis forces had been sufficiently softened up, the Allies prepared for the coup de grâce: a push through the Mareth line. On April 8, patrols from the U.S. forces in the east and the British Eighth Army from the west shook hands near Gafsa, signaling the official linkup that was to drive the Axis from North Africa for good. Rommel, who had become ill, had already been flown to Germany, where he would play an important role in designing the German defense of Normandy. But the Desert Fox would never set foot in Africa again.

The Axis forces were in no position to put up much of a fight once the Allies hooked up and started their push. Desperately low on food and supplies and exhausted from the long retreat from El Alamein, they established one last defensive position encompassing Tunis, Bizerte, and the Cape Bon Peninsula but were quickly overwhelmed. Tunis was captured by the British, Bizerte by the U.S. and French. The German and Italian forces laid down their weapons for good on May 13, and their generals arranged for mass surrenders that eventually totaled more than 240,000 soldiers. North Africa was finally under complete Allied control.

This fact would prove strategically important, as Allied forces gradually took control of the entire Mediterranean region.

Chapter 6

The Pacific

In the spring of 1942, Japan continued its campaign in the central Pacific with an attempt to take Port Moresby in New Guinea. Because Port Moresby was an important objective that would put northern Australia within range of Japanese land-based bombers, U.S. troops reinforced it in April 1942. The Japanese planned a landing for June but were stopped by the Battle of the Coral Sea. They began an assault on Port Moresby in July by landing troops at Buna and Gona on the northern coast of New Guinea. The Japanese came within 25 miles of the city, but the Australians pushed them back and retook their beachhead in a decisive series of battles in December 1942 and January 1943.

The Battle of the Coral Sea

While it was a naval battle in the sense that the opposing forces were on ships, the Battle of the Coral Sea in May 1942 was unique in that the ships did not fire on each other, relying instead on carrier aircraft. The Battle of the Coral Sea was important, too, in that it was the first Japanese setback of World War II.

The Coral Sea is located between Queensland, Australia, on the southwest, the New Hebrides and New Caledonia on the east, and Papua and the Solomon Islands on the north. The battle there resulted from the Japanese plan to take Port Moresby and then threaten the Australian mainland. Capture of Port Moresby would also end Allied attacks against Japanese bases at Rabaul and in the Solomon Islands.

ESSENTIAL

On April 18, 1942—just four months after the attack on Pearl Harbor— American bombers, later known as "Doolittle's Raiders," passed over Japan. An Allied attack on the Japanese mainland was thought to be impossible, yet it happened. That first bombing assault actually did little physical damage, but it succeeded greatly in raising American morale and puncturing, at least a little, the veneer of Japanese invincibility.

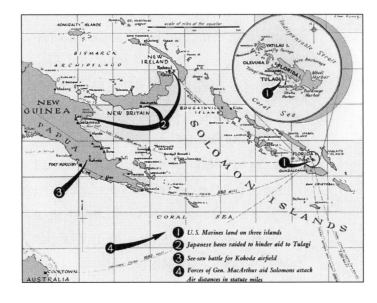

Map 6-1 The U.S. offensive in the Solomon Islands.

Map courtesy of the National Archives (Solomon Islands, RG 160, Vol. 1, No. 17)

For the invasion of New Guinea, the Japanese amassed seventy ships, including two large aircraft carriers, two smaller carriers, and a number of cruisers, destroyers, and supply ships. Thanks to luck in breaking the Japanese code, the U.S. Navy was well aware of the deployment, and plans were made to counter the invasion with a naval task force under the command of Rear Admiral Frank Fletcher that included the carriers *Lexington* and *Yorktown* and a handful of destroyers and cruisers. It was a force smaller than that of the Japanese, but it was all that was available at the time.

Cat and Mouse

On May 3, 1942, Japanese troops landed on Tulagi in the Solomons, off Guadalcanal. Planes from the *Yorktown* scouted the area in search of the Japanese fleet but found only a few isolated ships, including three minesweepers and a destroyer, all of which were quickly sunk.

Figure 6-1 A Japanese torpedo bomber explodes after being hit by antiaircraft fire.

Photo courtesy of the National Archives (80-G-415001)

For the invasion of New Guinea, the Japanese amassed seventy ships, including two large aircraft carriers, two smaller carriers, and a number of cruisers, destroyers, and supply ships. Thanks to luck in breaking the

Japanese code, the U.S. Navy was well aware of the deployment, and plans were made to counter the invasion with a naval task force under the command of Rear Admiral Frank Fletcher that included the carriers *Lexington* and *Yorktown* and a handful of destroyers and cruisers. It was a force smaller than that of the Japanese, but it was all that was available at the time.

At the same time, the Japanese force was searching for the American task force. Japanese planes came across an oiler and a destroyer, sinking both. On May 7, the U.S. force received a garbled message noting the presence of two Japanese carriers and four heavy cruisers. But the message was incorrect—the convoy actually contained two heavy cruisers and two destroyers. A total of ninety-three American aircraft went hunting for the misidentified Japanese carriers, while Japanese reconnaissance planes continued their search for the U.S. fleet.

American planes eventually came across the Japanese light carrier *Shoho* and its destroyer escorts. The carrier was hit with seven torpedoes and numerous bombs and sank within minutes.

FACT

The logistics of the first Tokyo bombing raid were astounding. The flight deck of an aircraft carrier was only 450 feet compared with the standard 1,200 feet or more generally used. Air force pilots practiced extensively on ground mockups of a carrier deck until they had every nuance down pat.

Meanwhile, poor weather prevented the Japanese planes from finding the U.S. carriers, so they dumped their bombs and torpedoes in the ocean and headed back toward their fleet. U.S. fighters on reconnaissance saw the Japanese planes and attacked, shooting down ten while losing two of their own. The air battle raged past sunset, and some of the surviving Japanese planes accidentally stumbled across the *Yorktown*, which, in the dark, they mistook for their own carrier. Several Japanese planes prepared to land on the *Yorktown* when the pilot of the lead plane suddenly realized his mistake and immediately throttled up in a desperate attempt to escape blistering antiaircraft fire. Shortly afterward, the surviving planes found their own carriers, which used searchlights to guide the pilots in.

Massive Aerial Recon on Both Sides

More than eighty U.S. bombers and torpedo planes went in search of the Japanese carriers the next day, while the Japanese fleet sent sixty-nine planes after the *Lexington* and the *Yorktown*. Astoundingly, the two aerial armadas didn't see each other as they headed for their respective targets. Torpedo planes attacked the *Lexington*, sending two torpedoes into its port side. Five bombs also struck the ship, but they did little damage. The *Yorktown* was also hit by a bomb, which plunged through the flight deck before exploding.

Figure 6-2
Troops and supplies heading into the invasion of Cape Gloucester, New Britain, December 24, 1943.

Photo courtesy of the National Archives (26-G-3056)

Numerous internal explosions rocked the *Lexington* as a result of the Japanese attack, which took 216 lives, and five hours later orders were given to abandon ship. After the crew of more than 2,700 was evacuated, the carrier was torpedoed by a U.S. destroyer to hasten its death.

As Japanese planes attacked the American carriers, bombers and torpedo planes from the *Yorktown* launched a massive attack against two Japanese carriers. But several torpedoes launched against the carrier *Shokaku* missed or failed to detonate. In addition, only two bombs found their target. Planes from the *Lexington* followed with a second attack but also inflicted minimal damage.

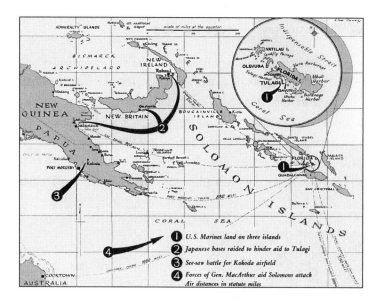

Map 6-2 The height of the Japanese power in the Pacific, China, and Southeast Asia.

Map courtesy of the National Archives (Japanese Empire August 1942, RG 160, Vol. 4, No. 19F)

Map 6-3 The range of Japanese power as the war ended.

Map courtesy of the National Archives (Japanese Holdings as War Ended, RG 160, Vol. 4, No. 19F)

It appeared that the Japanese were the victors in the Battle of the Coral Sea, but the Allies were the tactical winners because the assault damaged a sufficient number of Japanese ships and planes to delay the Japanese expedition against Port Moresby and thus prevented planned air attacks against Australia.

FACT

When the order was given to abandon the *Lexington* during the Battle of the Coral Sea, 2,735 men went over the side and were rescued without a single loss. Accompanying the crew was the captain's cocker spaniel, Wags.

Wake Island

Wake Island, a small coral atoll approximately 2,000 miles west of Hawaii, is notable as the site of the first lengthy battle between U.S. and Japanese forces.

The United States took possession of Wake Island in 1898, though the island meant little until 1935, when it became an important refueling stop for Pan American Airways Clippers flying between San Francisco and Manila in the Philippines. The U.S. military also took notice of Wake Island, and in 1938, funds were allocated to build air and submarine support bases there. Construction was delayed until 1941, when a civilian crew of 1,200 workers arrived, along with a small navy and marine contingent and an army communications unit. The base was completed by November, and a 388-man marine defense detachment was based there, supported by a variety of heavy guns, many of them scavenged from old World War I battleships.

The Japanese attacked Wake Island the same day they attacked Pearl Harbor. Japanese bombers out of Kwajalein destroyed seven F4F Wildcat fighters on the ground and heavily damaged the base. A Pan American Clipper loaded with tires for the P-40 Warhawks of the fabled Flying Tigers in China was caught on Wake at the time of the attack. Once the Japanese bombers left, the tires were unloaded and burned to keep them out of Japanese hands, and the plane took off.

The American defenders of Wake Island managed to get in a few good hits of their own on December 11 when they damaged three Japanese cruisers, two destroyers, and other ships that were part of an invasion force. The Japanese responded by bombing and shelling Wake Island for twelve consecutive days, then landing an invasion force on December 23. Unable to mount a defense, Navy Commander Winfield Cunningham surrendered.

The Japanese eventually placed 4,400 troops on Wake Island, but the island proved to be of little use. It was bombed repeatedly by U.S. planes, and ships commonly used it as an artillery range. Supplies were slow in reaching the men stationed there, and many suffered from malnutrition. Fewer than 1,200 were left alive when Rear Admiral Shigematsu Sakaibara, commander of the Japanese force on Wake, surrendered on September 4, 1945. Sakaibara was tried for war crimes and was executed on June 18, 1947.

Midway

Midway, a U.S. Navy base on two tiny islands that form a coral atoll in the central Pacific, was the site of unsuccessful Japanese attacks in December 1941 and January 1942. The Japanese attacked for the third time in June 1942, and the resulting battle was one of the largest of the war in the Pacific.

The Doolittle raid reached Tokyo just minutes after a practice air raid drill. As a result, most residents of the city thought the planes were part of the exercise. Later, when asked where the bombers had come from, President Roosevelt slyly replied, "Shangri-La." The U.S. Navy later named an aircraft carrier under construction at the time the *Shangri-La*.

The Japanese wanted Midway for several reasons. It would be an essential part of Japan's defensive line in the Pacific. It was also a necessary cog in Japan's strategy to invade the Hawaiian Islands.

The Battle Ensues

The U.S. naval presence in the Pacific was a constant threat to Japanese imperialism, and Admiral Isoroku Yamamoto, commander in chief of the Combined Fleet, believed that the U.S. Pacific Fleet had to be completely destroyed in 1942 or Japan would lose the war. A savvy strategist, Yamamoto rightly believed that an attack on Midway would pressure Admiral Chester Nimitz, commander in chief of the Pacific Fleet, into using everything at his disposal to protect the island, which was integral to the defense of Pearl Harbor.

The attack on Midway was to begin on June 5 with carrier aircraft destroying the island's ground defenses and aircraft. The next day, according to the plan, Japanese troops would take Kure Island, nearly 60 miles northwest of Midway, and create a base for seaplanes to support the Midway invasion. In addition, a fleet of Japanese submarines was dispersed to intercept U.S. ships sent to Midway and the Aleutians from Pearl Harbor.

Thanks to their code breakers, U.S. Navy officials were well aware of Yamamoto's plans. Admiral Nimitz decided to send his only three aircraft carriers—the *Enterprise*, the *Hornet*, and the recently repaired *Yorktown*—against the Japanese invaders.

The Japanese invasion force was identified on June 3, but air strikes by bombers out of Midway inflicted little damage. The next morning, bombers and fighters from Japanese carriers attacked Midway.

Aircraft armed with torpedoes were being held at the ready on the Japanese carriers to deal with any U.S. warships that might be seen by Japanese reconnaissance planes. Then a change of orders sent the crews scrambling to swap the torpedoes for bombs so Midway could be attacked a second time.

While crewmen struggled to make the switch, a Japanese search plane saw U.S. warships just 200 miles away. But Rear Admiral Frank Fletcher, commander of the U.S. carrier strike force, was already aware that two Japanese carriers were within easy striking distance. The battle of Midway was set in motion.

Surprise Assault

Acting quickly to maintain the element of surprise, Fletcher ordered Rear Admiral Raymond Spruance to attack the Japanese carriers with planes from the *Enterprise* and the *Hornet*. Fletcher planned to follow the two carriers aboard the *Yorktown* once his scout bombers returned.

Speeding toward the Japanese carriers at twenty-five knots, Spruance decided to launch his planes before the Japanese could launch another attack on the battered station at Midway. This required launching his planes 200 miles out—well short of the torpedo bombers' combat radius. Nonetheless, fourteen TBD Devastator torpedo bombers were launched from the *Enterprise*, along with thirty-three dive-bombers and an escort of ten Wildcat fighters. The *Hornet* launched thirty-five dive-bombers, fifteen torpedo bombers, and ten fighter escorts. Approximately an hour and a half later, the *Yorktown* delivered seventeen dive-bombers, twelve torpedo bombers, and six fighters.

The *Hornet*'s fifteen-plane Torpedo Squadron Eight lost contact with the other attack planes but came across four Japanese carriers. Though greatly outnumbered by Japanese Zeros and facing a blanket of antiaircraft fire from cruisers and destroyers, the planes engaged the ships in short-range battle. Plane after plane was shot down by the Japanese Zeros and the barrage of artillery, but the American pilots continued their futile attack. In the end, not a single plane escaped, and none of their torpedoes hit the intended targets. Only one man from Torpedo Eight survived the battle; he was rescued at sea the following day.

Torpedo Squadron Six from the *Enterprise* attacked next, but it, too, suffered greatly. Of the fourteen torpedo bombers to engage the Japanese, only four survived. And once again, none of the torpedoes hit their targets. Torpedo Squadron Three from the *Yorktown* suffered a similar fate: all twelve planes lost, with no damage to the Japanese.

But the loss of the torpedo squadrons opened the door for the destruction of the Japanese carriers. Because the planes came in low over the water, the guns on the Japanese ships and all Japanese fighters were drawn down low. As the attack continued, American dive-bombers from the *Enterprise* arrived on the scene unopposed.

While wave after wave of U.S. torpedo bombers attacked the Japanese carriers, the ships' crews were working to prepare planes for a counterattack, stacking bombs on the hangar decks of the *Akagi* and the *Kaga*. The first few Zeros were taxiing down the *Akagi*'s flight deck when an American bomb struck the carrier, causing more than sixty newly fueled and armed planes to explode. Four bombs also struck the *Kaga*, causing the bombs set on its deck to go off.

While the *Akagi* and the *Kaga* burned, seventeen dive-bombers from the *Yorktown* converged on the carrier *Soryu*, hitting it with three well-placed bombs that ignited the waiting, weapons-heavy planes and sending a fireball of destruction across the ship's flight deck.

The Battle Winds Down

The fourth Japanese carrier, the *Hiryu*, was able to launch its bombers against the U.S. carriers, stopping the *Yorktown* with three bombs. In a second attack, the carrier was hit in the port side by two torpedoes and began taking on water. The order to abandon ship was given, and the ship's survivors, numbering more than 2,200, crossed into the waiting destroyers and cruisers. The *Yorktown*'s dive-bombers, which were on the *Enterprise*, then hooked up with that ship's bombers to destroy the *Hiryu*. The job was done with four bombs, which ignited huge fires aboard the Japanese carrier, stopping it dead in the water.

The Battle of Midway is widely regarded as the turning point for the Americans in the Pacific, showing that the Japanese had greatly underestimated them.

Even with the loss of the *Yorktown*, the Battle of Midway was a decisive blow against the Japanese navy. In addition to the four aircraft carriers, a Japanese cruiser was sunk, and another cruiser and two destroyers were badly damaged. All of the carriers' 240 planes were lost, along with most of their pilots and support crews.

But all was not lost for the Japanese in the Pacific. The northern phase of the battle succeeded, with the Japanese continuing to the Aleutians because Admiral Nimitz had nothing left to stop them. Japanese carrier aircraft were able to inflict substantial damage on the American base at Dutch Harbor, and the Japanese were virtually unopposed when they landed at Kiska and Attu. They would hold these positions for another year.

The Philippines

This collection of some 7,000 islands, along with Guam and Puerto Rico, was ceded to the United States by Spain after the Spanish-American War. The battles of Bataan and Corregidor fought in the Philippines were two of America's greatest losses to Japan at the beginning of World War II, but the territory was eventually liberated in 1944.

As a commonwealth, the Philippines relied on the United States for its defense. Retired general Douglas MacArthur, former U.S. Army chief of staff and onetime commander of the army's Philippine Department, was made the territory's military adviser.

In July 1941, as the Japanese threat grew more imminent, MacArthur was recalled to active duty and made commander of all U.S. and Philippine troops in the Philippines.

MacArthur believed that the troops under his command were up to the task of keeping the Japanese at bay, and he pretty much ignored the official war plan for defense of the commonwealth, known as War Plan Orange, Revision Three. This plan called for forces to withdraw to the mountainous Bataan peninsula at the mouth of Manila Bay, which was protected at the rear by the fortified island of Corregidor, until reinforcements could arrive.

The plan looked good on paper, but the reality of the situation was quite different. After the attack on Pearl Harbor, Japanese forces immediately turned their attention to the Philippines with an unexpected air attack on U.S. bases that wiped out nearly half of the 200 aircraft stationed there. The following day, December 9, the Japanese made an amphibious landing on Bataan Island off Luzon and seized the airstrip. More Japanese forces arrived the next day, going ashore at two points on northern Luzon. Additional airstrips were quickly seized with almost no opposition because most of MacArthur's forces were 800 miles away in Mindanao at the southern tip of the Philippine chain.

The Japanese continued gradually increasing their control of the Philippines, finally landing at Mindanao on December 20. They were met by approximately 3,500 U.S. and Philippine troops, but they quickly overwhelmed them. Meanwhile, a major Japanese landing force went ashore at Lingayen Gulf on Luzon's west coast on December 22, with a secondary landing on the east coast, south of Manila. The Philippine capital became their next goal.

MacArthur hoped to save Manila from destruction by declaring it an open city (meaning it was undefended) on December 26; then he began a withdrawal to the Bataan peninsula, where he hoped to either be rescued or receive reinforcements. Meanwhile, the Japanese disregarded MacArthur's open-city declaration and began bombing Manila, which fell on January 2, 1942. Lieutenant General Masaharu Homma, the supreme Japanese commander, chose to take Manila as originally planned rather than chase MacArthur and his small army to Bataan. He wouldn't turn his attention to MacArthur until January 9. This delay gave MacArthur's troops time to establish a defensive perimeter, though the chances of a rescue were bleak because of the heavy losses the Pacific Fleet had suffered in the attack on Pearl Harbor.

On February 20, Manuel Quezon, president of the Philippines, and several other U.S. and Philippine officials were evacuated by submarine. Once in Washington, Quezon quickly established a government in exile. Meanwhile, President Roosevelt acknowledged the loss of the Philippines and ordered MacArthur to escape to Australia, which he did via PT boat on March 17.

The Battle of Bataan

MacArthur's forces put up a formidable defense in Bataan, but it wasn't enough to hold off the much larger Japanese army. On January 9, Homma unleashed a heavy artillery barrage on the defenders, then ordered his men across the Calaguiman River to within 150 yards of the defensive line. Then, he ordered a suicide run by his troops, which pushed the American and Philippine soldiers farther down the peninsula.

But MacArthur's troops didn't roll over. Instead, they fought with tremendous ferocity, throwing everything they had at the attacking Japanese. Though continually pushed back, the defenders were able to prevent the swift Japanese victory that Homma had anticipated.

Ordered to evacuate the Philippines by President Roosevelt, MacArthur placed Jonathan Wainwright, newly promoted to lieutenant general, in command of the Philippine army. Boarding the PT boat that would take him to Australia, MacArthur uttered his now-famous farewell: "I shall return."

FACT

Members of the Provisional Naval Battalion, who fought the Japanese during the battle of Bataan, tried to turn their white uniforms khaki for better camouflage using coffee. However, rather than turning brown, the uniforms came out yellow. As a result, one Japanese officer wrote in his diary of seeing "a new type of suicide squad dressed in brightly colored uniforms."

By this time, the defending army consisted of approximately 500 American sailors and their officers, who formed the Provisional Naval Battalion. Knowing that their task was ultimately futile, the men nonetheless vowed to do everything in their power to hold off the Japanese as long as physically possible.

Homma's forces received reinforcements in early April, and on April 3, he launched a brutal assault against the weakened American and Filipino defenders. Wave after wave of Japanese soldiers threw themselves at the defensive line with little regard for casualties. Yet despite overwhelming odds, the American and Filipino troops continued to defend themselves with everything at hand, fighting past the point of exhaustion. A week later, on April 9, the valiant fighters, exhausted and out of supplies, finally surrendered.

ESSENTIAL

Before the fall of Bataan, a handful of survivors, including Lieutenant General Wainwright, joined the small contingent of servicemen and nurses on the fortified island of Corregidor, which was next in the Japanese campaign for the Philippines. The Japanese won, but the victory was bittersweet for Homma, who had been given fifty days to take the Philippines. Because he went over schedule, Homma was relieved of command on June 9.

For the survivors of the Battle of Bataan, the worst was yet to come. Taken prisoner, they were forced by the Japanese to march sixty grueling miles from Bataan to San Fernando.

The Bataan Death March

The Bataan Death March—involving 76,000 American and Filipino soldiers taken prisoner after the capture of Bataan—is one of the most infamous atrocities committed by the Japanese against Allied servicemen.

FACT

During the Bataan Death March, an American prisoner—a former Notre Dame football player—had his 1935 class ring taken from him by a Japanese guard. It was later returned to him by an apologetic Japanese officer who politely explained, "I graduated from Southern California in thirty-five."

The march began on April 10, 1942, when thousands of prisoners were searched and stripped of personal belongings by Japanese guards. Some of the prisoners were summarily executed, supposedly because they possessed Japanese money. The prisoners were then placed in groups of 500 to 1,000 and forced to march without food or water to a camp under construction at San Fernando in Pampanga Province.

Figure 6-3
American POWs in the Bataan Death March, May 1942.

Photo courtesy of the National Archives (127-N-114541)

The march was an exercise in brutality. One soldier reported having his canteen confiscated, the water given to a horse, and the canteen discarded in the bushes. Prisoners who fell behind because of exhaustion were bayoneted and left at the side of the road. The stronger prisoners were not allowed to help.

According to the U.S. War Department, nearly 5,200 Americans died during the twelve-day march, and many more died after reaching the camp. Conditions were so harsh that the death rate at San Fernando reached 550 a day.

The Bataan Death March was a well-kept secret. Word of the atrocities didn't get out until three years later, when three American officers escaped from the prison camp and revealed the truth. After the war, General Masaharu Homma received much of the blame for the death march. He was convicted of war crimes and executed.

Philippine Resistance

The Japanese began the next phase of their conquest—reorienting Filipinos to view the Japanese not as enemies but as friends eager to help them against the colonialists. The teaching of Japanese became mandatory in Philippine schools, and radios were adapted so they could not pick up American broadcasts. All political parties were abolished, and a new party loyal to the Japanese was started to select members of a pro-Japanese puppet government.

The Japanese had hoped to bring the Philippines into the Greater East Asia Co-Prosperity Sphere after they conquered it. However, vehemently anti-Japanese forces took to the hills and began an aggressive guerrilla campaign against the invaders. The fighting forces were frequently reinforced and given weapons and supplies via submarine drops, and many of the secret military forces were led by U.S. officers under MacArthur's command. The movement solidified quickly, and by 1944, the guerrillas had a working recruitment program, communications system, political organization, and even their own currency. Nearly 60 percent of Philippine territory (most of it outlying regions) came under guerrilla control over the course of the war.

Figure 6-4
General MacArthur wades ashore during the initial landing at Leyte following the invasion to liberate the Philippines.

Photo courtesy of the National Archives (111-SC-407101)

MacArthur was eager to keep the promise he had made to the Filipino people on his evacuation to Australia, and after his forces made major gains in New Guinea, he started lobbying for the liberation of the Philippines. After much debate, President Roosevelt finally agreed.

The invasion began on October 20, 1944. With two assault forces and 500 ships at his disposal, MacArthur landed more than 200,000 troops on Leyte, which was an important steppingstone to Mindanao and Luzon. The U.S. forces wasted little time in their campaign to retake the island chain. On October 21, they captured the harbor and airfield at Tacloban, the provincial capital of Leyte.

MacArthur had wanted to make the liberation of the Philippines an army operation, but it was the navy that helped propel him to victory as a result of the decisive naval battle of Leyte Gulf, which devastated the Japanese fleet and left the Japanese forces in the Philippines with little air support or supply line protection.

During the naval battle of Leyte Gulf, which enabled General Douglas MacArthur to retake the Philippines by severing Japanese forces' supply lines, Commander David McCampbell of the carrier *Essex* shot down at least nine Japanese fighters. McCampbell became the navy's top fighter pilot in the war with thirty-four confirmed kills.

The Battle of Leyte Gulf

The three-day battle of Leyte Gulf, one of the greatest sea battles in history, was Japan's desperate attempt to disrupt the landing of American troops in the Philippines, as well as drive away the U.S. warships that supported them. Almost the entire Japanese fleet took part in the battle, which started badly for the Japanese with the sinking of two of the first cruisers sent to the region; the ships were torpedoed off the north coast of Borneo, claiming 582 sailors.

Both sides took heavy losses in the battle. When the American carrier *Princeton* was hit and sunk by a single Japanese bomb, the destruction was so massive and immediate that more than 500 sailors drowned. However, U.S. forces gained immediate and uncontested air superiority and quickly changed the course of the battle by sinking the Japanese battleship *Musashi*.

During the engagement, the Japanese lost thirty-six warships and the United States lost six. The battle signaled the end of Japanese aggression in the Pacific and introduced a last-ditch weapon from the Japanese: the suicide corps known as the *kamikaze*, or "divine wind." On October 25, the last day of the battle, one kamikaze pilot plunged his plane into the flight deck of the American escort carrier *St. Lo*, igniting the bombs and torpedoes stored below. The ship went down less than a half hour later.

Even though the invasion force met little resistance at Tacloban, the landing at Ormoc on December 7 was a different story. Japanese soldiers hiding in caves and carved-out pillboxes threw everything they had at the Americans while kamikaze raids inflicted heavy damage on U.S. support ships just off shore. A week later, nearly 16,000 U.S. troops and 15,000 construction and army air force personnel landed at Mindoro, quickly overwhelming the 500-man Japanese garrison there. Leyte was secured by Christmas, and MacArthur turned his attention to Luzon, which was being protected by nearly 250,000 Japanese troops.

The Landing at Luzon

The initial landing forces at Luzon met very little resistance, a situation that perplexed the U.S. commanders. It was later learned that the Japanese had opted to let the beach landing take place unopposed so the Japanese defenders would not lose men to the aerial bombardment that usually accompanied such an action. The Japanese, entrenched in a maze of tunnels and pillboxes, fought hard, hoping to prevent an invasion of Luzon and the Philippines' other main islands.

However, on January 31, 1945, U.S. troops pushed into Manila, beginning a battle that lasted more than a month and involved intense house-to-house and hand-to-hand combat with Japanese defenders unwilling to give up. In Manila, U.S. rangers, backed by Filipino guerrillas, freed a large number of American POWs, including many survivors of the Bataan Death March.

On March 3, MacArthur proclaimed Manila a secure city and returned civil control of the territory to the former Philippine government.

American forces liberated the Philippines piece by piece, with fighting that continued throughout the islands for several more months. General Tomoyuki Yamashita led his force of 65,000 into the hills around Luzon and continued to harass American and Filipino forces until the end of the war.

Aftermath of Occupation

Four years of war took a horrible toll on the Philippines. The Japanese destroyed countless homes, buildings, infrastructures, and farmland. Reconstruction had to be postponed because the Philippines were a primary staging area for a planned invasion of the Japanese mainland. (The Japanese surrender after the atomic bombing of Hiroshima and Nagasaki eliminated the need for the invasion.)

After the war, the United States gratefully thanked its ally with eight years of free trade, generous quotas on imports, and a $400 million fund for the payment of war-damage claims. The United States also provided a $120 million public works program and turned over $100 million in surplus properties to the Philippine government. The greatest gift of all came on July 4, 1946, when the Philippines was granted its independence.

The Battle of Guadalcanal

The battle of the Solomon island known as Guadalcanal, which started in August 1942, began the first U.S. offensive of the war in the Pacific. It would prove to be a vicious battle, with heavy losses on both sides.

The invasion, code-named Operation Watchtower, began on August 7 with marines going ashore at Florida and Tulagi Islands, located just north of Guadalcanal, and nearby Tanambogo and Gavuru Islands. Japanese opposition on these secondary islands was much stronger than what the marines landing on Guadalcanal itself faced. It was later learned that the Japanese forces on Guadalcanal had been taken by surprise because poor weather kept their surveillance planes on the ground.

Figure 6-5 U.S. Marine Raiders in front of a Japanese dugout on Cape Totkina on Bougainville, Solomon Islands, which they helped to take in January 1944.

Photo courtesy of the National Archives (80-G-205686)

It would take an entire day for the Japanese forces on Guadalcanal to realize they were being invaded. During that time, more than 11,000 marines stepped ashore, in addition to the 6,800 who landed on the other islands.

The Japanese finally reacted with a hasty air attack out of Rabaul, which inflicted little damage on the U.S. forces.

The goal of the Guadalcanal invasion was the nearly finished Japanese airfield there, an important element in Japan's planned invasion of New Guinea. The Japanese, outgunned and outmanned, quickly withdrew from the unfinished airfield as the marines approached, and the area was secured and renamed Henderson Field, in honor of Major Lofton Henderson, a marine pilot killed in the Battle of Midway.

Japan Fights Back

However, the Japanese were not about to give up Guadalcanal without a fight. Using barges and transports from Cape Esperance, they were able to quickly unload a considerable armed force. Japanese military leaders then turned their attention to U.S. naval forces in the area, engaging them in a number of battles that would play an important role in whether the marines would be able to take and control Guadalcanal.

FACT

The first Medal of Honor ever awarded to a marine went to Sergeant John Basilone. During the Battle of Guadalcanal, Basilone killed so many Japanese in one firefight that he had to send out fellow marines to clear his field of fire. The recommendation for Basilone's medal said he had contributed "materially to the defeat and virtually the annihilation of a Japanese regiment."

The Japanese won a decisive naval victory off Savo Island, sinking four Allied cruisers while experiencing minimal damage themselves. The victory allowed Japan to pour reinforcements into Guadalcanal, but Japanese military leaders grossly underestimated the number of marines on the island, and the first small detachment sent to the beach was quickly eliminated. The next wave of Japanese reinforcements was considerably larger, numbering nearly 1,500 men in five protected transports. However, the U.S. naval victory in the battle of the eastern Solomons helped destroy most of the invading force, and those who did make it ashore did so without heavy weapons.

It became increasingly difficult to bring supplies to the entrenched marines, and food, water, and other necessities quickly became scarce. Reinforcements arrived before the situation turned critical. The Japanese also received reinforcements from ships, almost always at night, in a relay that came to be known as the Tokyo Express. However, the added forces were never enough to regain control of the island.

Japan's Final Push Fails

The largest reinforcement effort by the Japanese occurred in mid-November, when an attempt was made to land 10,000 men. However, no matter what the Japanese tried, they couldn't establish a strong foothold on Guadalcanal, and by December a complete evacuation was considered. The order was approved by Emperor Hirohito (since Japanese forces were loath to retreat lest they lose face before their emperor), but the actual evacuation didn't take place until February 1943. So secretive had the Japanese been about the withdrawal that the marines didn't even realize they'd abandoned the island until they found empty boats and abandoned supplies on the beaches of Cape Esperance.

Figure 6-6 U.S. Marines with scouting dogs on the Solomon Islands, circa November 1943.

Photo courtesy of the National Archives (127-GR-84-68407)

The Battle of Guadalcanal was a costly defeat for Japan. More than 25,000 Japanese soldiers lost their lives (nearly 9,000 from starvation and disease) both defending and then trying to wrest the island from the marines. U.S. losses totaled 1,500 dead and 4,800 wounded.

The Battle of Iwo Jima

The Battle of Iwo Jima, memorialized for all time by Associated Press photographer Joe Rosenthal's inspiring photograph of marines raising the American flag atop Mount Suribachi, was one of the bloodiest engagements of the entire war. When it was over, almost all of the 21,000 Japanese defenders were dead. U.S. losses totaled 6,821.

Iwo Jima lies only 660 miles from Japan. Because of its relative proximity to the Japanese mainland, it was an essential target for U.S. forces. The Japanese knew this and created a tremendous defense on and beneath the island. More than 600 pillboxes and gun positions dotted Iwo Jima, which also contained a number of caves.

Because the Japanese were so well entrenched on Iwo Jima, U.S. forces spent seventy-four consecutive days softening it up with a constant barrage of shells and bombs from air and sea. The bombardment, which began in November 1944, was the longest of the war, but it was necessary if the island was to be taken.

Underwater demolition teams were used to survey the proposed landing sites and clear away anything that might impede troop carriers. But the Japanese misidentified the demolition teams as an actual landing force and opened fire, killing 170. The mistaken attack gave away hidden gun positions, which greatly aided the invasion planners.

Operation Detachment—the actual amphibious landing of U.S. troops—began on February 19, 1945, observed from a special amphibious command center by Secretary of the Navy James Forrestal. The first divisions to hit the beach were greeted with only sporadic gunfire. But once all seven battalions were on the beach, the Japanese let loose with a blistering defense. Antitank guns picked off marine tanks stationed on the beach while the troops pinned down on the volcanic sand were hit with machine gun fire. When the sun set, 566 marines had been killed and 1,854 wounded.

The goals of the invasion were 550-foot Mount Suribachi and an air-field directly inland. By the second day of the assault, the marines targeting Mount Suribachi had advanced just 200 yards, their movements impeded by incessant Japanese gunfire. Members of the Twenty-eighth Regiment of the Fifth Division spent three full days battling their way up the volcano, using flamethrowers and grenades to clear the Japanese ahead of them. On the morning of February 23, the marines reached the top of Mount Suribachi, where they planted an American flag.

Figure 6-7 The planting of the flag at Iwo Jima.

Photo courtesy of the National Archives (80-G-413988)

A total of twenty-seven Medals of Honor were awarded to the fighting men who risked their lives to take the tiny island of Iwo Jima. It was the largest number awarded for any single action of World War II.

The Battle of Okinawa

The Battle of Okinawa came late in the war, when Japan was down to its last defenses. Its fleet in the Pacific had been devastated by several strategic losses, and it had lost almost all the territory it had gained at the war's beginning. With the Allies practically knocking on their door, Japanese military leaders had become desperate. Okinawa had to be held or all was lost.

The 100,000 Japanese troops amassed on Okinawa fully understood the situation. To that end, they had vowed to eliminate as many of the enemy as they could through whatever means necessary. The motto of the Thirty-second Japanese Army confirmed the soldiers' dedication: "One plane for one warship. One boat for one ship. One man for ten enemies. One man for one tank."

Because of the passion of the Japanese defenders, Okinawa was a hard-fought and bloody engagement that resulted in huge casualties. When it was finally over in June 1945, more than 107,000 Japanese and Okinawan soldiers and civilians had been killed, and another 4,000 Japanese perished when the battleship *Yamato* was destroyed on its way to support the Japanese Okinawan defense. American losses on the island totaled 7,613 dead or missing in action and more than 31,000 wounded. An additional 4,907 sailors and marines were killed and 4,824 wounded aboard U.S. ships supporting the island assault.

The U.S. invasion fleet contained almost 1,500 combat and support vessels—the largest number of ships involved in a single operation over the course of the war in the Pacific. The British also contributed a carrier task force of 21 ships, with 244 aircraft on 4 carriers to supplement the nearly 1,000 U.S. carrier aircraft. The number of fighting men involved in the operation totaled nearly half a million, representing the U.S. Army, Navy, and Marines, and the Royal Navy.

Operation Iceberg

Operation Iceberg, as the invasion of Okinawa was code-named, was scheduled to begin on March 1, 1945. But it had to be postponed to April 1—Easter Sunday—because of delays in the Philippines campaign and at Iwo Jima, where the Japanese were forcing the marines to pay heavily for every yard they took.

A preinvasion bombardment of Okinawa started a week before the landings, and on March 26, U.S. forces captured five small islands in the Kerama Retto group west of Okinawa. This would help stop suicide boats based on the islands from being used against the invading forces.

The landing itself began at 4:06 A.M. on April 1 with a feint toward the southwestern shore of the island. This was designed to reduce the Japanese forces at the real landing site, a five-mile stretch on the southwestern coast near two strategic airfields. Marines and army troops went ashore as planned and achieved their immediate goals relatively quickly with a minimum of opposition.

Fatal Defense

The Japanese began their defense with kamikaze attacks against the naval task force supporting the invasion. Nearly 1,900 suicide sorties were flown from April to July, and more than 260 ships were sunk or damaged. According to military records, 2,336 Japanese aircraft were destroyed by U.S. planes and naval guns.

Figure 6-8 Transfer of wounded from the USS *Bunker Hill* to the USS *Wilkes-Barre*. The injuries were sustained as a result of a Japanese kamikaze attack off Okinawa, May 11, 1945.

Photo courtesy of the National Archives (080-G-328610)

The Japanese sacrificed the island's airfields so they could fortify their defenses along what came to be known as the Shuri line, named after a nearby castle. American forces first hit the line on April 4; the resulting battle lasted eight days as American soldiers struggled to take a ridge and clear Japanese fighters from the area's many caves. An offensive against the Shuri line was launched on May 11, but the Japanese were able to repulse the

American forces. The First Marine Division finally captured Shuri Castle on May 29.

FACT

Renowned combat journalist Ernie Pyle was killed by a Japanese sniper on the island of Ie Shima during the battle to take Okinawa.

Unable to hold the line, the Japanese evacuated Shuri and established another defensive line at Yaeju Dake and Yazu Dake to the south. Vicious fighting continued on Okinawa until the last week of June, with the U.S. campaign officially ending in a successful conquest on July 2.

The Battle of Okinawa is unique because of the high number of cases of "combat fatigue" (now known as posttraumatic stress disorder) that resulted. More than 26,000 American servicemen who fought on Okinawa were later treated for psychological problems due to the ferocity and intensity of the fighting and the almost nonstop artillery and mortar fire that accompanied it.

Part Three:
The Major Players

Chapter 7

The Political Leaders

Wars are won or lost based on the drive and abilities of the people who direct them. The leaders of the Axis—Adolf Hitler, Benito Mussolini, and Hideki Tojo—rose to power and led their nations into a campaign of global conquest. Focusing on national pride, they whipped their countrymen into a frenzied devotion, driving the belief that military conquest was not merely their right but their divine duty. The Allied leaders were not eager for war. Their nations, still reeling from the losses of World War I, favored peace. But when finally forced into battle by despotic rulers, they faced the challenge and pushed back the enemy.

Adolf Hitler

No other twentieth-century world leader achieved the degree of infamy that Adolf Hitler did. A power-mad dictator intent on world conquest, Hitler used Germany's tattered national pride and raging anti-Semitism as steppingstones to create one of the most heinous and morally repulsive governments in world history. Millions of people died as a result of Hitler's lust for power, and his name has justly become synonymous with hate, intolerance, and evil.

Adolf Hitler was born on April 20, 1889, in Braunau, Austria, the fourth child of Klara and Alois Hitler. His father worked for the Austrian customs service and was able to give his family a comfortable lifestyle.

Hitler's father died in 1903, leaving the family without a strong male figure. With no one to drive him, Hitler began skipping school, and his grades continued to drop. He left school in 1905 with a ninth-grade education.

When his mother died in 1908, Hitler pretended to continue his education in Vienna in order to receive an orphan's pension. However, he spent most of his days wandering the city streets and dreaming about his future. Hitler eventually ended up in a homeless shelter, where he was first introduced to the racist concepts that would be the cornerstone of his political ideology. He also developed an intense hatred for socialism, which he came to associate with Jewish people. From 1910 to 1913, he was able to eke out a meager living painting postcards and sketches. Then he moved to Munich, Bavaria, in Germany.

Hitler in the First World War

Hitler volunteered for a Bavarian unit during World War I and fought through the entire war. He returned to Munich after the war and was selected to be a political speaker by the local army headquarters, which trained him as an orator and allowed him to practice public speaking before returning prisoners of war. Hitler excelled as a public speaker and was selected as an observer of political groups around Munich. As part of his job, he investigated the German Workers' Party, a nationalist group steeped in racism. It was here that Hitler found his soul mates.

Birth of the Nazi Party

Hitler embraced the German Workers' Party and became an active member. He renamed the organization the National Socialist German Workers' Party (commonly abbreviated as the Nazi Party) and became its spokesman—despite the fact that he was still technically employed by the army.

Hitler used his deft speaking skills to promote the organization, drawing huge crowds wherever he lectured. When he presented the party's official program to a gathering in February 1920, more than 2,000 people were in the audience. Discharged from the army in March, Hitler threw all his energies into the new political party, quickly rising to become its leader. He learned early on how to use treachery and backroom scheming to eliminate opposition, a skill that would serve him well in the years to come. On July 29, 1921, Hitler was chosen Führer (absolute leader) of the growing political organization.

FACT

The swastika was adopted by Hitler as the emblem and primary flag motif of the Nazi Party during the organization's infancy. Hitler adopted the design as a symbol "for the victory of the Aryan man." However, the symbol is actually very old. Similar designs were used by ancient Greeks, Tibetans, and some Native American tribes and are widespread in India.

On November 8, 1923, Hitler attempted his infamous Beer Hall Putsch, a revolution designed to push out the current ruling party and install himself as leader of the German people. The "revolution"—in truth, a small riot—started at a beer hall in Bavaria and quickly spread to the streets, fanned by some 600 of Hitler's faithful followers. It was quickly put down by armed police, and Hitler was arrested for treason. Though he might have faced life in prison for his acts, he was sentenced to just five years and served only nine months. Though the revolt had failed, Hitler actually came out ahead. The act gained him tremendous publicity and convinced him that the most effective political change came not from an outside force but from maneuvering within. Hitler knew he would have to become part of the government in order to take it over.

Hitler returned to the helm of the Nazi Party after his release from prison in 1924 and spent the next several years creating a network of local party organizations throughout Germany in an attempt to bolster the party's political strength and influence. He also organized the black-shirted Schutzstaffel, or SS, an elite corps created to protect him, control the party, and perform certain police tasks.

Hitler's rise to power continued with the 1928 election. Though the Nazi Party garnered just under 3 percent of the vote, it received quite a bit of publicity, and its membership grew. Two years later, new elections increased Nazi representation in the Reichstag, the German parliament, from 12 to 107. Because of the Great Depression and the Nazis' campaign to cancel all of Germany's financial obligations, foreign investors fled the country, resulting in the collapse of the German banking system. As the nation's economic woes worsened, the simplistic appeal of the Nazis grew, and more and more people joined the party. In the 1932 elections, the Nazis received more votes than any other party, and Hitler demanded that President Paul von Hindenburg appoint him chancellor. Hindenburg was initially reluctant but finally agreed. Hitler had now achieved the political clout necessary to make him absolute ruler.

FACT

One of the most vivid and frightening film images of wartime Germany is of thousands of hysterical Nazi supporters raising their hands in stiff-armed salute to their Führer while screaming *"Heil Hitler!"* (Long live Hitler!) It's an image that, once seen, is difficult to forget. The salute was used by members of the Nazi Party and other civilians to show their allegiance.

Der Führer

After Hindenburg's death, Hitler became the Führer of Germany, consolidating his power with astounding speed. By that time, the Nazi Party was in complete control of the nation, and Hitler immediately began his despicable racial policies designed to eliminate all undesirables—particularly the Jewish people. Many prominent Jews, fearing for their lives, fled the country.

Hitler also started immediate rearmament and militarization of Germany, despite the fact that it violated the Treaty of Versailles. Though he was chastised, other nations did nothing to stop him. As his arsenal grew, Hitler planned four distinct attacks in his drive to conquer Europe and then the world: Czechoslovakia, Britain and France, the Soviet Union, and finally the United States.

Hitler wasted little time putting his military plan into action. He aligned himself with Italian dictator Benito Mussolini. By the middle of 1940, the German despot had taken much of Europe through political scheming and sheer military might. The USSR proved more difficult than originally assumed, however, and the tide of the war changed dramatically with the entry of the United States.

Figure 7-1 Adolf Hitler after the conquest of France, June 23, 1940.

Photo courtesy of the National Archives (242-HLB-5073-20)

The German military machine achieved tremendous victories but was hampered by Hitler's unwillingness to delegate authority where necessary and his "no retreat, no surrender" policies. Victory in war often comes from a strategic pullback and regrouping, but Hitler almost always refused to let his commanders do this, particularly during the Soviet campaign. As a result, a huge number of men and equipment were lost unnecessarily over the course of the war. In the big picture, the German army's worst enemy was its commander in chief.

The Allies were able to get an important foothold in Europe with the Normandy invasion in June 1944, and the push toward Berlin began in earnest. By this time, the German army was facing overwhelming defeat. A growing number of Germans believed that the only way to end the carnage was to assassinate Hitler, but several attempts failed.

Hitler launched his last desperate offensive of the war in the fabled Battle of the Bulge—in December 1944. The attack managed to push into the Allied defensive line, but the Allies rallied to drive the Germans back.

Hitler's Final Days

As Allied troops advanced on Berlin, it became apparent that the end was near. Hitler chose to take his own life rather than face trial and judgment in the world court.

Preparing for death, Hitler married his longtime girlfriend, Eva Braun. His marriage to Braun was performed on April 28, 1945, by a Berlin municipal councillor. During the ceremony, both Hitler and Braun swore they were "of complete Aryan descent." A party followed the ceremony, but few people felt like celebrating.

Hitler then set about dictating his will and political testament. He appointed Karl Dönitz as his successor and encouraged his countrymen to continue their opposition to "international Jewry." He also noted that his decision to die was made voluntarily, as was his decision to stay in Berlin.

Shortly after 2:00 A.M. on April 30, Hitler bade farewell to his two secretaries and about twenty other people as exploding Soviet artillery echoed above. He then retired to his room with Braun.

Hitler emerged alone the following day for lunch. Shortly after, he ordered his chauffeur, Erich Kempka, to get some gasoline from the Chancellery garage. Hitler and Braun then returned to their private quarters, where Hitler shot himself through the mouth and Braun took cyanide. Kempka and some aides carried their bodies into the Chancellery garden, doused them with gasoline, and set them on fire. Just hours later, Berlin fell to the Allies.

Benito Mussolini

Renowned both for his shaved head and for making the infamously bad Italian train system run on time, dictator Benito Mussolini plunged his nation into a global conflict for which it was woefully unprepared. Aligning himself with Adolf Hitler, he sought world domination—only to lose the support of his own people and ultimately his life.

Benito Mussolini was born on July 29, 1883, in Dovia di Predappio, Italy. His father was a blacksmith and his mother an elementary school teacher. Mostly self-educated, Mussolini became a teacher and socialist journalist in northern Italy. He married Rachele Guidi in 1910 and fathered five children.

Mussolini opposed Italy's 1912 war with Libya and was jailed for expressing his views. Shortly after his release, he became editor of *Avanti!*, the Socialist Party's newspaper in Milan. He initially opposed involvement in World War I, considering it "imperialist," but changed his mind and called for Italy to fight on the side of the Allies. He was expelled from the Socialist Party and soon started his own newspaper, *Il Popolo d'Italia* (The People of Italy), which would eventually become the voice of the Fascist movement.

Mussolini and several other young war veterans formed the Fasci di Combattimento in March 1919. The organization, which took its name from the fasces, an ancient symbol of Roman discipline, promoted a nationalistic, antiliberal, antisocialist position that attracted many middle-class Italians. The party, its members dressed in telltale black shirts, grew quickly, making a name for itself by attacking peasant leagues, socialist groups, and any others it deemed a threat to Italian nationalism.

Il Duce

In 1922, the Fascists—under direction from Mussolini—marched on Rome. A nervous King Victor Emmanuel III invited Mussolini to form a coalition government. He seized the opportunity, and within four years was able to maneuver the nation into a totalitarian regime, with himself as *Il Duce* (the leader).

Eager to create a modern Roman Empire, Mussolini defied the League of Nations and, in a very quick war, conquered Ethiopia in 1936. The populace supported this initiative, but Mussolini's popularity quickly plummeted when he backed Generalissimo Francisco Franco in the Spanish Civil War, developed an alliance with Nazi Germany, legislated anti-Semitism, and invaded Albania in 1939.

The relationship between Hitler and Mussolini was primarily one of convenience for both men. Hitler saw Mussolini as a role model who could teach him much about dictatorial control. However, as Mussolini made one mistake after another, Hitler lost his respect for the Italian leader. Mussolini, on the other hand, disliked Hitler from the beginning.

FACT

Promising to support Austrian independence, Mussolini described Hitler to an Austrian official as "a horrible sexual degenerate, a dangerous fool." According to Mussolini, fascism recognized the rights of the individual, as well as of religion and the family. Nazism, on the other hand, was "savage barbarism."

However, as much as Mussolini found Hitler foolish, he couldn't help but be impressed by Hitler's quick rise to power and his accelerating military might. In October 1936, Germany and Italy signed a secret alliance that promised a joint effort on issues of foreign policy. The pact was the beginning of the Axis.

In September 1937, Mussolini met Hitler on the Führer's home turf. He toured German military factories and attended a huge rally in Berlin. The two men joined hands before the massive crowds and pledged eternal cooperation.

The Puppet

Mussolini was eager to join the war in Europe after Hitler's conquest of Poland but was forced to wait until his own army could be strengthened. Italy officially entered the war in June 1940 after Germany had taken France. In quick succession, Italy attacked British territory in Africa, invaded Greece, and joined Germany in dividing Yugoslavia and attacking the Soviet Union. Italy eventually also declared war on the United States.

But Mussolini's Italy was not Hitler's Germany, and some early military successes were quickly countered by major defeats. The country's unprepared army was devastated by heavy casualties, and the Italian people began to question their role in the global conflict. On July 16, 1943, after the Allied invasion of Sicily, Italian Fascist leaders met with Mussolini and demanded a session of the Fascist Grand Council. Mussolini, sensing that his days as ruler of Italy were numbered, stalled with the excuse that he would soon be meeting with Hitler. Mussolini hoped to peacefully end his nation's alliance with Germany, but Hitler was able to talk him out of it.

On July 24, the Grand Council met for the first time since 1939. After Mussolini offered a lengthy speech on Italy's current position in the war, the council voted to depose him. King Victor Emmanuel deposed Mussolini on July 25, 1943, and replaced him with Marshal Pietro Badoglio, chief of the Italian General Staff. In September, King Victor Emmanuel and Badoglio brokered an armistice with the Allies—who had invaded southern Italy— that effectively removed Italy from the Axis.

Mussolini was arrested shortly after his removal from office, possibly because Italian authorities hoped to use him as a bargaining chip with the Allies. Though moved to a number of locations over the next couple of months, he was finally rescued by a German raid on September 12 and flown to Vienna, then to Munich, where he was reunited with his wife. On September 14, Mussolini met with Hitler at the Führer's compound in Rastenburg.

Hitler placed Mussolini in charge of a puppet state in northern Italy known as the Italian Socialist Republic. But the job came at a hefty price. In exchange for his freedom, Mussolini was forced to give Germany Trieste, the Istrian Peninsula, and South Tyrol.

Mussolini had little real authority over his nonexistent state, which was actually controlled by the Germans. However, in January 1944 he used what little power he had to order a public trial of his son-in-law, Galeazzo Ciano, who had been arrested by the Germans the previous August. Mussolini was enraged that Ciano had participated in his ouster as the leader of Italy and wanted to make examples of Ciano and four other former members of the Fascist Grand Council. Ciano and the others were found guilty of treason and executed by firing squad on January 11.

As the Allies swept through Italy in April 1945, Mussolini visited his wife in Milan and encouraged her to flee the country. He left Milan in a motorcade with his longtime mistress, Clara Petacci. On April 27, Italian partisan guerrillas stopped the motorcade at gunpoint near Dongo on Lake Como and yanked Mussolini and Petacci from their cars. The next day, Mussolini,

Petacci, and twelve other captured Fascist leaders were executed by the guerrillas and their bodies hung upside down from a gas station girder in Milan. Allied officials eventually ordered the bodies removed.

The bodies were buried in an unmarked grave. Later, Mussolini's body was removed and buried in Predappio next to his son Bruno, who had died in a 1941 air crash.

Winston Churchill

Few leaders had as much influence over the course of World War II as British prime minister Winston Churchill. With unflagging strength and vitality, he rallied his beleaguered people when things looked their bleakest, never wavering from his belief that the Allies would eventually emerge victorious. As a result of his tenacity and dedication, most historians consider him the greatest British leader of the twentieth century.

Churchill was born on November 30, 1874, at Blenheim Palace in Oxfordshire to an old and very aristocratic family. He was the oldest son of Lord Randolph Henry Spencer Churchill, a British statesman who rose to be chancellor of the exchequer and leader of the House of Commons. His mother, Jennie Jerome, was American by birth, the daughter of a New York financier.

In his youth, Churchill developed a deep interest in military affairs and warfare, and his later years at Harrow School prepared him for the Royal Military College at Sandhurst, from which he graduated with honors. In 1895, Churchill was commissioned a second lieutenant in the Fourth Queen's Own Hussars, a regiment of the British army. On military leave as a war correspondent for a London newspaper, he covered the Spanish army's attempts to quell a rebellion in Cuba. It was during this endeavor that Churchill came under enemy fire for the first time.

Churchill Enters Politics

Churchill resigned his army commission in 1899 and, in keeping with his family history, turned to politics. He ran for a seat in Parliament as a Conservative candidate but was defeated. Working as a journalist, he went to South Africa to cover the Boer War and was captured by the Boers and imprisoned in Pretoria. He escaped and caught a train to Portuguese East Africa, a feat that made him a hero back home. Churchill later returned to South Africa and sought another army commission. He fought during the Boer War and again wrote about his exploits.

Churchill's wartime activities made him famous in Great Britain and paved the way for his election to the House of Commons. Though a Conservative, he butted heads with the Conservative leadership over a number of issues and eventually took a seat with the Liberal Party. Churchill's political star continued to climb for the next several years. In 1908 he married Clementine Ogilvy Hozier, who bore him five children, one of whom died in childhood.

In 1911, as world events were leading to World War I, Churchill was appointed first lord of the admiralty by Prime Minister Herbert Henry Asquith. Churchill was instructed to create a naval war staff and to maintain the fleet in constant readiness for war. Under his guidance, the British navy became a formidable force, and when war broke out in 1914, its presence in the North Sea helped keep the German fleet under control. Churchill was an active participant during World War I, aiding the Belgians at Antwerp (though the port was lost) and working to develop armored tanks that he believed would help end the stalemate in Europe. His work greatly helped the Allied effort, though Churchill would later become the scapegoat for the failed land campaign at the Gallipoli Peninsula on the Dardanelles. (The campaign actually failed because of delays and incompetent leadership.)

After World War I, Churchill was appointed to the War Office and then to the Colonial Office. In the next election, he was defeated as the Conservatives returned to power, and he found himself cast from the House of Commons for the first time since 1900. Churchill turned again to writing, penning a comprehensive history of World War I, among other books. He won election in 1924, once again as a Conservative, and remained in the House of Commons for the next four decades.

Churchill's career and popularity ebbed and flowed over the next several years. He supported King Edward VIII in the controversy over his romance with Wallis Warfield Simpson, which eventually led to Edward's abdication from the throne, and this cost Churchill heavily in the opinion polls. It also widened the rift between Churchill and Prime Minister Stanley Baldwin. In addition, Churchill continued to sound frequent warnings about Adolf Hitler and the Nazis, though few people listened.

World War II Breaks Out

When World War II broke out, Prime Minister Neville Chamberlain asked Churchill to become a member of his war cabinet. He was again made first lord of the admiralty and immediately began efforts to bolster the Royal Navy, particularly in the area of antisubmarine warfare.

Public confidence in Chamberlain began to fade with the German invasion of Norway, and he resigned on May 10, 1940, the day Germans invaded the Netherlands and Belgium. King George VI asked Churchill to be prime minister, and the Labour and Liberal Parties immediately agreed to join the Conservatives in a wartime coalition government. Said Churchill during his first report to the House of Commons: "I have nothing to offer but blood, toil, tears, and sweat."

Churchill quickly proved to be a skillful prime minister. As commander in chief, he had direct control over the formulation of policy and the conduct of military operations. He and his staff supervised virtually every aspect of the war effort, working closely with the war cabinet secretariat. Through Churchill's efforts, Great Britain was able to arm itself and prepare for war with remarkable speed.

Churchill assumed power just as the Germans were invading France. The French begged him to send fighter squadrons, but he quickly realized that there was little Britain could do to stop the German war machine in France. In one of his most difficult decisions, he declined France's request. Great Britain's planes, he knew, would be needed for his nation's own air defense.

After the fall of France, Hitler turned his attention to Great Britain. His goal was a land invasion following massive bombing raids designed to weaken Britain to the point of helplessness. It was a dark time for the nation, but Churchill did all he could to protect its suffering populace. His frequent speeches did much to maintain public morale and rally his people to their own defense.

Early in the war, Churchill established a strong relationship with President Franklin Roosevelt, who did much to help the British war effort despite America's position of neutrality. When the United States officially entered the war in December 1941, the relationship between the two world leaders—based on mutual trust, respect, and admiration—grew closer still. However, as the war progressed and the United States became increasingly powerful, Churchill found himself having to accept American-imposed war plans. His relationship with Roosevelt began to deteriorate, and Churchill's ideas often went unheeded. In early 1945, for example, Roosevelt ignored Churchill's warnings about Joseph Stalin's plans to take over countries in Eastern Europe after the war, with dire consequences.

Churchill Re-elected Following the War

Churchill was re-elected to Parliament in the first postwar election in July 1945, but the Labour Party gained a majority and Churchill, who had run as a Conservative, was replaced as prime minister by Labour leader Clement Richard Attlee. Churchill was at the Potsdam Conference—the last meeting among the United States, Britain, and the USSR—when he received news of the election, and his chair at the conference was taken by Attlee. Churchill was extremely disappointed to be retiring as prime minister, having worked so hard to save the nation from German aggression.

Winston Churchill coined the phrase "iron curtain" during a 1946 speech in Fulton, Missouri. It defined the barrier constructed by the Soviet Union between its Eastern European satellites and the rest of Europe.

Winston Churchill continued to be involved in politics and international affairs. In 1951, his efforts to revitalize the Conservative Party were rewarded when he was again asked to assume the mantle of prime minister. The international nuclear threat was one of his primary concerns, and he tried unsuccessfully to broker a summit conference among the USSR and the Western powers. In 1953, Queen Elizabeth II conferred on him the Order of the Garter, Britain's highest order of knighthood, making him Sir Winston Churchill. He resigned as prime minister in 1955 but remained a member of the House of Commons.

Churchill continued to write and paint in his retirement, and his paintings were exhibited at the Royal Academy of Arts in 1959. He died in 1965, two months after his nintieth birthday and was buried near Blenheim Palace.

Emperor Hirohito

Emperor Hirohito, born in 1901, reigned as emperor of Japan from 1926 until his death in 1989. Revered as divine by his people, he had little to do with the actual governing of his country, his authority stifled by pomp and pageantry. During World War II, he held the title of commander in chief of the armed forces, though almost all military affairs were handled by others.

Hirohito was born in Tokyo, the eldest son of Crown Prince Yoshohito. Beginning in 1914, he was educated at a palace school created to prepare him for his future role as emperor.

Hirohito became the first Japanese crown prince to visit the West when he toured Europe for six months in 1921. During his trip, he expressed great interest in British culture and tradition and was particularly attracted to the concept of a constitutional monarchy as characterized by King George V. When Hirohito became emperor in 1926, he chose to call his dynasty *Showa*, meaning "peace and enlightenment."

Under the Japanese constitution of 1889, Hirohito held tremendous authority that derived from the belief that the Japanese imperial line descended from Amaterasu, the sun goddess of the Shinto religion, and had ruled the nation forever. However, Hirohito's authority was primarily symbolic; he was trained by his advisers to refrain from interfering in political decisions. He remained uninvolved in politics and avoided public controversy, refraining from taking a stand on almost any public issue. In most cases, Hirohito merely approved the policies of his advisers and ministers, which were then adopted in his name.

Because the day-to-day governing of his nation was controlled by militarists, it came as no surprise that Japan instituted an aggressive foreign policy as it sought new sources for needed natural resources. And though Hirohito had little influence on most military issues, he was not completely removed from his nation's aggression. He approved a number of important Japanese cabinet decisions, including the 1937 invasion of China and the attack on Pearl Harbor. (In an oral autobiography published after his death, Hirohito said he was powerless to stop the militarists because any dissent on his part would have led to his assassination. He also denied knowledge of many of the atrocities committed by Japan during the war, though Western biographers have uncovered evidence that he knew of—and did nothing to stop—the Bataan Death March and the execution of American airmen captured after the Doolittle raid on Tokyo.)

FACT

When Emperor Hirohito of Japan died in 1989, he was buried with several of his favorite possessions, including a microscope and a Mickey Mouse watch, which he had received during a 1975 visit to the United States.

Hirohito was as loathed by the Allies as Hitler and Mussolini during World War II, and many people expected the emperor to be tried for war crimes after the fighting was over. However, Allied officials felt it was necessary that Hirohito remain emperor to maintain political calm in postwar Japan, and neither he nor his immediate family (which included many high-ranking military officers) were ever questioned about their involvement in or knowledge of Japan's wartime activities.

Hideki Tojo

Hideki Tojo, along with Adolf Hitler and Benito Mussolini, personally represented the evil Axis to many people around the world. Though not a dictator like his Axis allies, Tojo ruled the military with an iron fist, and as prime minister was responsible for many of Japan's strategic successes during the early stages of the war.

Tojo was born in Tokyo in 1884, the son of an army general. He attended the Imperial Military Academy and then the Army Staff College, from which he graduated at the top of his class in 1915. From 1919 to 1922 he was a military attaché in Switzerland and Germany, and in the late 1920s he served in a section of the Army General Staff, monitoring mobilization preparations for full-scale war.

In the early 1930s, Tojo joined a group of officers known as the Control Faction, which was devoted to updating and modernizing the Japanese army, with an emphasis on military technology. However, his association with the group was viewed unfavorably by an opposing faction, and Tojo was punished with a series of posts far below his status and ability. His career took a turn for the better after 1935 when he was sent to Manchukuo, the puppet state established by the Japanese in Manchuria. Tojo eventually became the chief of staff of the Kwantung Army, the primary Japanese military force in the region.

While in Manchukuo, Tojo became known for his efficient and decisive manner and his aggressiveness as a staff officer. A tough disciplinarian, he was secretly called "The Razor" by his men. Tojo was ordered back to Tokyo in 1938 to serve as vice minister of war, and in 1940 he was promoted to war minister. He closely watched the war in Europe and became convinced that Germany would eventually triumph. In the fall of 1940, he actively supported an official alliance with Germany and Italy, making Japan the third member of the Axis triad.

Tojo strongly advocated Japanese expansion into East Asia through military force and the establishment of a regional co-prosperity sphere under Japanese control. When relations between Japan and the United States worsened in 1941 as a result of Japanese aggression, Tojo held firm, opposing any compromise that would undermine Japan's position in East Asia. By the fall of 1941, it appeared that Japan would have no choice but to enter the world war. Tojo, widely viewed by many as a man who could guide Japan to victory, was named prime minister in October. In December 1941 his cabinet decided to declare war on the United States by attacking the American naval base at Pearl Harbor.

Tojo's scope of authority widened over the course of the war. While retaining his position as war minister, he became head of the Munitions Ministry in 1943 and took over as army chief of staff in 1944.

Tojo's political power began to wane as Allied victories over Japan became increasingly common toward the end of the war. Forced to resign as prime minister in July 1944 when the United States took the island of Saipan (thus placing Japan within range of Allied bombers), Tojo remained in retirement for the rest of the war.

In September 1945, Tojo tried to commit suicide when he learned that he was to be arrested and tried for war crimes. After his recovery, he was tried as ordered by the International Military Tribunal in Tokyo and found guilty. He was hanged in December 1948.

Franklin Delano Roosevelt

During his unprecedented twelve years in office, Franklin D. Roosevelt faced national and international problems whose severity had not been seen since the presidency of Abraham Lincoln. It's a testament to Roosevelt's skill as a leader and a politician that he was able to successfully guide the nation—and the world—through these troubling times.

When Roosevelt was elected as the thirty-second president in 1932, the nation was well into the most devastating economic depression it had ever experienced. And nine years later he would be forced to ask Congress to thrust the United States into a war that would eventually envelop most of the world. No political weakling like many of his immediate predecessors, Franklin Roosevelt mustered all of his strength and courage to keep the world free from tyranny.

Franklin Roosevelt was born on his family's estate in Hyde Park, New York, on January 10, 1882. His father, James, was a successful businessman with a variety of interests, and his mother, Sara, was a prominent member of New York society. The family, conservative Democrats by belief, was deeply involved in politics and had already produced one president: Franklin's cousin, Theodore Roosevelt.

Political Career

Roosevelt entered politics in 1910 when he ran for the New York State Senate. He campaigned vigorously and won by a narrow margin. In Albany, he developed a reputation as an independent scrapper who followed his own ideals rather than the desires of the more established Democratic leadership. He quickly became known as a social and economic reformer and was re-elected in 1912—despite his inability to actively campaign because of a case of typhoid fever. Much of Roosevelt's political success must be attributed to his association with Louis McHenry Howe, a journalist and savvy political strategist who knew how to promote Roosevelt's career with maximum effectiveness.

Roosevelt managed to make a name for himself in national politics even before his state senate re-election by assisting in Woodrow Wilson's presidential campaign. When Wilson took the White House in 1912, Roosevelt was rewarded for his hard work with an appointment as assistant secretary of the navy. Roosevelt resigned his state senate seat and moved to Washington, D.C.

Roosevelt served as assistant secretary of the navy until 1920. He came to understand how Washington worked and how to manipulate the system to get things done, so when the United States entered World War I in 1917, the navy was ready and able to leap into action. Roosevelt's position required him to make frequent public speeches, which helped establish his image as a politician with a tremendous future. Roosevelt resigned his Navy Department post in 1920 to campaign for the vice presidency under Democratic presidential candidate James Cox, but they were defeated by Republicans Warren G. Harding and Calvin Coolidge.

In August 1921, Roosevelt was diagnosed with poliomyelitis (polio). In pain and no longer able to walk, Roosevelt might have thought that his political career was destined to end before it had really begun. His mother urged him to retire to Hyde Park and enjoy the peace and quiet there, but encouraged by both his wife, Eleanor, and Louis Howe, Roosevelt refused to let his illness keep him down. Though primarily confined to a wheelchair, he remained active, maintaining important political contacts and slowly rebuilding his career.

Franklin Roosevelt was very rarely photographed in a wheelchair or walking with the leg braces and canes he required, and the press almost never discussed his disability. As a result, many Americans remained unaware for years that Roosevelt was paralyzed from the waist down.

Throughout much of the 1920s, Roosevelt worked with Al Smith, helping him win his second term as governor of New York and later assisting with Smith's presidential campaigns. In 1928, at Smith's encouragement, Roosevelt ran for governor of New York, winning by a very slim margin. Smith, meanwhile, lost the presidency to Herbert Hoover. The following year, the United States slipped into a crippling economic depression when the stock market crashed, taking with it the fortunes of thousands of Americans and forcing the closing of many banks. In 1930, Roosevelt was re-elected governor of New York—a position that would quickly help him reach the White House.

Roosevelt Becomes President, Introduces the New Deal

As a result of his aggressive personality, his reputation as a social reformer, and his strong New York roots, Roosevelt was a natural for the 1932 Democratic presidential nomination. He worked vigorously to hold on to his status as party favorite and was nominated on the fourth ballot. In his acceptance speech, Roosevelt promised the American people a "new deal" that would help alleviate many of the social and economic ills forced on them by the Depression. He campaigned strongly, making numerous speeches throughout the country, and ultimately took forty-two of the nation's forty-eight states.

Roosevelt's first concerns were with helping the millions of Americans who were suffering as a result of the Depression. He instituted a number of domestic reforms, bringing the government more directly into people's lives than ever before. During his first 100 days in office, Roosevelt and Congress worked together to pass more bills than any previous administration had done in a similar time span. The Emergency Banking Act, which was introduced, passed, and signed by the president in just one day, gave the federal government remarkable power to deal with the banking crisis that had economically crippled the nation.

Roosevelt also worked hard and fast on relief legislation designed to temporarily assist out-of-work Americans while getting them back into the work force as quickly as possible. Under Roosevelt's Federal Emergency Relief Administration (FERA), large amounts of money were given to the states to assist those most in need.

Nearly one-sixth of the nation was still on government relief by the end of 1934. In 1935, the Works Progress Administration (WPA) was established by executive order and the FERA was abolished. The WPA (later renamed the Work Projects Administration) helped the nation by building or repairing roads, schools, libraries, and government buildings. Roosevelt also established the Civilian Conservation Corps to assist unemployed and unmarried young men and the National Youth Administration, which gave part-time jobs to needy high school and college students.

Roosevelt was a strong advocate of government-sponsored social and economic change. His administration enacted reform legislation that increased the federal government's regulatory activities as well as important banking legislation designed to bolster the flagging dollar.

Re-elections

Roosevelt did much to help the American people during his first term in office, and he was re-elected in 1936 with more than 60 percent of the popular vote. However, middle-class support for the Roosevelt administration began to erode in 1937 and 1938, primarily because of its support of increasingly militant labor unions. Roosevelt's armor also lost some of its sheen when he unsuccessfully tried to increase the size of the Supreme Court. The president argued that the change was needed to facilitate the high court's work, but in truth, Roosevelt hoped to pack the court with members who better supported his progressive program. Then, in 1937, the president cut spending to balance the budget, causing the Depression to worsen and further tarnishing Roosevelt's reputation.

Roosevelt scored better with his foreign policy. He instituted the Good Neighbor policy toward Latin America, which meant that the United States would no longer intervene in Latin America to protect private American interests. Later, he requested a huge government appropriation for naval expansion, then asked for yet more money to bolster American defense. After war broke out in September 1939, he called a special session of Congress to revise the Neutrality Act so that nations at war against Germany could buy arms on a cash-and-carry basis. Then, after his re-election in 1940, Roosevelt worked around national isolationist policies through congressional passage in March 1941 of the Lend-Lease Act, which allowed the United States to militarily aid Great Britain and other nations without actually having to declare war on Germany and Italy. Roosevelt's goal was to provide yet more aid to Great Britain and France, though deep in his heart he knew the United States was headed toward war whether it wanted to or not.

Entering the War

America entered World War II on December 8, 1941, the day after the Japanese bombed Pearl Harbor. Roosevelt found himself in the dual position of commander in chief of the U.S. armed forces and soothing father figure to the American people. Historians have long debated Roosevelt's effectiveness during the war years, though most agree he was a strong national and international figure who understood that the only way to protect the United States was to drive Germany and Japan into unconditional surrender.

Roosevelt was, for the most part, admired and respected by the other Allied leaders with whom he was aligned. Though the United States was slow to enter the conflict in Europe, once it was involved, Roosevelt offered everything in the American arsenal and then some. He consulted often with other world leaders and helped ease the hurt feelings and international misunderstandings that were sure to accompany a war effort of such remarkable scope.

Figure 7-2
President Roosevelt receives a Red Cross pin from a young volunteer.

Photo courtesy of the Franklin D. Roosevelt Presidential Library and Museum (ARC 196055)

Roosevelt's stint as assistant secretary of the navy under Wilson served him well during this period. Most historians agree that he ably directed the course of the war and worked closely with his Joint Chiefs of Staff in making important decisions. Very often, Roosevelt's final decisions went against those of his military advisers as he attempted to balance both military and political concerns. Examples include the decision to invade North Africa, the plan for Douglas MacArthur to retake the Philippines, and the decision to continue sending Lend-Lease ships to the Soviet Union.

Extraordinary Challenges

Roosevelt's job as commander in chief was extraordinarily difficult. At the beginning of the war, he found himself in the unenviable position of having to dramatically increase military production without creating inflation, and he had to oversee the allocation of goods throughout several theaters of war and to the various Allied powers. In addition, Roosevelt oversaw the immediate buildup of the nation's army and navy, recruiting servicemen (and women) and increasing production of needed materiel. Lastly, he had to stay in constant contact with the American people, explaining his decisions and their importance in ways that the average American could understand and support. Thankfully, this was a skill at which Roosevelt was adept. His frequent radio addresses, known as "fireside chats," helped calm a frightened populace during its most desperate and dire hours.

Franklin Roosevelt was the only president to be elected to four terms in office—and the only president who will ever hold such an honor. The Twenty-second Amendment to the Constitution, adopted after his death, limits a president to two elected terms.

Though Franklin Delano Roosevelt saw the United States into its second world war and worked tirelessly to support it, he died before an Allied victory could be achieved. The war took a terrible toll on his health, and he looked old and frail while campaigning for his fourth term. He defeated Thomas Dewey in 1944, and in the early spring of 1945, Roosevelt traveled to his vacation home at Warm Springs, Georgia, in an attempt to rebuild his strength. On April 12, Roosevelt complained of a severe headache; he died a short time later from a massive cerebral hemorrhage. Vice President Harry

Truman took the oath of office later that day to become the nation's thirty-third president.

Charles de Gaulle

Though forced to flee to Great Britain with the fall of France in 1940, Charles de Gaulle was not about to give up on his beloved country. Over the objections of Winston Churchill, he established a Free French movement that helped to liberate the nation.

Charles André Joseph Marie de Gaulle was born in Lille, France, on November 22, 1890. The son of a teacher, he attended the Saint-Cyr Military Academy, graduating in 1912. An infantry officer during World War I, de Gaulle was wounded three times and eventually captured by the Germans. After the war, he was appointed aide-de-camp to Marshal Henri Philippe Pétain. During this period, de Gaulle became a true student of war, conceiving doctrines and plans that conflicted with established military articles of faith. In his book *The Army of the Future*, de Gaulle recommended lightning-swift movements and use of armored forces that very closely mirrored Hitler's blitzkrieg strategy.

When the war in Europe began in September 1939 with the German invasion of Poland, de Gaulle was commander of tanks in the French Fifth Army. However, under the French army command structure, it was outside de Gaulle's authority to actually place the tanks into action. After Germany raced through Poland, de Gaulle requested—and was granted—command of an armored division. His division engaged the Germans in one of France's few offensives in Germany's campaign against France and the Low Countries.

FACT

Charles de Gaulle had a strong sense of self-purpose. While he was attending military school, a fellow student commented, "I have a curious feeling that you are intended for a very great destiny." To which de Gaulle replied, "Yes. So have I."

On June 6, 1940, de Gaulle was named undersecretary of state to the minister of national defense and war. Three days later he flew to London to meet with Prime Minister Winston Churchill about coordinating the strategy of the two nations' armies. But when de Gaulle returned home, he found the government on the verge of fleeing. He pleaded with Prime Minister Pétain to stay and fight or at least to evacuate troops to French North Africa and take a stand there.

But de Gaulle's pleas fell on deaf ears. By that point, France was on the verge of surrender, its army no match for the German juggernaut. De Gaulle returned to Great Britain, and in an address to his countrymen broadcast across the channel by the BBC he stated, "France is not alone!" The collaborationist Vichy government charged de Gaulle with treason and condemned him to death. Unbowed, de Gaulle formed a government-in-exile force known as the Free French movement, which later became the Free French National Council.

Later, de Gaulle aligned himself with General Henri Giraud in French North Africa, where another freedom movement had developed, becoming copresident with Giraud of the French Committee of National Liberation. After the crafty de Gaulle was able to facilitate Giraud's departure, he became the leader of both the French Resistance movement in German-occupied France and the Free French in North Africa.

Shortly before the start of the Normandy invasion, de Gaulle demanded that his provisional government be declared the rightful government of all liberated areas in France. General Dwight Eisenhower was able to placate de Gaulle by promising not to accept any ruling government except de Gaulle's and by making de Gaulle supreme commander of the French armed forces. On August 26, 1944, a triumphant de Gaulle rode into newly liberated Paris behind French and American troops.

At the war's end, de Gaulle was elected interim president of the provisional government by a newly elected constitutional assembly. He tried desperately to make France a part of the postwar planning but was rebuffed by Churchill, Roosevelt, and Stalin.

De Gaulle resigned as provisional president on January 20, 1946. He returned to politics in 1958 and was elected president of the newly created Fifth Republic under a revised constitution. He held the position until 1969, when he resigned after defeat in a national referendum. He retired to his estate in Colombey-les-deux-Églises, where he worked on his memoirs until his death in 1970.

Joseph Stalin

Few Allied leaders were as controversial as Soviet dictator Joseph Stalin. A valued ally in the war against Germany, Stalin quickly became the enemy by making a grab for much of Eastern Europe once the war was over.

Stalin was born Joseph Vissarionovich Dzhugashvili on December 21, 1879, in what would later become the Soviet Republic of Georgia. His father was a cobbler and his mother a house cleaner. In 1888, Stalin entered the Gori Church School. He was an excellent student and won a scholarship to the Tbilisi Theological Seminary. It was there that he was introduced to the political philosophies of Karl Marx, which caused him to rethink his dedication to the church. Because of his involvement with the underground revolutionary movement to overthrow the monarchy, Stalin was expelled from the seminary in 1899. Soon, he was arrested for distributing illegal literature (primarily Marxist propaganda) to rail workers and others, and was eventually exiled to Siberia. However, he managed to escape and returned to Georgia in 1904.

He took the name of Stalin ("man of steel") and eventually joined the Bolsheviks, who were being led by Vladimir Lenin. He married in 1905 (his wife, Yekaterina, died two years later). Between 1908 and 1912, Stalin was arrested several times but managed to escape. In 1912, he traveled to St. Petersburg (later Petrograd and then Leningrad) and joined the staff of a small newspaper titled *Pravda* (Truth), later the official Communist newspaper of the USSR. It was then that Stalin was encouraged by Lenin to write his primary theoretical work, *Marxism and the National Question*. In 1913, Stalin was arrested again and sentenced to life in exile. This time, he was not able to regain his freedom until the revolution of 1917 that instituted Communist rule.

Communist Takeover of Russia

Free again, Stalin traveled back to Petrograd, where he became deeply involved in the workings of the Bolshevik government and became a member of the party's Central Committee bureau. In 1919, he was elected to the

Politburo, the Communist Party's highest decision-making body. As a political commissar in the Red Army during the Russian Civil War, he oversaw military activities against the counterrevolutionary White forces led by General Piotr Wrangel.

Stalin was elected general secretary of the Communist Party in 1922, which helped solidify the base of his political power. Aggressive by nature, he often clashed with Lenin, who came to regret his association with Stalin. Lenin eventually called for Stalin's removal from office, but Stalin was able to hold on to his position through slick political maneuvering. After Lenin's death in 1924, Stalin used political connections, strategic alliances, and good old-fashioned back-stabbing to establish and maintain his power. By 1929, he had become the supreme ruler of the USSR.

Stalin as Supreme Ruler

A brutal and vicious leader, Stalin carried out a number of purges throughout the 1930s to eliminate anyone who might oppose him. His purge of the Red Army just before the onset of World War II removed nearly a third of the officer corps, hampering the nation's ability to defend itself early in the conflict.

Stalin would continue his campaign of terror throughout his life, sending as many as 25 million of his own people to squalid prison camps in Siberia before his death in 1953. People could be exiled to prison for virtually anything, causing the entire nation to tremble in fear under his iron-fisted rule. During World War II, Stalin sentenced his soldiers to prison camps for the crime of being captured by the Germans.

Entering the War

Though ideologically opposed to Nazism, Stalin saw value in aligning with Hitler, and in August 1939 the two leaders signed a nonaggression pact that essentially gave the Soviet Union a piece of Poland. However, Hitler turned on his ally and invaded the Soviet Union on June 22, 1941. The move stunned Stalin, who seemed unable to make a decision for the first few weeks of the German campaign in the Soviet Union.

Stalin's unwillingness to prepare for a German invasion despite overwhelming evidence that it was coming and the poor condition of the Red

Army meant quick victories for Hitler and placed the Soviet Union in a desperate defensive position.

Stalin guided the Soviet war effort from a bomb shelter deep below the Kremlin, directing his generals and rallying his people against the German invaders. Though Stalin was a vicious dictator who had ordered the deaths of millions, the Soviets looked to him to protect them from Hitler.

When the United States entered the war in December 1941, Stalin began pushing for a second front, arguing that a U.S.–British invasion of German-occupied Europe would help take some of the pressure off the Soviet Union. Stalin also demanded supplies from his Allied brethren, threatening to sue for a separate peace with Germany if help was not forthcoming.

FACT

When Stalin addressed his people on the radio in November, he offered fictitious statistics suggesting that the Red Army had the enemy on the run. In truth, it was the other way around: Soviet forces were taking a pounding. Stalin's lies were the result of concerns that the populace of the conquered territories would rise up against him.

Stalin met with Roosevelt and Churchill for the first time at the Tehran Conference in November 1943. By then, the Germans had pulled most of the way out of the Soviet Union and the Soviet offensive had begun. Sensing an Allied victory in Europe, Stalin plotted to gain control of as much territory as he could after the war. Months later, Stalin began his land grab by demanding concessions on Poland and the rest of Eastern Europe in exchange for a promise to declare war on Japan. Soviet participation in the war against Japan lasted all of five days; for his effort, Stalin was allowed to extend his influence into northern Korea, Manchuria, and the Kuril Islands.

The Start of the Cold War

With World War II over, Stalin immediately began his efforts to spread Communism around the world, resulting in icy relations with the Western powers. The Cold War was quick in coming, and it would last for decades.

Stalin's mental abilities began to deteriorate about 1950, and he was seen less and less around the Kremlin. His paranoia growing, Stalin ordered another purge in January 1953, this one aimed at Kremlin doctors who Stalin thought were plotting against high-level Soviet officials. Stalin died from complications of a stroke in March, just before his latest round of terror could begin. He was succeeded as general secretary of the Soviet Communist party by Nikita Khrushchev.

Harry S Truman

Truman had served as vice president under Franklin D. Roosevelt for less than three months when Roosevelt's death thrust Truman into the presidency. His administration would be rife with controversy, but the stalwart Missourian never backed away from the rigors of high office, and he assumed responsibility for all the decisions made by his administration. A small plaque on his desk confirmed Truman's conviction: "The buck stops here."

Truman was born on May 8, 1884, in Lamar, Missouri, the oldest child of John and Martha Truman. When he was six years old, his family moved to Independence, Missouri. It was there, while attending Sunday school at the local Presbyterian church, that Truman met five-year-old Bess Wallace, the girl who would later become his wife.

Political Beginnings

In need of a job, Truman turned to Mike Pendergast, organizer of the Democratic club Truman had belonged to years earlier, for permission to enter a four-way Democratic primary for an eastern Jackson County judgeship. Pendergast okayed Truman's entry but refused to endorse him. Truman campaigned on his war record and his deep Missouri roots, and he won both the primary and the general election. He was sworn into his first public office in January 1923.

When Truman's term was up, he hoped for renomination in the Democratic primary, but the influential Ku Klux Klan had other ideas. Almost as quickly as he had entered politics, Truman was out. For the next two years, he sold automobile club memberships and dabbled in banking.

FACT

Harry Truman's middle initial doesn't stand for any name. It was given to him when he was born to honor both of his grandfathers.

In 1926, Truman sought a four-year term as presiding judge of the county, a position that oversaw county roads, buildings, and taxes. This time, Truman was supported by Pendergast, who was boss of the local political machine. Most political machines maintained power and influence by rewarding supporters with lucrative government jobs, but Truman—never one to mince words—told Pendergast he would immediately fire anyone who wasn't doing his job. Truman won the position and immediately set about correcting the problems caused by years of graft and political cronyism. His hard work paid off with a second easily won four-year term.

Truman Joins the Senate

After his stint as county judge, Truman was asked by Pendergast to run for the U.S. Senate. Truman campaigned vigorously, capitalizing on the popularity of Franklin Roosevelt's New Deal, and beat his Republican opponent by a large margin. However, his stint in the Senate got off to a bad start. Despite his honesty, Truman's association with the Pendergast political machine tainted him, and some believed that he would be implicated in the government's investigation of the Pendergast organization. Truman managed to salvage his political career by impressing two important men: Vice President John Nance Garner and Arthur Vandenberg, the Republican senator from Michigan. With their assistance, Truman was named to two important Senate committees, where his political savvy was a valued asset.

Truman was challenged for his Senate seat in 1940 by two influential Missouri Democrats who had worked to bring down the Pendergast machine. He was the odd man out in the race, hampered by a lack of both money and big-name support. Still, he decided to make his best effort, canvassing the state and talking to the people in terms they could understand. Truman won the general election, and when he returned to the Senate, he received a standing ovation from his colleagues, many of whom were startled by his victory.

As the United States geared up for war in 1941, Truman began investigating allegations of waste in the defense program. He toured the camps and defense plants and found conditions that he called appalling. When he returned to the Senate, he denounced the defense program and demanded a full investigation. His colleagues agreed and put him in charge of the investigating committee.

The Truman committee spent the next two years investigating the defense program and producing detailed reports confirming allegations of fraud and waste. With a budget of just $400,000, the committee managed to save the nation an estimated $15 billion. The committee's success also served to make Harry Truman a national figure, and leading Democrats started mentioning his name as a contender for the 1944 vice presidential spot under Roosevelt.

The Call for a Strong VP

Few people doubted that Roosevelt would run for a fourth term in 1944, though Democratic leaders were increasingly troubled by his failing health. The need for a strong vice presidential candidate became paramount. At the Democratic convention, Truman was elected on the second ballot; together, he and Roosevelt won the election.

Truman had been vice president for just eighty-two days when Roosevelt died, in April 1945. He spent his first month as president meeting with Roosevelt's aides and advisers in an attempt to get up to speed on the war effort and to ensure the continuation of Roosevelt's plans and programs. As the Allies pushed into Germany and victory in Europe seemed guaranteed, Truman insisted that unconditional surrender was Germany's only option. V-E Day (Victory in Europe Day) was announced on May 8, 1945: Truman's sixty-first birthday.

From July 17 to August 2, Truman attended the Potsdam Conference in Germany along with Joseph Stalin and Winston Churchill (with Clement Attlee succeeding Churchill as British prime minister during the conference). The men discussed how best to implement the decisions reached at the previous Yalta Conference regarding the reconstruction of Europe after the war. As presiding officer, Truman suggested the establishment of a council of foreign ministers to oversee peace negotiations, settlement of reparations claims, and war crimes trials.

Figure 7-3 Harry S Truman and Winston Churchill at the Potsdam Conference, 1945.

U.S. Army, courtesy of Harry S Truman Library (ARC 198808)

Truman, backed by the other Allied leaders, issued the Potsdam Declaration on July 26, calling for Japan's unconditional surrender and listing peace terms. Ten days earlier, the first successful atomic bomb had been detonated near Alamogordo, New Mexico. The use of such a bomb, Truman's military advisers told him, could help prevent the loss of up to 500,000 American servicemen should the Allies be forced to invade the Japanese mainland. When Japan ignored the ultimatum set forth in the Potsdam Declaration, Truman authorized the use of the bomb, which was dropped on the city of Hiroshima on August 6. Two days later, Stalin sent troops into Manchuria and Korea, and a second atomic bomb was dropped on Nagasaki the day after that. Japan laid down arms on August 14 and officially surrendered on September 2.

Following the War

With the war over, Harry Truman turned his attention to converting the United States back to a nation at peace. However, many of his proposals received tremendous opposition from Congress, which felt he was trying to attain too much too soon. Controversy over his domestic policies followed Truman for much of the rest of his first term.

The end of World War II did not mean an end to international tension. The USSR, once America's ally, quickly became a feared enemy as it tried to take control of much of Eastern Europe. Truman vehemently opposed Stalin's actions, and both sides quickly broke wartime agreements. The ensuing hostility between the two world superpowers blossomed into what became known as the Cold War.

Truman was re-elected president in 1948, campaigning on a platform of civil rights and other social issues that angered Southern Democrats. The race was exceptionally close, and most people thought Republican candidate Thomas Dewey would win. The *Chicago Tribune*, in its belief that Truman would lose, ran the headline "Dewey Defeats Truman" on the front page of its early edition on November 2. However, when the votes were finally tabulated, Truman had won by nearly 2 million votes.

FACT

In 1950, Harry Truman survived an assassination attempt that killed a White House guard.

After his second term, Truman retired to his home in Independence, Missouri. He remained active in national and regional politics, though his influence had waned, and loyally supported the Democratic presidential candidates in subsequent years. He wrote memoirs and other books, and toured colleges and universities, lecturing on American government. Harry Truman died in 1972 and was buried on the grounds of the Truman Library in Independence.

Chapter 8

The Military Leaders

No individual can be credited, or in some cases blamed, with single-handedly altering the course of the war. However, the military leaders on all sides significantly influenced the results of all of the most major battles fought. The military leaders with the most knowledge of the situation at hand, the most control of the decision-making, and the keenest insight to plan ahead, proved to be among the most definitive factors in the results of the war.

Isoroku Yamamoto

Admiral Isoroku Yamamoto was commander in chief of the Japanese Combined Fleet and the primary architect of the attack on Pearl Harbor, which plunged the United States into World War II. A brilliant naval tactician, he spearheaded many of Japan's victories early in the war.

Yamamoto took command of the Kasumigaura naval air facility in 1924 and immediately began a program to increase and modernize Japanese naval aviation in the belief that combined air and naval support made for an extremely imposing and effective military force. In the early 1930s, Yamamoto commanded the First Carrier Division, doing all he could to sharpen its offensive capabilities. He was later promoted to vice minister of the navy but expressed reservations about engaging in a world war.

Figure 8-1 Admiral Isoroku Yamamoto, the primary architect of the attack on Pearl Harbor.

Getty Images/Keystone/Stringer

Yamamoto was appointed commander in chief of the Combined Fleet by Prime Minister Mitsumasa Yonai in 1939, just as Japan was headed for certain war. Though he still felt uneasy about engaging the United States, he realized that in order to win, Japan would have to cripple U.S. defenses before the United States had a chance to act. With that in mind, Yamamoto conceived a sneak attack on the naval base at Pearl Harbor and spent months putting the plan together.

The attack went just as Yamamoto had planned, with devastating results. However, he was gravely concerned about the fact that the attack had failed to take out any U.S. aircraft carriers, which happened to be out to sea the day of the assault, and he looked for future battles that he hoped would eliminate the carrier threat.

In April 1942, Yamamoto saw his opportunity in a surprise attack on Midway, which he hoped would lure the rest of the U.S. Pacific Fleet within range of Japan's aircraft and battleships. However, the Battle of Midway resulted in an unexpected American victory and the destruction of many Japanese ships and planes.

Yamamoto later engaged American naval forces at Guadalcanal, with both sides suffering huge loses. In February 1943, he was forced to withdraw the remaining troops from Guadalcanal. He tried to bolster Japanese defenses in the Solomon Islands by staging several air raids on U.S. forces, and he came away with a sense of victory. After the raids, he planned a tour of forward bases, unaware that U.S. intelligence had decoded a report of his itinerary. Armed with this knowledge, American fighter planes under Admiral Chester Nimitz ambushed Yamamoto's plane over Bougainville and shot it down on April 18, 1943. Yamamoto was killed in the crash.

Erwin Rommel

General Field Marshal Erwin Rommel came to symbolize in the eyes of many the amazing German war effort in North Africa. A brilliant tactician, Rommel received his nickname, the "Desert Fox," by guiding his elite Afrika Korps to several decisive victories against British forces before finally being pushed back by a cooperative Allied offensive. Rommel was later involved in planning the German defense of northern France.

Figure 8-2 German Field Marshal Erwin Rommel in Libya, November 1941.

Photo courtesy of the National Archives (242-EAPC-6-M713A)

Rommel was born in Heidenheim, Germany, on November 15, 1891. A sickly child, he was first schooled at home but later attended the military academy in Danzig and became an officer cadet in 1910. During World War I, Rommel saw combat in France, Romania, and Italy and was wounded twice. He received numerous decorations for bravery and decided to make the military his career.

Promotions

When World War II started in Europe, Rommel was commandant of Hitler's field headquarters in Poland. Later promoted to brigadier general, he was given command of the Seventh Panzer Division and fought in France and the Low Countries in May and June of 1940. Rommel's tanks led the German push near the Meuse, and he was almost captured when the British counterattacked on May 21. However, Rommel quickly took the offensive and nearly succeeded in overwhelming the British army—including Bernard Montgomery's Third Division. Rommel and Montgomery would meet again in Africa.

Rommel's reputation as a crafty desert fighter was made when he arrived with German divisions to support Italian forces in North Africa in February 1941. The Italian forces had been routed by the British, and it was Rommel's job to recapture the lost territory, then press on into Egypt. His efforts succeeded mightily, and Rommel was rewarded by Hitler with a promotion to field marshal. However, the weapons, supplies, and reinforcements he so desperately needed to continue his offensive never arrived as promised, and after a lot of give-and-take skirmishes between the British and Rommel's Afrika Korps, he was finally forced to retreat when pressed by the better-prepared Allied forces at the Mareth line.

Rommel was evacuated from Africa in March 1943 and sent to command German forces in northern Italy. He recommended that all German forces withdraw to a line north of Rome when Allied forces landed at Salerno in September 1943. A forward defense, suggested by General Field Marshal Albrecht Kesselring, slowed the Allies somewhat, but the Germans were ultimately unable to hold Italy.

Rommel Sees the End

Always a pragmatist, Rommel had started to believe that, despite Hitler's rhetoric, Germany would not be able to survive the coming Allied onslaught, and his once-strong support for the Führer started to wane. Meanwhile, his next appointment was to upgrade the defenses along the Atlantic coast of France in preparation for an anticipated Allied invasion. Rommel firmly believed that victory could be had only if German forces met the invaders on the beaches during the first confusing hours of the invasion, and he asked for mobile reserves at the suspected invasion points and the authority to use them at his discretion. Hitler refused, preferring to make such strategic decisions himself. This decision by Hitler severely hobbled Rommel's defensive plan and, as history later showed, ultimately enabled Allied forces to break the German defensive line.

On July 20, 1944, an assassination attempt was made on Hitler. Rommel had known of the plot and had argued against assassination in favor of having Hitler arrested by the army and tried in a civilian court. On October 14, SS troops surrounded Rommel's house, and a general gave him two options: face trial for treason or take his own life by poison. Rommel chose the latter, having been told that if he opted for a public trial, the Nazis would go after his family following his certain execution. The government publicly attributed Rommel's death to wounds received in an air attack on July 17, and he was given a hero's funeral.

Dwight Eisenhower

No other Allied military commander had as much influence or control over the war in Europe than Dwight David Eisenhower. His military savvy and the ability to hold together a sometimes tenuous military coalition helped guide the Allied forces to victory over Germany and Italy. His reputation as a war hero helped get him elected to the White House in 1952.

Eisenhower was born in 1890 in Denison, Texas. An average student in school, he excelled at sports, particularly baseball. Eisenhower wanted a college education, but his family couldn't afford the tuition, so he sought, and won, an appointment to the U.S. Military Academy at West Point, graduating in 1915.

Figure 8-3 General of the Army Dwight D. Eisenhower at his headquarters in Europe.

Photo courtesy of the National Archives (80-G-331330)

When the United States entered World War I in 1917, Eisenhower was promoted to captain and assigned to training duty. He begged to be transferred overseas so he could see action, but his superiors declined, sending him to Camp Colt in Gettysburg, Pennsylvania, where he trained the army's first tank corps. He continued his work at Camp Meade, Maryland, where he became close friends with George S. Patton.

Eisenhower's Role in World War II

At the onset of World War II, Eisenhower was put in charge of the War Plans Division. He favored the "Europe first" strategy, which dictated a strong Allied push against Germany before launching a major offensive in the Pacific. In March 1942, Eisenhower was promoted to major general and made head of the Operations Division. In June, he was promoted to lieutenant general and placed in command of the army's European theater of operations, headquartered in London. His job was to lead U.S. forces in the offensive against Germany. Eisenhower wanted to start in the spring of 1943, but Winston Churchill suggested an invasion of North Africa instead, arguing that U.S. soldiers were still a little too green for an immediate invasion of German territory. Eisenhower was then placed in charge of Allied forces for the North African campaign. Though his troops were initially overrun by Erwin Rommel's army, Eisenhower recovered and eventually drove Germany out of North Africa.

Figure 8-4
General Eisenhower surrounded by fellow American Generals Simpson, Patton, Spaatz, Bradley, Hodges, Gerow, Stearley, Vandenberg, Smith, Weyland, and Nugent.

Photo courtesy of the National Archives (208-YE-182)

In July 1943, Eisenhower launched the successful invasion of Sicily, and in September he commanded the invasion of the Italian mainland, which was under German control. In December, while the Italian campaign was still under way, Eisenhower was chosen to command the Allied invasion of Normandy, with the goal of retaking German-occupied France and then pushing on to Berlin. It was a massive undertaking and a huge responsibility, but Eisenhower was ready. He pushed his staff and his troops tirelessly, requiring the invasion force to train with live ammunition. The offensive was a success, though casualties were high.

On December 15, 1944, Eisenhower was promoted to General of the Army, the U.S. military's highest rank. The next day, Germany began a final offensive in Belgium: the Battle of the Bulge. The Germans caught the Allied line by surprise and made a startling advance, though Allied forces eventually regrouped and pushed the German forces back in heavy fighting. It was one of Eisenhower's greatest moments as a military leader and strategist.

After the War

Eisenhower served as Chief of Staff of the U.S. Army from 1945 to 1948 and as Supreme Commander of NATO from 1950 to 1952. In April 1952, Eisenhower announced that he would seek the Republican nomination for president. He won the nomination and ran against Democrat Adlai Stevenson of Illinois. Eisenhower, a war hero, achieved an easy victory, taking thirty-nine of the forty-eight states and receiving 34 million popular votes. He was elected to a second term in 1956 with 57 percent of the popular vote.

FACT

General of the Army Omar N. Bradley was the highest-ranking American field commander in the European theater and a major influence in determining the course of the war. Eisenhower relied on him heavily during the North Africa campaign, the Normandy invasion, and the Battle of the Bulge, among other events.

Eisenhower eventually retired to his farm in Gettysburg, Pennsylvania, though he remained active as a government adviser; because of his vast experience, both John Kennedy and Lyndon Johnson called on him during various crises. Eisenhower died in 1969 after an extended illness.

Bernard Montgomery

Few Allied military leaders were as controversial as Field Marshal Bernard Law Montgomery. Though he played an integral role in several key Allied victories in North Africa and Europe, many of his fellow Allied officers disliked Montgomery because of his tendency to hog the spotlight and take credit for the contributions of others. Nonetheless, no one can question his combat and strategic skills.

Figure 8-5
British Field Marshal Bernard Montgomery watches his tanks advance during battle in North Africa, November 1942.

Photo courtesy of the National Archives (208-PU-138LL-3)

Montgomery was born in London on November 17, 1887, the son of a Protestant minister. He attended the Royal Military College and entered the British army in 1908. Montgomery showed great aptitude for leadership when he served as an infantry captain on the French front during World War I. He was wounded during an infantry attack at Ypres in October 1914 and spent the rest of the war as a staff officer. Military life suited Montgomery, who quickly decided to make a career of it. After the war, he rose as a commander and became well known as an instructor of military tactics and strategy.

In 1940, Montgomery led the British Third Division into the battle of France during Germany's conquest of France and the Low Countries, and he was one of the thousands evacuated at Dunkirk. He was later promoted to major general, and in 1942 he was appointed commander of the British Eighth Army in Africa. Two months later, he initiated an offensive at El Alamein, Egypt, that successfully drove the German-Italian forces led by Erwin Rommel all the way back to Libya. A year later, he again defeated Rommel at the Battle of the Mareth Line in southern Tunisia.

After his return to Europe, Montgomery was named commander in chief of the British armies on the western front. He served under Dwight Eisenhower, who was supreme commander of the Allied forces, from December 1943 to August 1944, when he was promoted to field marshal in command of British and Canadian troops. He ably participated in the invasion of Sicily and the Italian campaign, and helped contain the 1944 German counteroffensive in the Ardennes known as the Battle of the Bulge, though he irritated his fellow Allied commanders by taking much of the credit during a press briefing.

After the war, Montgomery was made viscount and named chief of the imperial general staff. He was deputy supreme commander of NATO forces from 1951 to 1958. Montgomery did some writing after his retirement, including his memoirs, which were published in 1958. He died at his estate in Alton, Hampshire, on March 25, 1976.

George Patton

Like Bernard Montgomery, General George Smith Patton Jr. was both a skilled and a controversial soldier. His aggressiveness on the field of combat helped him win many decisive battles, particularly in Italy and North Africa, but his problems with authority and his obvious lack of people skills (including an incident in which he slapped a soldier he thought was wasting time in a field hospital) nearly cost him his career. In the end, however, history proved Patton to be an invaluable asset to every Allied campaign in which he participated.

George Patton was born in San Gabriel, California, in 1885 and attended the U.S. Military Academy at West Point. After his graduation in 1909, he was commissioned a second lieutenant. Patton served as aide-de-camp to General John J. Pershing on Pershing's 1917 expedition to Mexico and proved the usefulness of armored tanks during World War I, eventually establishing a tank training school and commanding a tank brigade.

Patton's work with armored vehicles led to his receiving command of the Western Task Force that landed in Morocco as part of the North Africa invasion in November 1942. As a lieutenant general commanding the U.S. Seventh Army in the July 1943 invasion of Sicily, he made headlines around the world by capturing Palermo with what was considered just a reconnaissance force, pushing ahead despite contrary orders from his superiors.

Media reports that he had belittled his men nearly resulted in his termination, but General George Marshall and General Dwight Eisenhower knew Patton's value as an aggressive commander and intervened on his behalf. However, Patton was given little to do after the Sicily invasion until he was called to Great Britain and placed in command of the fictitious First U.S. Army Group, which was created to confuse the Germans for the impending Normandy invasion.

Patton was then placed in command of the Third Army, which was activated just six days after the American breakout following the Normandy landing. Under his direction, the Third Army cut a wide swath through German-occupied territory, devastating German defenses. Within weeks, Patton was at the Seine River, German forces encircled. With the enemy on the run, he was eager to push on to the Rhine River and keep pushing forward. However, his plans were set aside in favor of a similar action proposed by Montgomery, and Patton was forced to sit and fume while a lot of his fuel and supplies were given to Montgomery for his own offensive.

Patton was able to reclaim much of his glory during the Battle of the Bulge, though, when he rerouted the Third Army to save the town of Bastogne from a German siege. The speed of Patton's movement was astounding, and many historians consider his counterthrust one of his greatest military achievements.

Patton continued his aggressive move against Germany and crossed the Rhine in late March 1945—a day before Montgomery's crossing farther north. He was able to move his army through southern Germany and into Czechoslovakia before Germany finally surrendered. When the war was over, Patton was transferred to command of the Fifteenth Army Group.

Unfortunately, on December 9, 1945, just months after the end of the war, Patton broke his neck in a freak automobile accident near Mannheim, Germany. He died twelve days later. In 1970, his exploits were turned into a motion picture starring George C. Scott, who received an Academy Award for Best Actor for his portrayal of the flamboyant and controversial general.

Douglas MacArthur

Douglas A. MacArthur's name is almost synonymous with the war in the Pacific. He lost the Philippines to the Japanese early in the conflict but—true to his promise—returned as liberator. MacArthur's postwar career was marked by controversy, but his influence and impact on the Allied fight in the Pacific cannot be underestimated. In many ways, he was the ultimate soldier.

During World War I, MacArthur achieved the rank of general and won several honors for his heroism and leadership of the Forty-second (Rainbow) Division. In the years after the war, he was appointed superintendent of West Point. In 1930, MacArthur was made army chief of staff—one of the youngest men ever to hold the position. During his service as chief of staff, he received a lot of bad publicity for his decision to use tanks against homeless World War I veterans who had created a camp in Washington, D.C., as part of their campaign to receive government bonus money they felt was due them. In 1935, MacArthur retired from the army to serve as chief military adviser to Philippine President Manuel Quezon.

Reactivated for War

In July 1941, just months before the Japanese invasion, MacArthur was recalled to active military service and named commanding general of U.S. army forces in the Far East. Japanese aggression had accelerated, and war with Japan seemed a near certainty. The Japanese had bolstered their military force dramatically in the years before the war, but MacArthur was confident he could defend the Philippines from a Japanese invasion. He was wrong, as the battles of Bataan and Corregidor and MacArthur's last-minute evacuation on March 23, 1942, proved.

MacArthur and his family fled to Australia, where he was awarded a Medal of Honor. There, he began planning to retake the Pacific from the Japanese, often clashing with his superiors, including Admiral Ernest King, Admiral Chester Nimitz, and General George Marshall. MacArthur's strategy was to begin with the liberation of New Guinea, but his long-term goal was to return to the Philippines; he began that leg of his campaign in October 1944 and quickly fulfilled his promise by driving out the Japanese.

After the Philippine campaign, MacArthur—by then commander of all U.S. Army forces in the Pacific—was selected to lead troops, in collaboration with Nimitz's combined navy-marine forces, in the planned invasion of the Japanese mainland. However, the Japanese surrendered in August 1945 after the atomic destruction of Hiroshima and Nagasaki, and the planned offensive was canceled. MacArthur accepted the official Japanese surrender on the deck of the battleship *Missouri* on September 2.

Following World War II

MacArthur was named supreme allied commander in Japan and played a prominent role in the conquered nation's postwar occupation. He instituted a wide variety of reforms in the country, including important social changes and the creation of a constitutional monarchy.

MacArthur's career after World War II was marked with controversy. In 1950, he was named commander in chief of the United Nations force in South Korea, where his military acumen and strategic skill proved most useful. But in 1951 he butted heads publicly with President Truman regarding U.S. strategy in the war (he wanted to extend the limited war into a general war against China) and was dismissed.

MacArthur retired from the military and became chairman of the board of the Remington Rand Corporation. He died on April 5, 1964, in Washington, D.C.

Chester Nimitz

As commander in chief of the Pacific Fleet, Admiral Chester W. Nimitz was instrumental in disabling the Japanese Pacific Fleet over the course of the war. His aggressive strategy helped stop the Japanese advance at the Battle of the Coral Sea and secured a U.S. victory in the Battle of Midway. Nimitz is also credited with developing the strategy of island hopping, in which each island that was captured became the base from which to attack the next, with islands known to be Japanese strongholds avoided in favor of easier targets. The battle plan saved countless American lives and much time during a period in which U.S. naval forces in the Pacific could afford to lose neither.

Nimitz was born in Fredericksburg, Texas, in 1885 and received his military education at the United States Naval Academy. During World War I, he was chief of staff to the commander of the Atlantic Fleet's submarine force. Nimitz slowly rose through the ranks and in 1938 was appointed rear admiral.

Rear Admiral Chester W. Nimitz Jr., son of Fleet Admiral Chester Nimitz, was a submarine commander during World War II. His submarine, the *Haddo*, is known to have sunk at least five Japanese ships.

In December 1941, after the U.S. entry into World War II, Nimitz was appointed commander in chief of the Pacific Fleet with the rank of four-star admiral. As commander of the Pacific war zone, he directed both the navy and the marines.

Nimitz was known for his cool self-control, ability to quickly assess a battle situation, and dedication to his staff. (When a subordinate made a mistake, Nimitz was quick to give him a second chance.) He also had a keen eye for talent and promoted a number of officers who would play a decisive role in the war in the Pacific, including William Halsey and Thomas Kincaid.

Nimitz was promoted to admiral of the fleet in 1944 and was the official U.S. representative who signed the Japanese surrender in 1945. After the war, Nimitz served as chief of naval operations, until he retired from the navy in 1947. Chester Nimitz died in 1966.

FACT

When Hitler was named chancellor of Germany in 1933, he put Hermann Goering in charge of the German air force, which Goering secretly rearmed and greatly expanded. He also developed the effective bomber/fighter strategies used in the blitzkriegs against Poland, Norway, Denmark, the Netherlands, Belgium, and France. Under Goering's direction, the Luftwaffe became one of the most formidable air war machines in the world, often employing "terror bombing"—the leveling of entire cities—to destroy civilian morale.

Masaharu Homma

General Masaharu Homma was one of the most complex military leaders in the Japanese army. Intelligent and introspective, he vehemently opposed going to war with the United States and Great Britain in the belief that Japan could not win an extended conflict against such a dedicated military force. However, when instructed in November 1941 to take the main Philippine island of Luzon, he did so—reluctantly. The abuse of prisoners after that campaign would eventually lead to Homma's being tried for war crimes.

Homma was born in Niigata Prefecture in 1887 and entered the military at an early age. He developed strong leadership qualities and was known for his creative, emotional side as well as for his military bearing. Homma served with British army units from 1918 to 1925 and was appointed military attaché to London in 1930.

Homma was not an advocate of the extreme nationalism that infected the Japanese military in the 1930s, and this led to his being sent to China to command the Tientsin Defense Army, then to Formosa. During this period, Homma continued to crusade against a war with the United States. When such a war seemed inevitable, Homma blamed Hideki Tojo, for whom he felt nothing but contempt.

When ordered to take Luzon, Homma was told he had two divisions and fifty days to accomplish the task. It was assumed that the U.S. and Philippine troops there would stand and fight, so Homma's schedule was thrown off when they instead retreated to Bataan and then Corregidor. Unwilling to deviate from his orders, Homma ordered his troops to follow and eliminate the retreating defenders, a decision that added several weeks to his assignment. Homma's troops took Manila as scheduled on January 2, 1942, but he did not receive the surrender of Bataan until April 9 and that of Corregidor until May 6. Though his campaign ultimately succeeded, Homma was relieved of command for going over schedule and ordered home to Japan, where he spent the rest of the war with little to do.

At the end of the war, Homma was arrested and charged with war crimes related to atrocities committed during the Bataan Death March. He maintained that the atrocities had been committed by underlings (primarily his chief of staff, Colonel Masanobu Tsuji) who were assigned to handle the large number of prisoners after the capture of Bataan and that he had not known about the Bataan Death March until after the war. Nonetheless, Homma was found guilty and sentenced to death by hanging. However, a plea from his wife to General Douglas MacArthur resulted in a change to execution by firing squad, which was considered more honorable for a man of his stature. Homma was executed on April 3, 1946.

Karl Dönitz

Admiral Karl Dönitz achieved two distinct claims to fame during World War II: He was commander of the German U-boat force that terrorized Allied convoys in the Atlantic; and during the final days of the Third Reich, he was chosen to succeed Adolf Hitler as president of the Reich and supreme commander of the armed forces.

Dönitz's Military Career Between the Wars

After World War I, Dönitz rose through the ranks of the German navy. He was an early admirer of Adolf Hitler and one of the first members of the Nazi Party. (Dönitz's loyalty and support garnered him the prestigious Golden Party Badge in January 1944). In 1936, he was made commander of the relatively insignificant German submarine force and immediately set about increasing its numbers and capabilities. During this period, Dönitz also developed the "wolf pack" strategy of submarine warfare that would serve him so well during the Battle of the Atlantic. He was promoted to Kontradmiral in 1939 and received the rank of full admiral in 1942.

After the resignation of Erich Raeder in January 1943, Dönitz was appointed commander in chief of the navy. Raeder hadn't recommended Dönitz as his replacement, but Hitler no doubt based the decision on the fact that the U-boats were one of the few offensive weapons in the Atlantic that Germany could still count on. Raeder had resigned because Hitler had ordered that all surface warships be retired. Raeder felt this was a bad move and Dönitz agreed, arguing that surface warships had proven extremely effective against the Russian convoys.

Over the next two years, Dönitz watched his esteemed submarine fleet suffer a number of devastating defeats in the Atlantic and elsewhere as a result of the Allies' improved technology and antisubmarine techniques. He struggled to maintain Germany's superiority at sea, but by May 1943 the battle had been lost. German U-boats continued to damage Allied convoys but not nearly to the extent they had done earlier in the war.

FACT

German Admiral Karl Dönitz lost both of his sons in naval engagements during World War II, one in a U-boat and the other in a torpedo boat. Dönitz's son-in-law also died when Allied ships sank the submarine on which he served.

The End of War and Beyond

In April 1945, as the Allied advance cut Germany in two, Dönitz was given command of forces in the northern sector. He established his headquarters at the Baltic town of Plön on April 22, and just a little more than a week later he was told that, because of his loyalty to the German cause and the Nazi Party, Hitler had personally selected him as his successor—an honor almost everyone thought would go to Hermann Goering. On the morning of May 1, Dönitz received a call from Hitler's bunker in Berlin—he was now the new president and supreme commander of the armed forces. (Dönitz didn't find out for another couple of days that Hitler had committed suicide.)

ESSENTIAL

Dönitz and his cabinet were taken into custody by British forces on May 23, and he was ordered to be tried for war crimes, specifically the murder of shipwreck survivors. He was found guilty and sentenced to a relatively light ten years at Spandau Prison. After his release in 1956, he wrote several books and lectured on the Nazi movement and submarine warfare. Dönitz died in 1980.

Dönitz assumed control of the collapsing nation and tried valiantly to hold the army together from his headquarters in Flensburg-Murwik. He worked hard to continue the war and slow the Allied advance, but it was too late; his war machine was now almost nonexistent, and Germany was in complete chaos. On May 4, he instructed his representatives to sign the German surrender documents presented by Field Marshal Bernard Montgomery, followed by subsequent surrenders to General of the Army Dwight Eisenhower and the Soviets.

George Marshall

Though George Marshall was not a field commander on the front lines of the war, as General of the Army he played a vital role in determining how the United States would confront World War II, how the military and the civilian population would work together as a fighting team, and how certain delicate international issues should be handled when the war was over. Many military historians compare him to George Washington in his remarkable ability to exercise military strategy within a civilian democracy.

In the years after World War I, Marshall commanded a regiment stationed in China and also taught at the infantry school at Fort Benning, Georgia. In 1939, President Roosevelt named Marshall the army chief of staff, a position he would hold until the end of World War II.

Figure 8-6
General George
Marshall.

Getty Images/Keystone/Stringer

One of Marshall's greatest prewar achievements was convincing Congress to change the laws regarding the retirement of older officers and to accept selective service. As a result, he was able to place several capable younger officers in positions of authority throughout the army—a move that would serve the military well during the war. Marshall also successfully lobbied the president to significantly increase military spending immediately before the United States was forced into the war.

Marshall knew that the American public would not tolerate an indecisive war for long, and he pushed for quick action in Europe. He backed the "Germany first" strategy and opposed the British plan of creating a second threat to Germany by invading North Africa and then moving into Italy. Marshall felt a landing in northern France was the best way to press Germany and suggested such a plan at every Allied strategic conference; however, British strategists didn't approve his ideas until late 1943. Marshall hoped to lead the Allied force into France, but Roosevelt, who relied heavily on Marshall's counsel, felt his skills were more needed in Washington.

FACT

After the war, Marshall worked as secretary of state and secretary of defense. As secretary of state, he was the leading architect of the European Recovery Program, more commonly known as the Marshall Plan, through which the United States provided economic assistance to strengthen anti-Communist governments in Western Europe. He received a Nobel Peace Prize for his work in 1953. George Marshall died on October 16, 1959, in Washington, D.C.

As the war progressed, he was successful in building a tremendous American fighting machine that seemed capable of almost anything. During his tenure, the army increased dramatically in terms of fighting men and war materiel. One of Marshall's greatest skills was identifying and promoting uniquely gifted officers, a trait that ensured strong command on all fronts.

William Halsey

Fleet Admiral William F. Halsey served on destroyers during World War I and continued to serve on surface ships until 1935 when, as a captain, he received his naval aviator's wings and was placed in command of the aircraft carrier *Saratoga*. He realized the tremendous offensive potential of carriers, and by the time the United States entered the war in 1941, he commanded all the carriers in the Pacific Fleet.

During the first months of the U.S. Pacific campaign, Halsey conducted numerous raids on the Gilbert and Marshall Islands, in addition to supporting the American reinforcement of Samoa. His task force also carried the sixteen bombers for the Doolittle raid on Tokyo in April 1942.

Halsey missed participating in the Battle of the Coral Sea because his force was out of position, and a skin ailment landed him in the hospital just before the Battle of Midway. In October 1942 he was back in action, and Admiral Chester Nimitz appointed him commander, South Pacific, as a replacement for Vice Admiral Robert Ghormley, who had become exhausted from extended action.

Halsey was promoted to full admiral in November 1942 and worked with General MacArthur to coordinate the liberation of the Solomon Islands and New Guinea. In June 1944, Halsey was assigned command of the Central Pacific Force.

William Halsey and Raymond Spruance were both considered for five-star rank in late 1944. Halsey received the promotion because he was the more senior of the two, but Congress voted to reward Spruance with special compensation and benefits.

From August 1944 to August 1945, Halsey alternated with Admiral Raymond Spruance as commander of the U.S. Navy's main striking force in the Pacific theater, participating in the Battle of Leyte Gulf and MacArthur's recapture of the Philippines. In January 1945, Halsey turned over command to Spruance, partly as a result of his failure to take sufficient precautions against a December 1944 typhoon that heavily damaged his fleet. Halsey regained command of the Third Fleet in May 1945 and led it on a series of carrier raids against Japan until the end of the war, though failure to take sufficient precautions against another typhoon in June 1945 almost caused him to be relieved of command. William Halsey died in 1959.

Chapter 9
Other Prominent Figures

Amid all the horror stories, success stories, and outright miracles surrounding the political and military leaders during wartime, the lower-ranking figures sometimes fall between the cracks. There were several people who may have stood just outside the spotlight but whose actions contributed to our awareness of the details involved in every aspect of the war.

Adolf Eichmann

At the end of World War II, few names evoked as much revulsion as did that of Adolf Eichmann, one of the primary architects of the so-called Final Solution and the man ultimately responsible for the deaths of millions of Jews in Nazi-occupied nations.

Eichmann became an early supporter of Hitler and the Nazi movement. Under the guidance of Austrian Nazi official Ernst Kaltenbrunner, Eichmann became one of the Nazis' foremost "authorities" on Jews.

Figure 9-1 Adolf Eichmann.

Getty Images/David Rubinger/Contributor

Eichmann knew how to play politics and quickly became chief of the Reich Central Office of Jewish Emigration. In 1940, he was instructed to develop a plan to deport 4 million Jews to Madagascar, which was controlled at the time by the Vichy French. The plan never came to fruition because the Nazis found it easier to imprison and kill the Jews than to move them out of the country.

In January 1942, Eichmann attended the Wannsee Conference on the "Final Solution of the Jewish Question," which involved discussion of the most effective ways to eliminate large numbers of people. Eichmann's notes on the genocide conference were recovered after the war and used as evidence at the Nuremberg war crimes trials. Throughout the war, Eichmann authorized the deportation of countless Jews to concentration camps and supervised the SS action groups.

FACT

Eichmann managed to slip away from the authorities and escaped from Germany before he could be tried. Eichmann was finally located in Buenos Aires in May 1960 and secretly returned to Israel. Eichmann tried to convince the court that he had merely been following orders. His pleas fell on deaf ears. Eichmann was found guilty of war crimes, crimes against humanity, and crimes against the Jewish people, and was hanged on May 31, 1962.

Eichmann was one of numerous high-ranking Nazis who were tried for war crimes. He apparently felt no remorse for his actions. According to an associate, as Allied forces bore down on Berlin, Eichmann said he would leap laughing into the grave because the feeling that he had been instrumental in the deaths of 5 million people would be for him a source of extraordinary satisfaction.

Joseph Goebbels

The Third Reich flourished under a constant bombardment of public propaganda—almost all of it the work of Nazi Party propaganda chief Joseph Goebbels. Goebbels understood very well the impact and influence of the right image, and early on he designed and orchestrated an ongoing media campaign that emphasized Hitler's importance as the Führer and the 1,000-year reign of the invincible Third Reich.

ESSENTIAL

In 1933, Hitler appointed Goebbels minister of propaganda and public enlightenment and gave him the task of providing Germany with "spiritual direction." This meant complete government control of every form of media. Almost immediately, every book, radio program, newspaper, and motion picture became imbued with Nazi rhetoric. Opposing viewpoints were censored.

Goebbels was a slight, sinister-looking man who walked with a noticeable limp. He joined the Nazi Party in 1925 and was soon writing its propaganda leaflets. In 1926, Hitler made him district leader in Berlin, where he displayed an innate talent for turning political rallies into outright brawls against any group (but particularly Communists) that disagreed with the Nazi doctrine.

Goebbels was rapidly promoted to be Hitler's political manager, and it was here that his talents as a propagandist came to the forefront. Under Goebbels's direction, political rallies became impressive multimedia events complete with huge posters, documentary films, loudspeakers, and massive crowds of faithful supporters. The swastika—the Nazis' grand symbol—was clearly visible throughout.

Hitler rewarded Goebbels's devotion in 1944 with a promotion to the post of Reich trustee for total war. Goebbels took the title to heart and during the final days of the Reich endorsed Hitler's wish that Germany go down in flames rather than submit to its invaders. As the Allies approached, he read to Hitler from his favorite books and continued to feed the Führer's demented ego.

On May 1, 1945—the day after Hitler and Eva Braun committed suicide—Goebbels and his wife, Magda, ordered Hitler's dentist to give their five children a dose of morphine. Once the children, ranging in age from three to twelve, were asleep, Goebbels placed cyanide capsules in their mouths. He and Magda then walked into the Chancellery garden, where Hitler's charred remains were still evident, and ordered an SS underling to kill them. They were both shot in the back of the head; then their bodies were doused with gasoline and set afire. That night, the entire Führerbunker was torched, incinerating all that lay within.

Heinrich Himmler

Few men were as feared within the Nazi regime as Heinrich Himmler, leader of the Nazi secret police known as the SS. A Bavarian chicken farmer before joining Hitler and rising through the ranks of the Nazi Party, Himmler was responsible for some of the Nazis' most heinous activities, including the creation of concentration camps and the mass slaughter of "inferior" individuals, specifically the Jews, the physically infirm, and the mentally handicapped.

Himmler was an early supporter of Hitler and his National Socialist German Workers' Party. Originally commander of political police in Bavaria, he worked his way up through the party until he was second only to Hitler in power and authority.

Himmler firmly agreed with Hitler's desire to rid Germany of inferior people, and one of his first tasks was the creation in 1933 of the Dachau concentration camp, which was originally built to house dissidents. A year later, Himmler cemented his power within the Nazi Party with the orchestration of the "Night of Long Knives," a rapid series of assassinations that eliminated the increasingly powerful SA police apparatus and replaced it with the SS. Himmler put the SS in charge of Dachau, and the dreaded agency oversaw all concentration camps and death camps throughout the war.

When Germany went to war in 1939, Hitler appointed Himmler commissar for consolidation of German nationhood. As the title suggests, Himmler's job was to purify Germany by eliminating all "undesirables," "misfits," and "inferior races." Over the next several months, he supervised the forced eviction of Poles so their land could be taken over by ethnic Germans, ordered the systematic murder of concentration camp inmates at Auschwitz, and instigated the slaughter of hundreds of sick and starving civilians in the Warsaw ghetto. Himmler also was said to have established a program in which unwed German women could bear the children of pure Aryan soldiers on their way to battle.

In August 1943, Himmler was made minister of the interior, which placed him in complete charge of all concentration camps. His duties also included forcing the residents of conquered nations to work in German war factories and authorizing horrifying medical experiments on concentration camp inmates. In addition, Himmler established special action groups designed to enter conquered territories specifically to eliminate the Jewish population.

FACT

Himmler tried to escape Germany in disguise as the Allies entered Berlin, but he was captured by British troops near Bremen. Facing trial for war crimes, Himmler took his own life by poison on May 23, 1945.

Himmler's SS was instrumental in uncovering and rounding up the conspirators of the failed assassination plot against Hitler in July 1944. Hitler was pleased with Himmler's work and rewarded him by placing him in command of the reserve army Hitler had formed to make one last desperate offensive against the approaching Allied forces. However, the offensive was a failure, and Germany was soon in ruins. In the spring of 1945, Himmler tried to broker a peace settlement through the Swedish Red Cross, but his efforts were unsuccessful. Hitler found out about Himmler's "treason" and, in one of his last acts before committing suicide, expelled Himmler from the Nazi Party and stripped him of all authority.

Rudolf Hess

The saga of Rudolf Hess is a strange one indeed. A devoted follower of Hitler from the very beginning, Hess had a tremendous future in the Nazi Party. Then, in 1941, he threw it all away by flying to Scotland in a cockeyed attempt to work out an unauthorized peace treaty. The stunt landed him in prison for the rest of his life.

Hess and Hitler served in the same infantry regiment during World War I, and it was there that they forged a strong friendship. After the war, Hess became enamored of Hitler's political rhetoric and joined the Nazi Party. He was by Hitler's side during the ill-fated Beer Hall Putsch in 1923 and went to prison with the future Führer. While incarcerated, Hess transcribed and edited much of Hitler's autobiography, *Mein Kampf.*

When Hitler's political career started to take off, he made Hess his personal aide. In 1933, when Hitler assumed the position of chancellor, he made Hess deputy führer. Six years later, on the eve of World War II, Hess became a member of the Ministerial Council for the Defense of Germany and the third most powerful man in the German government, after Hitler and Hermann Goering.

During the Olympic Games in 1936, Hess had made the acquaintance of the Duke of Hamilton. When war broke out in Europe, Hess wrote the duke a letter—apparently without Hitler's knowledge—inquiring about the possibility of a peace treaty between Great Britain and Germany. The British government told the duke to ignore the letter.

FACT

Hess and six other convicted Nazis were incarcerated at Spandau Prison in western Berlin. Hess's fellow prisoners either died or were released over the years, and by 1966 he was the prison's sole inmate. Hess remained in Spandau until his death in 1987, at which time the prison was torn down.

But Hess wasn't about to be put off. With the help of aviator Willy Messerschmitt, he learned how to fly a fighter plane and took off, unarmed, for the Duke of Hamilton's estate on May 10, 1941. When he got lost, Hess bailed out over Scotland and was promptly taken into custody by British authorities, who thought he was crazy.

When Hitler found out what had happened, he flew into a rage, instantly removing Hess from the Nazi Party. The British held Hess in the Tower of London for the rest of the war. At the war's end, he was tried for conspiracy to commit crimes and for crimes against humanity. Hess pretended he had amnesia but did not convince the tribunal, which sentenced him to life in prison.

Eleanor Roosevelt

Eleanor Roosevelt, wife of President Franklin D. Roosevelt and niece of President Theodore Roosevelt, was a prominent figure during World War II. Not content to observe the war from the White House, she did much to improve the morale of her fellow countrymen and the troops overseas.

Anna Eleanor Roosevelt was born on October 11, 1884, to Elliott and Anna Hall Roosevelt. Both of her parents died by the time she was ten, and she lived with her maternal grandmother until being sent to a boarding school in Great Britain at age fifteen. When she returned home, Eleanor did social work in New York until she married her distant cousin, Franklin Roosevelt.

Eleanor played the role of faithful wife while Franklin pursued his political career, but their relationship changed drastically when she discovered that he had been having an affair with her social secretary. The couple reconciled, but Eleanor decided that she no longer wanted to be simply a housewife and started to pursue outside interests, including the League of Women Voters and the Women's Trade Union League. When Franklin was crippled by polio, she helped keep his political career alive by becoming active in the Democratic Party. When her husband assumed the presidency, Eleanor often acted as a springboard for his programs and proposals.

During World War II, Eleanor Roosevelt often donned a Red Cross uniform and visited wounded servicemen in military hospitals throughout the United States and overseas. During one trip, she traveled a remarkable 25,000 miles in just five weeks. After she returned home, she spent countless hours making hundreds of reassuring phone calls to the concerned parents, wives, and girlfriends of the servicemen she had met. She also championed the cause of desegregation in the military.

Eleanor Roosevelt served as a member of the U.S. delegation to the United Nations from 1945 to 1953 and chaired the commission that created the Universal Declaration of Human Rights. She died in New York City on November 7, 1962.

Chiang Kai-shek

One of two important Chinese leaders during the years of Japanese aggression and occupation was Chiang Kai-shek, the leader of the Kuomintang and of the Republic of China. Chiang inherited the mantle of government from Sun Yat-sen and was in charge of the country's rebuilding for a time, but was soon faced with two enemies: Japan and the Communists. Under the slogan "first internal pacification, then external resistance," Chiang led a significant armed force against the Communist forces, under Mao Tse-tung. This internal struggle cost China many men and much momentum in the early years of the Japanese invasion. However, by 1937, the two bitter rivals had agreed, at least on the surface, to put aside their differences and fight a common foe.

Years of bitter fighting between the Chinese and Japenese followed, with horrendous casualties on both sides, but especially Chinese forces. China lost 200,000 in the capture of Shanghai alone. Another 300,000 died in the Rape of Nanking. Chinese soldiers resisted Japanese aggression as much as possible. The country received a large amount of aid from the Allied powers, especially the United States, which sent the famous Flying Tigers to beef up

China's air defenses. China also provided landing space to those pilots who were lucky enough to escape after dropping bombs on Japan in James Doolittle's famous raid.

Chiang emerged as the national leader and a friend of the Allied powers, who made him one of the "big four" and invited him to the historic Cairo Conference in 1943. He remained the nominal leader of the country after the Japanese surrender but soon lost his position in the Communist Revolution. Chiang fled China for Formosa (Taiwan) in 1950 and ruled there until his death in 1975.

Marshal Philippe Pétain

Philippe Pétain had quite a dichotomous reputation, going from one of France's military heroes to one of its most villainous personalities. A hero of World War I known as the "Savior of Verdun," Pétain gradually and reluctantly assumed more powerful roles in the French government. As France's secretary of state, he urged appeasement of Germany and later signed the armistice that handed over control of much of the country to the Germans.

During the rest of the war, Pétain was the head of the Vichy government and provided much food, land, and war materiel to the Axis cause. His willingness to help the Nazi cause waned as the war went on, and he eventually lost his dictatorial powers as the Germans assumed greater control. Pétain was vilified for his actions by Charles de Gaulle and other leaders of the Free French.

After the war, Pétain was seized and named a traitor to his people. He was tried and convicted of war crimes and sentenced to death; De Gaulle commuted his sentence to life imprisonment because of Pétain's age, which was eighty-nine. He died in prison in 1951.

Henry L. Stimson

Secretary of state Henry L. Stimson, was a former U.S. attorney who brought great political and economic experience to the government. He served as secretary of war under President William Howard Taft and helped organize the military expansion during World War I, even seeing combat time in France. Stimson then served as secretary of state under president Herbert Hoover. He retired to private life when Roosevelt was elected.

Stimson issued the famous Stimson Doctrine in response to Japan's invasion of Manchuria. This doctrine was the official U.S. position against the Japanese invasion, which was a refusal to recognize the territorial claims of the aggressor.

In 1940 Stimson accepted FDR's invitation to re-enter the cabinet and assumed his old post as secretary of war. In this capacity, Stimson built the American military up to an eventual force of 10 million. His leadership during the war was invaluable in maintaining an overwhelming demand for men and raw materials.

A strong advocate of containing Japanese aggression, he was a prime supporter of the design and eventual use of the atomic bomb. He also played a leading role in determining the postwar fate of Germany and its leaders. Stimson retired from the cabinet not long after the war ended and died just four years later.

Anne Frank

Many fifteen-year-olds keep a diary, but none has influenced the world quite like Anne Frank's. Through her poignant words, the world learned what it was like to be an adolescent Jewish girl living in fear of Nazi persecution.

Anne was born in Germany in 1929, and her family moved to Amsterdam in 1933. The Germans invaded the Netherlands in 1940, and the roundup of Dutch Jews began shortly thereafter. At great risk to themselves, Christian friends saved Anne, her family, and four others by housing them in a hidden area of what had been a warehouse. There, the group lived for two years in constant fear of discovery by the Nazis, who were sending Dutch Jews to concentration camps by the thousands.

Figure 9-2 Anne Frank writes at her desk.

Getty Images/Anne Frank Fonds—Basel/Anne Frank House/Contributora

During her time in hiding, Anne kept a detailed diary describing her life, hopes, dreams, and fears. Foremost was the agonizing question of how people could treat others so brutally—a question that remains unanswered today. She started the diary on June 12, 1942; her final entry was dated August 1, 1944.

On August 4, 1944, Gestapo agents, tipped off by a Dutch informer, burst into the warehouse and arrested all who were living inside. The agents ransacked the room but considered Anne's precious diary inconsequential and threw it in a corner. Anne and her family were separated and sent to concentration camps. Her mother died at Auschwitz, while Anne and her sister, Margot, eventually died at Bergen-Belsen. (This camp was liberated by the British in April 1945, just a month after Anne died.)

FACT

A new edition of Anne Frank's diary was published in 2001 with five previously omitted pages describing her parents' loveless marriage and Anne's troubled relationship with her mother.

At the end of the war, the only family member still alive was Anne's father, Otto. He returned to the family's secret hideaway in Amsterdam and found Anne's diary in the corner where it had been tossed by the Gestapo agents. The diary, published under the title *Diary of a Young Girl*, was an international bestseller and became required reading in many U.S. schools. It was also adapted for theater and a motion picture.

Oskar Schindler

Until director Steven Spielberg brought his story to the big screen in the 1993 movie *Schindler's List*, most people had never heard of Oskar Schindler. Today, Schindler is renowned worldwide for his efforts to protect Jews from German persecution.

Schindler, a Catholic, was born in what is now the Czech Republic in 1908. He held a number of jobs before becoming a sales manager for an electrical products manufacturing company. In the late 1930s, the German government asked Schindler to spy against Poland during his frequent business trips there.

After the German conquest of Poland, Schindler moved to Krakow to run an enamelware factory that primarily employed low-paid Jewish workers. Jews flocked to his factory begging for work because Schindler could use his business connections in the German government to prevent his laborers from being taken to concentration camps. Schindler was both self-serving and compassionate in his efforts to protect his Jewish workers—he was irritated by the fact that Nazi brutality adversely affected his factories' production, but he was also morally repulsed by Germany's anti-Jewish campaign.

In 1943, the Nazis decided to send all the Jews living in the Krakow ghetto to a concentration camp at nearby Plaszow. Schindler managed to save a great many who would otherwise have been doomed by building a camp on his factory grounds and convincing German officials to let his employees stay there.

FACT

In 1961, Israel commemorated Schindler's efforts with a memorial that was unveiled on his fifty-third birthday. Germany also rewarded Schindler's efforts with the Cross of Merit in 1966 and a state pension in 1968. Oskar Schindler died in 1974. His story first became widely known as a result of Thomas Keneally's 1982 book *Schindler's Ark*.

A year later, as Soviet troops approached Krakow, the German government ordered all Jews in both the Plaszow concentration camp and Schindler's company camp sent to Auschwitz for extermination. Schindler used a combination of personal charm, bullying, and bribes to convince the Nazis to let him move his factory (and his workers) to Czechoslovakia instead. He created a registry—the now-famous Schindler's List—of more than 1,000 employees he wanted to accompany him to his new factory. Had Schindler not done so, those individuals almost certainly would have been killed. Schindler and his workers remained in Czechoslovakia until the end of the war.

Chapter 10

Ground Weapons

A tremendous variety of weapons—from small arms and artillery to mines and flamethrowers—were used by both the Allies and the Axis during the ground fighting in Europe, Africa, and the Pacific. Some weapons had changed little since World War I while others had evolved greatly. All were effective at destruction and killing people.

10

Personal Guns

For American soldiers and marines, the M1 Garand semiautomatic rifle was the standard issue weapon for most of the war. It was developed in 1930 and came into common use among army infantrymen six years later. The marines began issuing the M1 in 1942.

The M1 was, at 9.6 pounds loaded, a relatively light .30-caliber gas-operated rifle that used an eight-round clip. It had an effective range of 550 yards and a maximum range of 3,000 yards. American servicemen liked the M1 because it was reliable and accurate under even the worst conditions. Similar types of semiautomatic rifles were used by German, Japanese, and Italian forces.

Servicemen also sometimes carried sidearms for close-range fighting, though the rifle was the preferred weapon. The principal sidearm among U.S. servicemen was the M1911 .45-caliber pistol.

Figure 10-1
PT marksman off the coast of New Guinea.

Photo courtesy of the National Archives (80-G-53871)

Though powerful, the gun was not particularly accurate, and it packed quite a kick.

Among German infantry and naval personnel, the 9-mm Luger was standard issue from 1904 until 1938, though it was still commonly used throughout World War II.

Particularly effective in close- and medium-range fighting were the many types of machine guns and submachine guns, which were used to great effect by both sides. American tank crewmen and others who could not carry a carbine or M1 rifle were keen on the M3 grease gun, a .45-caliber submachine gun similar in design to the British Sten submachine gun. The M3 was a fully automatic weapon, though experienced marksmen could fire off a single round when necessary. It weighed 10¼ pounds and was fed from a thirty-round magazine that served as the forward handle. The M3 had a maximum range of about 100 yards and could fire more than 350 rounds per minute.

The British Sten submachine gun, introduced in 1941, was unique because of the simplicity of its design; it was made with a minimum of machined parts and thus was less prone to jamming and other mechanical problems. It was a favorite among British paratroopers and guerrilla fighters throughout Europe.

Before the introduction of the Sten gun, the Thompson was the military's most widely used submachine gun. It was popularized by gangsters and FBI agents in the 1920s and 1930s, and the effectiveness of the Thompson was first proved by U.S. Marines in Nicaragua in 1926. The Thompson weighed a little over twelve pounds, fired .45-caliber bullets, and could be used with a twenty-, thirty-, or fifty-round magazine. It had a range of about 600 yards and could fire up to 100 rounds a minute. The Thompson was particularly popular among airborne troops and commandos.

Artillery

Artillery—large weapons such as cannons and rocket launchers—came in many forms during World War II and were widely used as offensive weapons of tremendous destructive power by both the Allies and the Axis on land and sea. Artillery weapons included:

- Big guns, or cannons, that fire projectiles from a long barrel in a low, flat trajectory. A charge in the projectile detonates on impact. During World War II, big guns were widely used on warships, armored combat vehicles, and tanks to soften up an invasion site or eliminate enemy resistance. A prime example was the use of big guns against German fortifications along the Normandy coast before the Allied landing on D-Day.

- Mortars are cannons that fire exploding shells in a high, arcing trajectory that lets them travel over obstacles such as hills or enemy defenses. Most mortars are drop-fire weapons, meaning that the shells were dropped into the barrel of the weapon and propelled via a charge. The standard U.S. Army and Marine Corps mortars were the 60-mm M2 and 81-mm M1, which could be disassembled and carried by backpack. Mortars could also be carried by and fired from half-track vehicles. The 60-mm mortar could fire a maximum of nearly 2,000 yards. The 80-mm mortar could send its projectiles more than 3,200 yards.

- Howitzers fired a mid-velocity projectile along a curved trajectory. By firing at a low angle, they could achieve good range, like guns. When fired at a high angle, they could launch shells over obstacles as mortars do.

- Rocket launchers, which fire unguided missiles as both weapons and signals.

FACT

During World War II, mortars were particularly useful in rough, mountainous terrain because they were easy to use and transport, extremely accurate, and very effective at inflicting damage. Mortars were commonly used by both sides.

Rockets

Rockets were used by both sides because they were simple to make, easy to launch, and very effective. Ground and naval forces commonly used rockets to bombard enemy-held territory because, though they were unable to penetrate fortifications, they would easily saturate a specific area and inflict heavy casualties on unprotected troops. Rockets also provided excellent protection for troops during amphibious landings.

The United States relied on two main rocket launchers during World War II. One was the so-called calliope system, a sixty-tube launcher fitted on a Sherman tank. It fired 114-mm rockets individually or in a salvo. Sets of multiple 114-mm rocket tubes could also be attached to trucks for easy transportation.

Fire support ships used by American and British forces were usually converted landing ships. The finest of the line was the U.S. Navy's LSMR series, which had twenty automatic-loading, rapid-fire 127-mm rocket launchers in addition to a 127-mm gun.

Rockets were also launched from planes, primarily to attack ground troops and surface-riding submarines. American fighter planes typically used 5-inch (127-mm) rockets, as did Allied antisubmarine aircraft patrolling the Atlantic. The American 5-inch rocket had a 50-pound explosive charge, which created a huge crater when used against ground forces. In 1944, the navy introduced an 11-inch aircraft rocket known as Tiny Tim, which carried a 150-pound warhead.

Germany also made extensive use of rockets as ground artillery, air-to-ground, and air-to-air weapons. The most commonly used German rocket system was the six-tube smoke thrower. Originally created to launch blinding smoke shells, the system eventually became an antipersonnel weapon that was also effective against tanks and other armored vehicles. Americans came to refer to the rockets as "Screaming Meemies" because of the sound they made in flight.

Antiaircraft Weapons

Because much of World War II was fought in the air, antiaircraft weapons were widely used by both Allied and Axis forces in Europe and the Pacific.

Antiaircraft guns ran the gamut in size. Some were as small as machine guns while others, such as the German 128-mm Flak, were huge cannons. The 128-mm Flak was the largest antiaircraft weapon of the war and was usually mounted on a large tower. The guns were used to protect German-occupied territory from Allied bombing raids and inflicted quite a bit of damage on Allied planes.

U.S. ground troops in Europe and the Pacific relied on six antiaircraft weapons to bring down enemy planes. They included:

- Quad .50-caliber machine gun. Capable of firing 2,300 rounds per minute, it was quite effective against low-flying planes.
- 37-mm gun. A large weapon, it was usually towed by truck and could fire 120 rounds per minute with an effective ceiling of 10,500 feet.
- Bofors 40-mm gun. This was the most widely used antiaircraft gun in the war. Also towed by truck, it could fire 120 rounds a minute with an effective ceiling of 11,000 feet.
- 3-inch gun, also known as the 76-mm. Towed by truck, it could fire 25 rounds per minute and had an effective ceiling of 27,900 feet.
- 90-mm gun. A towed weapon, it could fire up to 25 rounds per minute in short cycles, with an effective ceiling of 33,800 feet.
- 120-mm gun. Used primarily for city defense, it had an effective ceiling of 56,000 feet.

Most of these guns were not used exclusively as antiaircraft weapons. With the exception of the 120-mm gun, they were also used against enemy troops during close-range fighting.

FACT

U.S. forces generally referred to antiaircraft guns as AA, while the British called them ack-ack. German forces called them flak, as did Allied bomber pilots who wore protective flak jackets against their bursting shells, which were also called flak. (This is where the phrase "to take flak" comes from.)

The U.S. Navy had seven primary antiaircraft guns on large ships, as well as .30-caliber and .50-caliber machine guns on smaller ships and submarines. Antiaircraft cannon (meaning they fired explosive shells) ranged from 1.1-inch guns capable of firing up to 600 rounds per minute to 5-inch guns capable of firing up to 22 rounds per minute, with an effective ceiling of 37,200 feet.

One of the most important advances in antiaircraft weaponry during the war was the proximity fuse, also known as the Variable-Time (VT) fuse. Introduced in 1943, the VT fuse detonated a shell when it was close to the enemy plane, dramatically increasing the effectiveness of antiaircraft fire. Ammunition equipped with the VT fuse could be fired from guns that were three inches and larger.

Radar also aided antiaircraft gunners by providing accurate information about the range, speed, and altitude of incoming enemy planes.

Tanks

Germany proved the effectiveness of tanks in combat during the invasion of France and held superiority in this area throughout much of the war. For a variety of reasons, the United States was slow to produce a heavy tank that equaled the German Panther or Tiger, though heavy Allied tanks did appear late in the war.

When German tanks crossed the border into France in 1940, the United States had just 464 tanks, most of them light tanks armed with .50-caliber machine guns. By comparison, the German Pzkw IV tank was armed with a 75-mm gun.

Figure 10-2
A tank moves forward on the island of Bougainville with infantry following in its cover.

Photo courtesy of the National Archives (111-SC-189099)

In July 1940, the U.S. War Department—inspired by the tremendous success of German armored units—created an armored force consisting of the First and Second Armored Divisions and the nondivisional Seventieth Tank Battalion.

Realizing the need for a heavier, better-armed tank, the army's Ordnance Department adapted the TS medium tank to carry a 75-mm gun on the right side, though the main turret still had a 37-mm gun. The new tank, called the M2 Grant, was widely used to great effectiveness by the British in North Africa.

Following was the M4 Sherman tank, the first to be armed with a primary 75-mm gun. It went into production in July 1942 and was widely used by U.S. Army and Marine Corps forces in the Atlantic, Pacific, and North African theaters. The Sherman was also used by the British and Free French forces.

As strong as the Sherman tank was, it was still no match for the German Panther and Tiger tanks, both of which carried larger guns. The Ordnance Department was eager to place a 76-mm long-barreled gun on the Sherman, but the plan was continually hampered by army officials who instead stressed the need for faster light tanks that could keep up with fast-moving infantry. Finally, in February 1944, the Ordnance Department was instructed to begin adding a 76-mm gun to the Sherman chassis. These hybrids were produced in small numbers but proved effective against opposing forces. A still stronger tank—the M26 Pershing, which featured an impressive 90-mm gun—followed; it was the heaviest tank mass-produced by the U.S. military.

Because of the widespread use of tanks in Europe, special tank destroyers—tank-type vehicles with open turret tops and thin side armor—were quickly put into action. By late 1942, the U.S. Army had thirty-six tank destroyer battalions, each with thirty-six guns, in addition to reconnaissance and antiaircraft weapons. Approximately half the tank destroyer battalions towed antitank guns. The other half had self-propelled tank-destroying vehicles such as the M10 Wolverine and the M18 Hellcat, both of which featured a 76-mm gun, and the M36, which boasted a 90-mm gun.

Land Mines

One of the most destructive weapons used in the war was the land mine, millions of which were placed throughout Europe, North Africa, and the Pacific islands. Every participant in the war used mines, and they came in dozens of shapes, sizes, and designs. The Germans used more than forty types of antivehicle mines over the course of the war, most of them buried just below the ground and detonated by the weight of a man or a vehicle. Direct contact with a land mine usually resulted in instant death or, at a minimum, the loss of both legs. One particularly deadly German mine, known as the Bouncing Betty, propelled upward three to six feet before blasting shrapnel in all directions. This type of mine could eliminate many soldiers with a single explosion.

Mine detection ranged from the very primitive (men searching the ground on their hands and knees or prodding suspected mines with a long stick) to the relatively sophisticated (tanks fitted with special mine-exploding equipment). A device known as the bangalore torpedo was often used to carve a path through a known mine field. It consisted of a metal tube packed with explosives that detonated all mines in its vicinity. The bangalore torpedo was also used to cut through thick barbed wire and blow up railway tracks.

Other Land Weapons

A wide variety of miscellaneous land weapons were used over the course of World War II, many of them first tested more than two decades earlier during World War I.

Grenades—both thrown and fired from rifles—were also widely used by both sides throughout the war. In most armies, infantrymen carried them in addition to their sidearms. The M2A1 and M3A fragmentation grenades were standard issue in the U.S. Army and Marine Corps. Both types of grenade had a ring-shaped safety pin and handle; the grenade would not explode until the pin was pulled out and the handle was released. The fuse time for both devices was about five seconds. Because of their design, grenades were commonly used in the creation of booby traps.

FACT

Napalm—a long-burning jellied gasoline—was first used during the air attacks that supported the U.S. invasion of Tinian in June 1944. The word is derived from the aluminum salts of naphthalenic and palmitic acids.

German and Japanese soldiers commonly used grenades known as "sticks" or "potato mashers" by Allied soldiers because they had a long handle at the top, which made them easier to carry and throw. The Germans and Japanese also used egg-shaped grenades that were similar in design to the M3As.

One of the most unique weapons introduced during the war was the bazooka, a shoulder-mounted rocket launcher commonly used against enemy tanks. The bazooka was so effective during tank warfare that General Dwight Eisenhower called it one of the four weapons that benefited the Allies the most in winning the war, the other three being the C-47 Skytrain/ Dakota transport, the Jeep, and the atomic bomb.

Almost every World War II movie has a scene in which a soldier removes the safety pin of a grenade with his teeth. In truth, this was extremely difficult to do and posed a tremendous safety hazard. Real World War II soldiers never removed a grenade's firing pin with their teeth.

The bazooka was introduced in 1942 and proved only minimally effective against the German Panther and Tiger tanks when fired at their armored fronts. However, it was extremely effective at blowing out a tank's tracks and rendering it immobile. (Some weak areas on the tanks' armor were also vulnerable to bazooka fire.)

The typical bazooka was 54 inches long, fired a rocket projectile weighing about 3.5 pounds, and had an effective range of about 300 feet. Two men were usually involved in using a bazooka, with one loading it and the other firing. The bazooka tube folded in half for convenient storage. Nearly a half million bazookas were produced during World War II, and they were also widely used in the Korean War.

One weapon invented during World War I and used by almost all forces in World War II was the flamethrower, which proved especially effective in eliminating entrenched troops in bunkers and other fortifications. The U.S. Marines in the Pacific often used flamethrowers to drive Japanese soldiers from caves, trenches, pillboxes, and other defensive positions.

Flamethrowers were coveted by ground troops because they were portable and easy to use. The M1 flamethrower consisted of a four-gallon fuel tank carried on the user's back and a handheld hose that directed the length and intensity of the flame. Fully loaded, the device weighed about seventy pounds and could shoot a flame up to ninety feet. Many Sherman tanks were also equipped with flamethrowers capable of sending a stream of fire up to 300 feet. These were sometimes called Ronsons, after the popular cigarette lighter.

Chapter 11

Air Weapons

Air warfare played an integral role in World War II. This certainly wasn't the first use of aircraft in war, but it was the first war in which aircraft were used with such devastating effectiveness. Aircraft evolved dramatically between World War I and the onset of World War II in 1939. In the first war, before effective bombsights and standardized bomb fittings were developed, bombs were dropped by hand from the cockpit. During World War II, heavy bombers could rain bombs on targets, destroying several city blocks at a time. Fighter planes provided protection for bombers and attacked enemy planes, ships, and ground troops.

Bombers

The development of high-speed offensive bombers really took off in the 1930s. All sides of the war made extensive use of bombers in terrifying air assaults.

Allied Bombers

One of the most influential bombers to come out of that era was the B-17 Flying Fortress, which was widely used by the Allies in both the European and Pacific theaters throughout the war. The B-17 was popular because it had a formidable defensive gun armament (hence the name Flying Fortress) and could also sustain considerable damage and still make it home.

Fig 11-1 The Avengers flying in formation, September 1942.

Photo courtesy of the National Archives (80-G-417475)

Equally important in the overall war effort was the B-24 Liberator, a heavy bomber produced in greater numbers than any other U.S. military aircraft. The B-24 was used primarily as a long-range bomber and saw service as such in Europe, the Pacific, and North Africa. However, it was also used as an antisubmarine plane, for reconnaissance, and to haul cargo.

The *Memphis Belle* was the first U.S. bomber to successfully complete twenty-five missions over Europe, and as a result it became one of the best-known aircraft of the war. The *Memphis Belle*, a B-17 Flying Fortress, was named by Captain Robert Morgan for Margaret Polk of Memphis, Tennessee. In addition to their bombing runs, the crew shot down eight German fighters.

The B-29 Superfortress was the next step in the evolution of American-designed heavy bombers and was by far the most advanced bomber to see action in the war. The B-29 was used extensively in bombing raids against Japanese industrial and urban targets during the latter months of the war. In addition, the B-29 was the first U.S. bomber with a radar bombing system, which replaced the popular Norden bombsight for precision bombing.

The B-32 Dominator was created just in case the B-29 failed to live up to expectations. Also a heavy bomber, it saw limited action (only fifteen actually flew in combat in the Pacific before the end of the war) because the B-29 proved to be so reliable and effective. However, the B-32 was a very solid plane with tremendous defensive capabilities. In one incident in August 1945, two B-32s on a photo mission over Tokyo were attacked by fourteen Japanese fighters. One Dominator was damaged in the ensuing battle, but both managed to return safely to their base in Okinawa.

FACT

Enola Gay, the plane that dropped the atomic bombs on Hiroshima, was a B-29.

The B-36 Peacemaker was a long-distance bomber designed to attack European targets from bases in North America. The plane was also considered for duty in the Pacific as a result of problems with the B-29 and B-32. However, the first B-36 didn't roll off the assembly line until August 1946—

a year after the end of the war and nearly five years after the prototype was first ordered.

Even more distinctive in concept was the B-35 Flying Wing, a long-range bomber that, as its name implies, looked like a flying wing. The plane was conceived of as a transatlantic bomber, and the order for a prototype was received by Northrop in 1941. The first B-35s took to the air in June 1946, too late to participate in the war.

QUESTION?

Who painted the noses of fighter planes during the war?
The job usually went to the crewman with the most talent. Lacking that, crews would often offer to pay others to do the job, though usually it was done for free. The farther from headquarters a crew was based, the more daring it made its nose art. Air crews were encouraged to keep their nose art inoffensive when close to home.

Medium-range Allied bombers included the B-25 Mitchell (which was flown by Lieutenant Colonel James Doolittle and his raiders during their famous attack on Tokyo in April 1942) and the B-26 Marauder (which Allied pilots disliked because of its high accident rate and difficulty in bailing out).

Axis Bombers

Germany and Japan also had very effective medium- and long-range bombers, as well as other craft. In the German Luftwaffe, the Ju 87 Stuka dive-bomber was most commonly used for air support and tactical bombing. Thousands of the planes were produced over the course of the war, and the Ju 87 participated in all early blitzkrieg attacks, as well as almost every major battle in which air support was needed. The plane carried bombs under the wings and fuselage and was unique in its use of an autopilot if the pilot blacked out during a dive. The use of sirens on the undercarriage made its natural scream even more terrifying to enemy troops.

Germany, like the Allies, experimented with a number of intriguing war plane prototypes. The Ju 390, a transatlantic bomber, was originally conceived of for strategic bombing missions against the United States from bases in Europe. In January 1944, the Ju 390 was tested with a mission that took it across the Atlantic to within twelve miles of New York City and back again. The plane was never mass-produced and did not see action during the war.

The Ju 88 was one of Germany's most commonly used medium-range bombers. In fact, the plane was so popular because of its versatility that more Ju 88s were produced than any other German bomber. Like the Ju 87, it participated in nearly all German aerial campaigns and inflicted tremendous damage on enemy targets.

The most effective dive-bomber used by the Japanese was the D3A Val, which inflicted tremendous damage during the attack on Pearl Harbor. A workhorse of the Japanese air force, the plane saw action throughout the Pacific and Indian Oceans. By mid-1944, however, the Val had largely been replaced by the A6M Zero fighter-bomber and to a lesser degree by the D4Y Suisei (Comet) bomber (code-named "Judy" by the Allies). The D4Y Suisei was most commonly used for kamikaze attacks against Allied ships.

Torpedo Bombers

One of the weapons most feared by seamen during wartime was the torpedo bomber, which was used by both sides against surface ships. The primary U.S. torpedo bomber at the start of the war was the TBD Devastator. Though capable of inflicting tremendous damage on enemy ships, the Devastator was slow and extremely vulnerable to attack by other planes. Devastators helped sink the Japanese light carrier *Shoho* at the Battle of the Coral Sea in May 1942 but proved useless during the Battle of Midway the following month; all three flights of U.S. Devastators were destroyed by Japanese defenses without hitting a single Japanese carrier. However, aerial torpedoes helped sink the Japanese battleships *Yamato* and *Musashi*.

Captain Robert Morgan, the pilot of the *Memphis Belle*, also flew the first B-29 Superfortress to bomb Japan.

In May 1943 Allied aircraft started using the acoustic antisubmarine torpedo known as Fido, which homed in on the sound of a submarine's propeller. Similar devices were used by German submarines against Allied surface ships. Torpedo bombers were used throughout the war, but dive-bombers eventually took over as the navy's primary striking force.

Bombs

Thousands of aircraft bombs were dropped by both sides over the course of the war, devastating entire cities and killing hundreds of thousands of people. A wide variety of bombs were used by the U.S. Army Air Forces, including high-explosive, fragmentation, and incendiary warheads. Bombs were also developed for chemical and biological warfare, but they were not deployed during World War II.

U.S. high-explosive bombs ranged in size from 100 to 4,000 pounds, though the larger sizes were seldom used. (An experimental 42,000-pound high-explosive bomb was created by the Army Air Forces in 1945 but was never used in the war.) Fragmentation bombs—also known as antipersonnel bombs—came in 20-, 23-, and 30-pound sizes and were dropped on enemy ground troops.

Incendiary bombs, which used chemicals to start fires, were usually fifty pounds in size and were often dropped in clusters to create a fast-moving blaze. Sometimes demolition bombs were dropped first to blow off roofs so the incendiary bombs that followed would be more effective in destroying target buildings. According to bomb experts, incendiary bombs were far superior to explosives for wholesale destruction, and entire cities, such as Dresden, Germany, were burned to the ground as a result of their use.

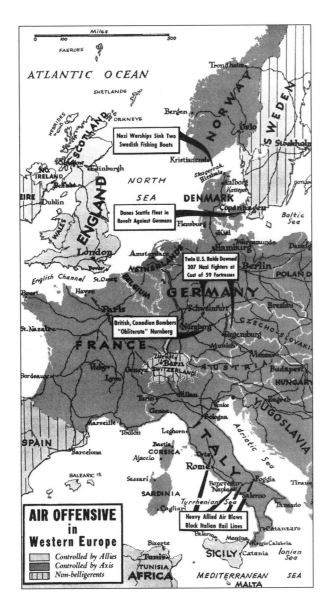

Map 11-1 Air offensive in Western Europe as of September 6, 1943.

Map courtesy of the National Archives (RG 160, Vol. 2, No. 20)

Toward the end of the war, the Japanese sent incendiary bombs to the United States and Canada via balloon. Few reached their targets, and damage from the balloon bombs was minimal. The only casualties were Elsie Mitchell and her five children, who found a balloon bomb while fishing in Lake County, Oregon. The bomb detonated while they were examining it.

The Mitchells were also the only casualties from enemy action on the U.S. mainland.

Fig 11-2 Pilots aboard a U.S. Navy aircraft carrier receive last minute instructions before taking off to attack industrial and military installations in Tokyo.

Photo courtesy of the National Archives (208-N-38374)

The British created a number of large bombs, including a 4,000-pounder that could level an entire city block. This "blockbuster" bomb was first used against the German port of Emden on April 1, 1941. The largest bombs used during the war were British-made 12,000- and 22,000-pound "earthquake" bombs known, respectively, as Tallboy and Grand Slam. These bombs were used against German submarine pens and other heavily fortified targets and proved quite effective. A Tallboy bomb was also used to sink the German battleship *Tirpitz*, which had survived blasts from smaller bombs.

FACT

Some large bombs were equipped with parachutes to slow their fall so aircraft could safely escape the blast area before they detonated.

The largest Axis bomb used was the German 5,511-pound SB 2500, which carried an explosive charge of more than 3,700 pounds. The bomb was effective, but few were dropped during the war. The most destructive

Allied bombs, of course, were the atomic bombs used to destroy Hiroshima and Nagasaki.

Fighter Planes

Bombers were not the only offensive planes used by Allied and Axis forces during World War II. Equally effective were fighter planes, which were used to defend bombers and attack other planes, ships at sea, and ground troops.

Fighters played an extremely important role in defending Great Britain during the Battle of Britain. Hermann Goering was confident his Luftwaffe would be able to make short work of the Royal Air Force, but the British Hurricane and Spitfire fighters quickly proved that Great Britain was not about to roll over. The planes were extremely successful in defending the British coast, and the RAF downed considerably more planes than it lost.

Fig 11-3 Pilots pleased over their victory during the Marshall Islands attack grin across the tale of an F6F Hellcat on board the USS *Lexington*, after shooting down seventeen out of twenty Japanese planes heading for Tarawa.

Photo courtesy of the National Archives (80-G-470985)

The Hurricane became part of the RAF's air arsenal in December 1937. The Spitfire followed in 1939 and quickly became one of the foremost Allied fighter planes of the war; it was even used during the Normandy invasion to direct gunfire from nearby warships.

FACT

The U.S. military was racially segregated during the war, with African-American servicemen serving in special units. The most famous was the Ninety-ninth Pursuit Squadron, the first African-American combat unit in the Army Air Forces. The unit was established in Tuskegee, Alabama. The so-called Tuskegee Airmen completed more than 500 missions in its first year of action. More than eighty members were decorated.

Fighter Plane Evolution

The United States also produced a wide variety of fighter planes during the war. The first fighter aircraft to see combat was the P-36, which was produced primarily for use by foreign air forces, though a few were flown by the U.S. Army at the start of the war. A variant of the P-36 was the Hawk 75, which was first flown in 1937. It, too, was primarily sold to other nations. (A handful of captured Hawk 75s were flown by the Germans after the fall of France.)

The P-47 Thunderbolt was the most widely flown American fighter of the war. In fact, in 1944 and 1945, the Thunderbolt was flown by more than 40 percent of all army air force fighter groups overseas. The plane was widely used in both Europe and the Pacific and was surpassed in performance only by the P-51 Mustang, which was considered the most reliable and effective land-based fighter of the war. Because of its long-distance and defensive capabilities, the Mustang allowed U.S. heavy bombers to fly over Europe during daylight rather than under the cloak of night.

Other effective American fighter planes included the P-38 Lightning, which had the longest range and greatest performance of any American fighter at the beginning of the war; the P-39 Airacobra; the P-40 Warhawk; the P-61 Black Widow, which was the first American plane developed specifically as a night fighter; and the P-80 Shooting Star, the first U.S. jet-propelled combat aircraft. Though the Shooting Star came out of development too late to see service in World War II, it was one of the first U.S. jet aircraft put into combat in the Korean War.

Probably the most feared Japanese fighter plane was the A6M Zero, which created havoc in the Pacific for the first two years of the war. Developed by Jiro Horikoshi, the Zero was the first plane to prove that a carrier-based aircraft could hold its own against land-based fighters. The Zero, which reached speeds of more than 300 miles per hour, was used in the attack on Pearl Harbor and in almost all Japanese naval air battles after that. It wasn't until the introduction of the Navy's F6F Hellcat in 1943 that an Allied fighter could defeat the Zero under all combat conditions.

The Dreaded Kamikaze

Allied naval personnel serving in the Pacific faced numerous hazards every day, but few were more dreaded than the Japanese naval suicide squads known as kamikaze.

The Japanese navy began organized suicide attacks against Allied forces on October 25, 1944, in the Battle of Leyte Gulf, though individual Japanese pilots had routinely aimed their planes at U.S. ships when their craft was damaged and they had no hope of returning safely to base.

The idea of organized crash-dive attacks was conceived of by Captain Motoharu Okamura, commander of the 341st Air Group, who felt such a program was the only way to prevent a U.S. advance on the Japanese mainland. "Provide me with 300 planes, and I will turn the tide of the war," Okamura told Vice Admiral Takijiro Onishi in June 1944.

The first Japanese Zero to fall into American hands was found in the Aleutian Islands, where it had crashed, killing its pilot. The plane was repaired by American technicians, who marveled at its unique design, and made its first flight with U.S. markings in October 1942.

The Japanese called the suicide squads "kamikaze" after the super-strong "divine winds" that were said to have destroyed Mongol fleets sailing to invade Japan in 1274 and 1281. The first kamikaze attacks in October 1944 were flown by twenty-four volunteers of the Japanese navy's 201st Air Group on Leyte. Using A6M Zero fighters, the pilots focused their efforts on U.S.

escort carriers that had engaged Japanese warships in the Battle of Leyte Gulf. The first U.S. ship to be hit was the escort carrier *St. Lo*, which went up in flames after being struck by a Zero filled with explosives. The carrier went down in less than half an hour, taking 100 members of its crew with it. Two other escort carriers were damaged by kamikazes on October 25 but stayed afloat.

After that, the Japanese sent more than 1,250 aircraft on organized kamikaze attacks against U.S. forces during the battles for the Philippines, Iwo Jima, and Okinawa. The suicide squads sank 26 combat ships and damaged nearly 300 more. The largest U.S. ships sunk were 3 escort carriers, 13 destroyers, and a destroyer escort. Several U.S. aircraft carriers were damaged by suicide attacks, but none was sunk. An estimated 3,000 Allied personnel (primarily American and British) were killed in kamikaze attacks, and another 6,000 were wounded.

The Japanese also used small, piloted suicide submarines (actually torpedoes) called *kaiten*, which sank a U.S. tanker and a destroyer escort, and damaged several other ships. Overall, however, the kaiten program was a failure.

Gliders

Gliders were used by both sides to deliver troops and equipment to locations where traditional aircraft couldn't go. Because they were unpowered, gliders were particularly good at delivering their cargo undetected behind enemy lines.

The Treaty of Versailles prevented Germany from having an air force, so German aviators formed glider clubs to retain their flight skills and train new pilots. From that came increased interest in gliders as military weapons. Large gliders were found to be superior to parachute landings in efficiently delivering large numbers of troops and equipment to a specific site.

One of the first significant German military gliders to be developed was the DFS 230, which could carry nine men. It was first test-flown in 1937 and proved to be quite useful. A glider commando force was formed in 1938, and production of the DFS 230 was greatly increased. By 1943, more than 1,500 of the craft had been made. During the German campaign of 1940 in France and the Low Countries, gliders were used to take Fort Eben Emael on the Belgian border. Gliders were also used during the German invasion of Crete in 1941, to bring supplies to besieged German troops in the Soviet Union, and to rescue Benito Mussolini in September 1944.

Larger and better gliders were soon created by the German air force, including the Gotha Go 242, which could carry 21 men, and the massive Messerschmitt Me 321 Gigant, which could carry 130 soldiers, though it was used primarily to transport cargo.

The U.S. Army Air Forces ignored the glider concept until Germany proved the planes' usefulness in a number of important airborne assaults in 1940 and 1941. Military aviation experts began to explore glider design in February 1941, and two distinct designs were eventually mass-produced: the CG-4A, which could carry thirteen men, and the CG-13, which could carry thirty. More than 14,000 of these gliders were produced over the course of the war.

The Allies used gliders to deliver troops and equipment during several crucial campaigns, including the capture of Sicily in 1943, the Normandy invasion in June 1944, and the Rhine crossings in 1945. Gliders were used sparingly in the Pacific because of the distances between bases and their objectives, as well as a shortage of transport craft.

Britain, the Soviet Union, and Japan all used gliders to varying degrees over the course of the war. The Soviet Union even designed a glider-bomber known as the PB, though the craft never left the drawing board.

Guided Missiles and Rockets

Both the Allies and the Axis explored the use of guided missiles—unmanned craft controlled by radio signals from nearby aircraft—as offensive and defensive weapons, with mixed results.

In 1944, the U.S. Army Air Forces and Navy worked together to refine the use of worn-out bombers packed with explosives as a weapon against German submarine pens, oil refineries, and other targets. The results of the top secret project, known as Aphrodite, were less than spectacular, and the concept was not implemented during the war. The use of radio-controlled fighters packed with bombs or napalm was also explored in 1945, but the war ended before the project could reach the development stage.

Specialized guided missiles were also widely researched. One concept involved fitting bombs with wings or controllable fins. A variety of glide bombs were developed, and in May 1944, bombers flying out of England dropped more than 100 of these GB-1s on Cologne, Germany. However, the results were disappointing, and no more attacks were approved. Improved GB-type weapons were tested in Europe over the course of the war, though they, too, had little success.

The Army Air Forces had better luck with vertical bomb weapons. The VB-1 Azon was a 1,000-pound bomb with a radio-controlled tail that allowed for much greater accuracy. It was used successfully against German targets throughout Europe and the Mediterranean in 1944 and 1945, as well as against Japanese bridges in Burma.

German Advances

Germany conducted extensive research into guided missiles and had its greatest success with the V-1 rocket, commonly known as the buzz bomb because of its distinctive drone. The V-1 was the first guided missile to be launched in large numbers against an enemy, and it inflicted tremendous damage and huge casualties on Great Britain starting in June 1944. In fact, during an eighty-day period, a nonstop rain of V-1s damaged or destroyed nearly 1 million buildings, killed 6,184 Britons, and injured more than 17,980 others. The city of Antwerp was also targeted with V-1s.

The U.S. Army Air Forces created its own version of the V-1 rocket in August 1944, using parts from recovered V-1s as a guide. The American version was called the JB-2 and was successfully tested in October 1944. General H. H. Arnold, head of the air forces, ordered the weapon into mass production. However, the initial numbers were scaled back because the high demand was exhausting production capability. Germany and Japan both surrendered before the guided missiles were put into wide use.

Many of the V-1s launched against England were duds though, and a large number were thwarted by planes and barrage balloons. V-1 production and launch sites in Germany became primary targets of Allied bombing raids.

Allied ships were another common target of German guided missiles. The primary guided bomb was the Kramer X-1, which carried a 1,300-pound armor-piercing bomb. The Luftwaffe successfully sank the Italian battleship *Roma* with a single X-1 on September 9, 1943. Many other Allied warships were heavily damaged by X-1s.

The V-2 Missile

Germany led the way in rocket research during the war, with deadly results. One of its most impressive rocket missiles was the dreaded V-2, a forerunner of the contemporary intercontinental ballistic missile.

At 46 feet in height, the V-2 was an impressive missile. Fueled by a mixture of liquid oxygen and alcohol, it weighed 28,373 pounds at launch and carried a 2,145-pound explosive warhead. Variations included a winged model called a glider, a two-stage rocket that would have been able to hit the United States from Europe, and a model that could be launched from a submarine. However, none of these was developed in time to have much of an impact on the war.

FACT

The V-2 was developed by a team of German rocket scientists led by Dr. Werner von Braun. After the war, he and many of his associates were brought to the United States, where they were instrumental in establishing the U.S. ballistic missile and space programs. Other German scientists aided the Soviet Union.

The experiments that led to the development of the V-2 started in the 1930s. The first operational launches occurred on September 6, 1944, when two V-2s were fired at Paris from the Peenemünde rocket facility on the shores of the Baltic Sea. Two days later, two more V-2s were fired at England. Over the next several months, England was hit by hundreds more. More than 2,700 Britons were killed by the rockets, and more than 6,500 were injured. Antwerp and Brussels were also frequent V-2 targets.

Unlike successful efforts to down the V-1 buzz bomb, no countermeasures could be taken against the V-2 once it had been launched. Fired from hundreds of miles away, the missile reached a terminal velocity of nearly 4,000 miles per hour; a flight of 200 miles took just a few minutes from launch to impact.

Airships

The U.S. Navy relied heavily on blimps for a variety of functions during the war and was the only service branch among all the war participants to use lighter-than-air ships.

When war broke out, the United States had only 10 operational blimps; by the end of the conflict, 167 were in service, most of them K-type airships. The blimps' primary function was to search for U-boats and lead aircraft and surface ships to them, and the airships were highly effective in that role. No Allied convoys accompanied by a blimp experienced serious damage from enemy ships. Blimps were also used for rescues at sea.

Blimps were often equipped with machine guns and other weapons, and sometimes they engaged enemy ships. Only one Allied blimp was ever shot down. The *K-74* discovered a surfaced submarine on July 18, 1943, and attacked it with machine guns and depth charges. The sub responded with a barrage of antiaircraft fire, and the *K-74* was struck multiple times, forcing it down in the ocean. Amazingly, all but one crewman survived. The German submarine *U-134* escaped but was later sunk in the Bay of Biscay by an RAF bomber.

Blimps were filled with nonflammable helium and propelled by two reciprocating engines. The K-type blimps had a cruising radius of approximately 1,500 miles and a top speed of about 75 miles per hour.

Chapter 12

Weapons
and Vessels at Sea

Control of the world's oceans was a crucial aspect of World War II, and a huge array of warships and seaborne weapons was used by both sides over the course of the conflict. Most vessels were involved in naval warfare, though warships also supported troop activity during amphibious landings.

Aircraft Carriers

Aircraft carriers were generally the largest ships in any nation's fleet and replaced battleships as the primary support vessels of the U.S., British, and Japanese navies during the war because their bomber aircraft were more flexible and could reach more-distant targets than the big guns of any battleship.

Most U.S. aircraft carriers saw action in the Pacific. When war first broke out, the navy had seven aircraft carriers in operation. They were the primary target of the Japanese attack against Pearl Harbor, but all were out to sea when the Japanese struck. Aircraft carriers played decisive roles in several important battles in the Pacific, including the battles of the Coral Sea and Midway. Though massive and heavily protected, aircraft carriers were not invincible, and several U.S. carriers were destroyed in combat. The *Lexington*, for example, was sunk at Coral Sea, the *Yorktown* at Midway, and both the *Wasp* and the *Hornet* during the campaign to take Guadalcanal and the Solomon Islands. At one point in 1942, the *Enterprise* was the only operational carrier in the Pacific Fleet, and it was limping as a result of enemy attack.

FACT

In the motion picture *Jaws*, fisherman Quint, played by Robert Shaw, admits that his hatred of sharks stems from watching many of his shipmates get eaten alive after the sinking of the cruiser *Indianapolis* on July 30, 1945. That scene, rewritten by Shaw, was later called one of the movie's best by its director, Steven Spielberg.

New carriers began joining the fray in 1943. By the middle of 1945, thirteen 27,100-ton Essex-class and nine 13,000-ton Independence-class light carriers were in service. These ships, capable of carrying large numbers of aircraft, conducted much of the Allied offensive against the Japanese, whose own fleet of carriers had been heavily damaged in fighting.

From the Battle of Midway until the end of the war, only one U.S. light carrier was sunk by enemy fire: the *Princeton*, which was hit by Japanese bombs during the Battle of Leyte Gulf in October 1944.

Only two American aircraft carriers saw action in the Atlantic. The *Wasp* was briefly part of the British Home Fleet and made two voyages into the Mediterranean Sea in April 1942 to unleash fighter planes during the campaign to take Malta. And the *Ranger*—kept out of the Pacific because of its slow speed and lack of torpedo planes—also aided the British in the Atlantic, particularly during the invasion of North Africa in 1942.

Figure 12-1
USS *Iowa* firing its 16-inch guns during a drill in the Pacific, circa 1944.

Photo courtesy of the National Archives (80-G-59493)

The German navy did not have any aircraft carriers, though it did have some formidable battleships, including the 41,700-ton *Bismarck* and the 42,900-ton *Tirpitz*.

Battleships

The U.S. Navy had seventeen battleships in service when the Japanese attacked Pearl Harbor. Fifteen of them had been put into commission from 1912 to 1923; the other two—the *North Carolina* and the *Washington*—were more modern, having joined the fleet in early 1941.

When the Japanese attacked, nine of the older ships were in the Pacific Fleet. Eight were stationed at Pearl Harbor, and two of them (the *Arizona* and the *Oklahoma*) were destroyed in the attack. Five others were heavily damaged but were quickly repaired and put back into action. At the time of the

Japanese attack, six of the older battleships and the two newest were in the Atlantic.

Over the course of the war, eight additional battleships were delivered to the fleet: four ships of the *Iowa* class and four of the *South Dakota* class. All of the modern battleships were equipped with nine 16-inch guns and a variety of smaller weapons. The four ships in the *Iowa* class were the largest and most heavily armed battleships on the seas with the exception of the Japanese *Yamato* and *Musashi*, both of which were eventually sunk by U.S. carrier aircraft. A larger class of battleship, to be known as the *Montana* class, was considered, but the program was canceled in 1943.

Figure 12-2 The crew of the U.S. Coast Guard Cutter *Spencer* watch charges explode while searching for German U-boats.

Photo courtesy of the National Archives (26-G-1517)

The primary role of U.S. battleships was to provide antiaircraft defense for carrier task forces and shore bombardment to reduce enemy resistance before amphibious landings. However, there were two major battleship-to-battleship fights off Guadalcanal in 1942. In one of them, the *Washington* sank a Japanese battle cruiser while suffering no damage itself, though another U.S. battleship was heavily damaged by Japanese cruisers and destroyers.

In addition, six U.S. battleships—four of them survivors of the Pearl Harbor attack—engaged Japanese ships in an impressive night battle during the Battle of Leyte Gulf in October 1944. Two Japanese battleships were sunk during the fighting.

No U.S. battleships were sunk by enemy fire after the attack on Pearl Harbor.

Destroyers

Destroyers were some of the most plentiful surface ships in the war and were used to great advantage by both the Allies and the Axis. Smaller and faster than battleships, destroyers were used primarily to intercept enemy destroyers and other warships and disable them with torpedoes. If necessary, crippled enemy ships were then finished off by larger battleships or cruisers.

The U.S. Navy had 171 destroyers in service when America entered the war. Of that number, 71 had been built during or immediately after World War I and the rest put into commission after 1934. (Several older destroyers were also used as light minelayers, minesweepers, and transports.) All U.S. destroyers had banks of torpedo tubes, and the newer ships were also equipped with 5-inch guns to defend against—and attack—planes and surface ships. American destroyers also had sonar for tracking other ships, depth charges for use against submarines, and machine guns.

The first destroyer action of the war involved the *Ward*, which sank a Japanese midget submarine as it tried to enter Pearl Harbor just minutes before the Japanese air attack. (Three destroyers were heavily damaged during the attack but were completely rebuilt and placed back in service.) After that, destroyers saw action in all theaters of combat. Like battleships, they were also used to soften up enemy coastal defenses before amphibious landings.

FACT

Two U.S. destroyers lost during a typhoon off Luzon provided the setting for Herman Wouk's novel *The Caine Mutiny*, which was turned into a popular motion picture starring Humphrey Bogart.

Production of destroyers escalated dramatically over the course of the war, with American shipyards delivering nearly 400 of the versatile ships.

A total of 71 U.S. destroyers were lost during the war—more than any other type of warship. Most were sunk by enemy planes and ships (including 9 by Japanese kamikazes), though 3 U.S. destroyers went down as a result of accidental collisions, and 2 were lost during a typhoon off Luzon.

Submarines

The submarine was one of the most effective offensive naval craft of the war and was used to great advantage by the United States against the Japanese in the Pacific and by the Germans against Allied convoys in the Atlantic and the Mediterranean.

At the start of the war, the United States had 114 submarines. In the Pacific, 22 fleet boats operated out of Pearl Harbor, and 23 fleet boats and 6 older S-boats were based at Manila Bay in the Philippines. Sixty-three additional submarines of various classes were based along both U.S. coasts.

Figure 12-3
An American submarine officer scanning the surface.

Photo courtesy of the National Archives (80-G-11258)

The fleet boats were large, long-range submarines built in the decade before the war to protect surface ships. They were more than 300 feet long and equipped with ten 21-inch torpedo tubes and a stock of up to twenty-four torpedoes. They were also armed with a single 76-mm deck gun and several machine guns. The smaller S-boats were not as spacious as the larger subs, could not dive as deep, and were armed with only four torpedo tubes.

At the onset of the war in December 1941, U.S. submarines in the Pacific were ordered to search for and destroy Japanese merchant ships rather than support the surface fleet, as originally intended. But the mission was impeded by recurring problems with faulty torpedoes, a situation that was not completely remedied until 1943.

The first successful U.S. submarine attack occurred just a week after Pearl Harbor, when the *Swordfish* sank the Japanese merchant ship *Atsutasan Maru* off Indochina. On January 27, 1942, the *Gudgeon* became the first U.S. submarine to sink a Japanese warship when it successfully torpedoed the submarine *I-173*. The attack was one of many based on information derived from decoded Japanese naval communiqués. Over the course of the war in the Pacific, U.S. subs sank nearly 1,300 Japanese merchant vessels, 4 fleet and 4 escort carriers, a battleship, 12 cruisers, 42 destroyers, 22 undersea craft, and 2 Soviet merchant ships mistaken for Japanese vessels.

Smaller older American submarines patrolled the east coast of the United States and the Panama Canal Zone during the early days of the war, though they saw little action. Then, in the summer of 1942, Roosevelt responded to a request by Winston Churchill and ordered six fleet-type submarines to the Atlantic, to be based in Scotland. The subs participated in the invasion of North Africa, but poor weather and confused recognition signals resulted in the *Gunnel* and the *Shad* being attacked by friendly fire.

FACT

U.S. submarines fired an estimated 14,750 torpedoes at 3,184 enemy ships over the course of the war. More than 1,300 enemy vessels were sunk, and submarines received "probable credit" for another 78 ships.

German submarines—called U-boats—patrolled the Atlantic during the early months of the war, sinking a great many Allied supply ships and dramatically affecting the European war effort. They played an integral role in the Battle of the Atlantic and were slowed only after the development of radar and increased use of antisubmarine ships and planes.

The first U-boats were launched in 1935 in direct violation of the Treaty of Versailles. When the war began, Germany had fifty-seven U-boats in commission, twenty-six of them large enough for ocean patrol. Their numbers increased quickly, and the German U-boat soon became the scourge of the Atlantic, which it easily accessed after the fall of Norway and France in 1940. By the end of 1942, nearly a hundred U-boats were in operation, with more to follow.

Germany and the Allies played a continual game of catch-up when it came to the U-boat, with every new submarine advance being met with a countermeasure. Germany also designed larger, better armed, and better equipped submarines such as the Type XXL, but few were produced, and they had little influence over the course of the war.

Other Sea Weapons

Warships weren't the only sea weapons to be used during the war. A wide variety of other weapons were also employed including:

- **Torpedoes.** Launched from submarines, destroyers, or aircraft, torpedoes were effective against both surface and undersea ships. Numerous sizes and designs were used throughout the war, with improvements occurring regularly. Japanese torpedoes were far superior to Allied torpedoes, with the Japanese Type 93 being the largest torpedo used in the war.
- **Mines.** Several hundred thousand naval mines were placed over the course of the war. Four basic types of mines were used: acoustic mines, which were detonated by the sound of a ship's engine or propeller; contact mines, which exploded when struck; magnetic mines, which detonated when disturbed by a steel-hulled ship; and pressure mines, which reacted to changes in water pressure caused by a passing ship. Some mines had multiple capabilities.
- **Depth charges.** Developed and first used during World War I, depth charges were surface ships' primary method of defense against submarines. They typically consisted of a metal cylinder filled with explosives and fitted with a fuse that caused the canister to explode

at a specific depth. Because surface ships often did not know exactly where or at what depth a submarine was, depth charges were often scattered in a fan pattern and set to go off at incremental depths. Depth charges were also dropped from submarine-hunting planes and blimps.

Liberty Ships

The workhorse of the combined Allied navies was the mass-produced "Liberty" cargo ship. More of them were made during the war than any other ship in history. Sturdy and reliable, they served in every theater of action.

The Liberty ship design was based on the old British "tramp" steamer, with modifications for wartime use. Each ship measured 441 feet long and could carry nearly 11,000 tons of cargo. Powered by steam engines, they had a maximum speed of 11 knots.

More than 2,700 Liberty ships were produced at nineteen American shipyards from 1941 to 1945. By December 1943, a complete Liberty ship could be built and delivered in twenty-seven days, with fourteen days for fitting out.

Chapter 13

The Horrors of War

The men and women who fought in World War II faced a combat situation unlike any other in history. Larger, more powerful weapons, difficult combat conditions, and a heavily armed, extremely tenacious enemy plunged soldiers into the horrific situation of kill or be killed. While most commanders were battle-hardened veterans who had honed their skills in World War I, the overwhelming majority of grunt soldiers were inexperienced young men. Most managed to cope fairly well under these difficult conditions, but some did not. Combat fatigue was a common problem—particularly among those who were involved in long campaigns in which heavy fighting was a daily occurrence.

Battlefield Conditions

Because World War II was a global conflict, the servicemen who fought in it faced astounding extremes on the battlefield. Soldiers stationed in Europe watched the pleasant spring and summer weather give way to numbing, incapacitating cold in the winter—particularly German soldiers engaged in the Soviet campaign of 1941–1943. For most German troops, the bitter Soviet winter was made worse by a lack of appropriate cold-weather clothing, heaters, and other supplies. In addition, heavy equipment that worked fine in warmer temperatures ground to a halt as internal parts froze solid and vehicles sank axle-deep in the slick winter mud. Soviet soldiers didn't have it much better, though for the most part they were better dressed for and acclimated to the winter temperatures.

The European winters were also a harsh surprise for many American troops, particularly those from the South who were unused to such temperature extremes. But unlike the German soldiers on the eastern front, most Allied soldiers in Europe were issued high-quality cold-weather gear.

The servicemen who fought in the Pacific experienced a host of different problems. Rather than bitter cold, they faced suffocating heat and humidity, as well as a wide variety of insects and wildlife that seemed to go out of their way to make life miserable. The combination of heat, humidity, and extreme physical exertion during combat caused many soldiers to become dehydrated. Unfortunately, water reserves were initially limited at many Pacific battle locations, such as Guadalcanal, and soldiers suffered because of it, often going a full day or more without a drink of water.

The Pacific rains, rather than bringing relief, only added to the average soldier's long, hard days. During the monsoon season, it rained almost every day, often heavily. As a result, it became next to impossible to stay dry, resulting in fungal infections and disease from mosquitoes and other insects. For many soldiers who saw long-term duty in the Pacific, a dry pair of socks was more coveted than a pinup of Betty Grable.

Extreme heat was also a hazard for Allied and Axis forces in North Africa, though it was a more insidious dry heat than that experienced in the Pacific. Sweat evaporated as quickly as it formed, reducing its cooling effect and increasing the need for additional fluids. As a result, water was a precious commodity among soldiers doing battle in the desert. Other serious concerns were sunburn and heat stroke, both of which could drop a soldier as quickly as an enemy bullet.

Temperature extremes weren't the only hazards facing soldiers on the battlefield. An astounding array of new weapons—many developed after World War I—posed tremendous threats to exposed soldiers and even those in bunkers. Most devastating were long-range artillery, which could wipe out an army in minutes, and planes equipped with bombs and machine guns, which could be equally devastating.

War has a way of affecting the senses, and soldiers quickly learned that even small battles could be deafeningly loud and frighteningly disorienting. Fear and panic were common emotions in the throes of combat, and it took all the willpower a soldier could muster to keep from fleeing in the face of enemy fire. Some Allied soldiers, unable to take the strain, deserted their posts or shot themselves in the foot to avoid being sent to the front. When discovered, soldiers with self-inflicted wounds were typically court-martialed, and many served time in prison for their actions. German and Japanese soldiers who deserted their posts faced far harsher punishment from unforgiving commanders.

Casualties

People die in war, and a lot of people—servicemen and civilians—died during World War II. Bombs probably took the most lives, but bullets, illness, accidents, weather extremes, starvation, incarceration in prison and concentration camps, and other factors also took a huge toll.

The exact number of people killed or seriously injured over the course of the war will never be known. Relatively good records were kept for Allied and Axis servicemen, but civilian deaths and injuries were so widespread and so frequently unreported that they were nearly impossible to tabulate with any accuracy. Tens of thousands of people in all theaters remain missing and unaccounted for to this day.

Figure 13-1 Two Coast Guardsmen pay silent homage to the memory of a fellow Coast Guardsman who lost his life in action in the Ryukyu Islands.

Photo courtesy of the National Archives (26-G-4739)

According to a report compiled by several neutral international relief agencies and released in 1946 by the Vatican, military and civilian casualties in World War II are estimated at 22,060,000 dead and 34,400,000 wounded. However, exact numbers were difficult to determine because of inadequate information and differences among nations in the ways the dead and wounded were tabulated.

FACT

The Sullivan family of Waterloo, Iowa, lost five members in one tragic event, the sinking of the USS *Juneau*. On November 1942, the ship was hit by three torpedoes off Guadalcanal and sank in less than a minute. After that, close relatives were no longer allowed to serve on the same ship.

Many casualty figures remain in conflict. For example, the U.S. Strategic Bombing Survey reported in December 1945 that Allied bombs had killed approximately 500,000 German civilians. However, a German report the following year put the figure at more than 4 million. The issue is made more difficult still by the fact that the Soviet Union refused to release information regarding prisoners of war and other wartime captives.

The U.S. military kept comprehensive casualty records throughout the war and reported a total of 294,597 battle-related deaths from December 7, 1941, to December 31, 1946. (In 1946, U.S. military officials officially declared dead all servicemen previously counted as missing in action in World War II.) In addition, there were 113,842 nonbattle-related deaths, and a total of 670,846 who suffered nonmortal wounds.

Allied military casualties were:

- **British Commonwealth** (including the United Kingdom, Australia, New Zealand, Canada, India, and South Africa): 544,596
- **USSR:** 7,500,000
- **France:** 210,671
- **China:** 2,200,000 (These are deaths after 1937 and do not include losses from earlier Japanese aggression.)

Germany lost an estimated 3,250,000 soldiers, sailors, and aviators over the course of the war; Italy lost 300,000, and Japan lost more than 1,506,000 from 1937 to 1945.

Suffer the Children

Few populations suffered more during World War II than the children of the many war-torn nations. Tens of millions of children were displaced over the course of the war, and millions died from enemy attacks, incarceration, disease, starvation, accidents, and exposure.

When war with Germany appeared imminent, Great Britain started a massive effort to evacuate children from potential target areas such as London to rural areas, the United States, or Commonwealth nations such as Australia, New Zealand, Canada, and South Africa. The move no doubt saved thousands of young lives, though a great many British children still perished in German bomb attacks and many more were orphaned.

Figure 13-2
Children of an
eastern suburb of
London wait out-
side the wreckage
of what was their
home.

*Photo courtesy
of the National
Archives
(306-NT-3163V)*

German children were well fed and cared for during the early months of the war, but the situation changed dramatically once the Allies began extensive bombing of Germany. There were a few brief evacuation efforts to remove children from target areas, but because Hitler felt the idea of fleeing civilians reflected poorly on the Third Reich, mass evacuations were never ordered. As a result, thousands of innocent German children were killed during Allied bombing raids and the devastation that followed.

Children in Japan suffered similarly as a result of the bombing of the Japanese mainland late in the war. Evacuation efforts started in 1944, but many children were still harmed. In one extensive U.S. raid on Tokyo, more than 30,000 children are known to have been killed.

The Holocaust also took a tremendous toll on the youth of Europe. Children of Jewish descent were routinely rounded up and sent to concentration camps or labor camps, where they died by the thousands. According to a 1947 report by the Child Study Association of America, only 10 percent of the Jews who survived the Holocaust were children. By 1946, the study added, "there were practically no children between the ages of six and twelve years among the displaced Jews of Germany."

Children in the United States, while spared the horrors of combat in their own backyard, still suffered as a result of the war. Many, known as "door-key children," were forced to raise themselves because both parents were involved in the war effort. (Typically, Dad was fighting overseas while Mom worked in war production.) The lack of parental supervision also resulted in a dramatic increase in juvenile delinquency.

Prisoners of War

Hundreds of thousands of male and female military personnel on both sides were captured as prisoners of war during World War II. Despite the 1929 Geneva Convention agreement, which provided for humane treatment of prisoners of war, atrocities still occurred. Mistreatment by German and Japanese captors is well documented, but Allied troops also committed acts of brutality against captured enemy soldiers.

Prisoners captured in World War II were the first to be detained under the Geneva Convention. The agreement, signed and ratified by forty-eight governments (Japan signed, but its government did not ratify the agreement), noted among other things that food served to prisoners should be equal in quality to that served to the detaining troops, that prisoners should not be placed in solitary confinement, and that officers should be paid the same amount as comparable officers in the detaining country. The agreement also noted that prisoners could be put to work but that the work must not be a form of brutality, nor could it be connected with the war effort. Despite the Geneva Convention agreement, Germany used a great many prisoners of war, as well as residents of occupied countries, as forced laborers in war production facilities.

Prisoners were instructed to give captors only their name, rank, and military serial number. According to the Geneva Convention agreement, captors were allowed to question prisoners but were not allowed to use force or brutality to extract military information. Of course, that didn't prevent both sides from applying pressure on POWs, including torture, when they felt it necessary.

POW Mistreatment by Japan

Indeed, mistreatment of POWs was common, particularly among the Japanese, who viewed surrender as a punishable dishonor. The Bataan Death March is a particularly glaring example of Japanese brutality against

Allied POWs. During that forced march, American and Philippine prisoners were routinely abused, beaten, starved, and executed without reason. At its end, more than 5,000 soldiers had died.

The forced construction of a military railway along the River Kwae Noi between Burma and Thailand was another example of Japanese mistreatment of prisoners of war and residents of occupied nations. In this case, more than 250,000 Asians and an estimated 61,000 Allied POWs, most of them British and Australian, were forced to build the 265-mile railway by hand, often using primitive tools and under brutal conditions. Tens of thousands died from mistreatment, malnutrition, and disease. The event was dramatized in Pierre Boulle's compelling novel *The Bridge on the River Kwai*.

FACT

At the end of the war, Germany held nearly 95,000 U.S. military personnel and about 200,000 British. Japan held almost 15,000 Americans and approximately 100,000 British. An estimated 2 million German prisoners were held by American forces at the end of the war and were turned over to the British and French as postwar laborers. An additional 2 million German POWs were also believed to have been held by the Soviets, who refused to release detailed records of prisoners of war.

The Japanese also routinely transferred prisoners of war without international supervision, as dictated by the Geneva Convention (which the Japanese government said in January 1942 that it would follow). As a result, thousands of Allied POWs were accidentally killed when unknowing Allied submarines sank the Japanese ships on which they were being carried.

German POW Camps

Germany usually complied with the Geneva Convention at its POW camps, but Allied servicemen still faced peril, and there were numerous reports of German atrocities against Allied soldiers who surrendered. In an event that came to be known as the Malmédy massacre, approximately

100 American prisoners were gunned down with machine gun fire by German SS troops near the Belgian town of Malmédy during the Battle of the Bulge. Those not instantly killed by machine gun were then shot in the head. Miraculously, a handful of soldiers escaped the massacre and were able to report it.

Many Axis POWs were held in Great Britain and elsewhere in Europe, but a large percentage—some 400,000—were brought over for incarceration in the United States. The German, Japanese, and Italian prisoners were gawked at by the locals and often forced to perform farm and ranch work but were generally well treated.

In another documented atrocity, nearly fifty British airmen were executed in 1944 after escaping from a German POW camp. And at the German concentration camp in Mauthausen, Austria, approximately fifty Allied officers of various nationalities were beaten and kicked to death by guards. Similar massacres are known to have involved Soviet POWs.

Late in the war, Hitler declared that Allied airmen were "terror fliers" and approved the execution of any Allied airman found on the ground. An unknown number of Allied fliers were killed as a result of the decree, many of them hanged by Nazi sympathizers. Hitler also approved the execution of any Allied prisoner caught trying to escape.

Allied Prisoners

The Allies also had the blood of enemy POWs on their hands. In one well-known incident, thirty-six Italian soldiers surrendered to Allied forces in Sicily on July 14, 1943. On orders from the American company commander, John Compton, the Italian prisoners were lined up along a ravine and shot, presumably in retaliation for the wounding of twelve American infantrymen by sniper fire.

Figure 13-3 German prisoners captured after the fall of Aachen.

Photo courtesy of the National Archives (260-MGG1061-1)

That same day, another American infantry company ordered forty-five Italian and three German POWs to be sent to the rear for interrogation. After the group had walked about a mile, the sergeant of the escort, Horace West, ordered them to halt, then mowed down the POWs with a submachine gun. On orders from General Omar Bradley, Compton and West were court-martialed. West was sentenced to life in prison, but Compton was found not guilty. An outcry regarding unfair discrimination between officers and enlisted men led to West's being released after a year and returned to active service. Compton died in action.

QUESTION?

Did any German POWs escape while in the United States?
According to FBI reports, 1,607 Axis prisoners escaped from POW camps in the United States. Most were quickly recaptured, but the number of those who escaped permanently remains unknown.

Battlefield Injuries and Medicine

Battlefield medicine evolved considerably between World War I and World War II. In the former, approximately 4 out of every 100 wounded men could expect to survive; in the latter, the rate improved to 50 out of 100.

Survival depended on a variety of factors: the type, severity, and location of the wound; the proximity of medical care (soldiers in the jungles of the Pacific typically fared worse than those in metropolitan Europe); and the availability of new "miracle drugs" such as penicillin. In general, however, a soldier who received treatment within an hour of being seriously wounded had a 90 percent chance of recovery. After eight hours, his chances slipped to 25 percent. Those most at risk were forces involved in amphibious landings, which were particularly hazardous. The beachhead casualty rate was often as high as 25 percent, and the rapid evacuation of men wounded during a beach landing was usually made doubly difficult by enemy fire and successive waves of incoming forces.

Figure 13-4
A medic treats a wounded American soldier in France, 1944.

Photo courtesy of the National Archives (208-YE-22)

During World War I, most soldiers were wounded by enemy bullets and chemical agents such as mustard gas. During World War II, artillery and bombs inflicted the most injuries—and the most severe. Head wounds and traumatic amputations were common, and medics strove to get the wounded into surgery within six hours, when the survival rate was highest (in the European theater, nearly 21 out of 100 who were wounded received treatment during this golden period).

The practice of triage increased the survival rate by sorting the wounded according to degree of injury, with the most severely wounded receiving treatment first. Men who were mortally wounded and likely to die were given drugs to ease their pain and were attended to only after those more likely to survive were seen.

A number of new drugs and medical techniques developed in the years between the world wars dramatically improved the survival rate among the sick and injured. For example, combat medics (and even men in the field) carried packets of sulfanilamide and sulfathiazole to coat wounds as a first line of defense against infection. Antibiotics such as streptomycin and penicillin also helped save the lives of countless soldiers.

Combat wasn't the only thing to fell soldiers during World War II; environment-related illnesses were also a common hazard. In the Pacific, for example, mosquito-borne malaria was a serious threat. To reduce the chances of infection, areas surrounding permanent bases were treated with insecticides such as DDT, and servicemen were routinely dosed with a quinine substitute known as atabrine. (Quinine itself was in short supply because many tropical countries that produced the raw materials for its manufacture had fallen to the Japanese.)

American servicemen were also inoculated for a wide variety of diseases before being shipped overseas. The most common vaccinations were for smallpox, typhoid, and tetanus, though soldiers assigned to tropical or extremely rural areas were also vaccinated for cholera, typhus, yellow fever, and, in some cases, bubonic plague.

Lastly, American military personnel also received numerous lectures—and viewed several graphic documentaries—about the risks of contracting a venereal disease such as gonorrhea or syphilis. "Fraternization" was strongly discouraged, but a great many men still became infected. Treatment usually consisted of a regimen of strong antibiotics.

Chapter 14

The Axis Giants Fall

Both the German and Japanese forces fell in 1945. During the January 1943 Casablanca Conference, attended by President Roosevelt and Winston Churchill, it was decided that the only acceptable end to the war would be unconditional surrender. This resolve was reinforced many times in the waning years of the war.

Germany Surrenders

The Allied victory over Germany—celebrated on V-E Day, or Victory in Europe Day, on May 8, 1945—was hard won, with political complications arising in the weeks and months leading up to Germany's unconditional surrender.

The beginning of the end for Germany came on many fronts, though it could be argued that it started with the fall of Benito Mussolini in July 1943 and Italy's surrender and withdrawal from the war in the following months. At first, Hitler showed little concern over the developments in Italy, believing that everything could be fixed by pouring more troops into the country and treating it like another occupied nation. He had little reason to feel otherwise, since this plan had worked so well in the past. However, the fall of Italy was the first in a long line of dominoes that would ultimately cost Germany the war.

FACT

No one in the German High Command dared suggest to Hitler that the end was near. In his madness, Hitler remained convinced that the Third Reich would still triumph.

Another domino was the successful invasion of Normandy, which planted Allied troops in occupied Europe and gave them the foothold they would need to push German forces all the way back to Berlin. By the time the primary Allied leaders—Roosevelt, Churchill, and Stalin—met at the Yalta Conference in February 1945, the writing was on the wall. A lot remained to be done, but Germany was doomed. The Allies knew it, and the German High Command knew it, too.

A New German Leader

In April 1945, several important events came together to ensure the defeat of Germany. The first was the linkup of U.S. and Soviet troops at Torgau on the Elbe in the very center of Germany. The second was the surrender of German forces in occupied Italy. The third, and most important, was the suicide of Adolf Hitler on April 30. With a single bullet, Nazi Germany had lost its guiding light.

With Hitler's death, Karl Dönitz became president of Germany and commander in chief of its armed forces. Hitler had instructed Dönitz to continue the war, but for all intents and purposes, it was already lost. Two months earlier, Heinrich Himmler had initiated talks with Count Folke Bernadotte, representing the Red Cross, on the release of some Scandinavian prisoners being held in concentration camps. These discussions quickly turned to the issue of Germany's surrender.

Himmler wasn't the first German official to send out feelers regarding an end to the war. Also in February, Karl Wolfe, the German military governor of Italy, contacted associates of Allen Dulles, the representative in Sweden of the U.S. Office of Strategic Services, to discuss the surrender of German troops in northern Italy. Wolfe and Dulles met face-to-face the following March, when Dulles stated emphatically that unconditional surrender was the only term the Allies would accept. Wolfe reluctantly agreed, and secret plans were set in motion to work out the details. On April 29, the day before Hitler killed himself, the German Southwest Command surrendered all forces in Italy to a combination of American, British, and Soviet officers.

Next to lay down arms was the German state of Lower Saxony, which on May 4 surrendered to British field marshal Bernard Montgomery, acting on behalf of Dwight Eisenhower, supreme commander of the Allied Expeditionary Force. The surrender agreement included German infantry and naval forces in Denmark, the Netherlands, and northwest Germany.

Germany Seeks Terms for Surrender

Dönitz knew the end was at hand. On May 6, he instructed Alfred Jodl, chief of the operations staff in the High Command of the Armed Forces, to negotiate an armistice with Eisenhower's Supreme Headquarters Allied Expeditionary Force (SHAEF). Dönitz hoped to work out a separate peace with Eisenhower without having to also surrender to the Red Army, which Dönitz rightly feared was preparing to enact a horrible vengeance against Germany. However, Eisenhower would have none of it and refused everything except an unconditional surrender that met all the Allied requirements set forth earlier.

Dönitz had to agree. On May 7, around 2:40 A.M., Jodl and two other German officers met with Lieutenant General Walter Bedell Smith, SHAEF chief of staff, and other military representatives from the United States, Great Britain, France, and the Soviet Union in the SHAEF war room in the Professional and Technical School at Reims in northeastern France. The Germans and the Allies—with the exception of the Soviet Union—signed a surrender document; Eisenhower was not present because he refused to meet with German military officials until they had formally surrendered.

That document was not the formal surrender agreement, however. The official document, supervised by Roosevelt, Churchill, and Stalin, had been under revision since July 1944. Prepared by the European Advisory Commission (EAC), it was to spell out all the details of an unconditional surrender and offer possible solutions to the inevitable economic and political problems that were sure to follow.

FACT

The surrender didn't officially take effect until 11:01 P.M. on May 8. The extension was given to allow as many German troops as possible to surrender to American forces rather than to the Red Army, which was out to exact revenge. Soviet officials demanded that a second ceremonial signing take place on May 9 because the Soviet observer at the first signing was too low in rank to sign on behalf of the nation.

Unfortunately, political difficulties prevented the Allies from presenting the EAC document at that time. France had not been included in the creation of the 1944 draft, and the word *dismemberment*, which had been added at the Yalta Conference to underscore the division of Germany, was not included. A revised draft was quickly written, but Eisenhower decided that the military surrender document, which officially ended hostilities, was sufficient for the moment and that all other problems could be worked out later.

The Axis Lays Down Its Arms

The first order of business was the question of how the Germans were to surrender. A second document addressed this issue with specific instructions on how, where, and when German forces were to lay down their arms. The document also stipulated that Germany was to immediately surrender all naval forces and provide maps of all minefields in European waters.

The Dönitz government remained in power for just over two more weeks. Dönitz, Jodl, and many other German officials were then taken into custody to be tried for war crimes at Nuremberg. Dönitz received a ten-year prison sentence for his role in the war. Jodl, who remained faithful to Hitler even during his trial, was hanged. However, a West German de-Nazification court concluded in 1953 that as a soldier, Jodl had not broken any international laws and posthumously cleared him of earlier charges.

Japan Surrenders

By mid-1944, the Japanese war machine was crumbling at a frightening rate, and a growing number of Japanese officials were in favor of ending hostilities. However, it would ultimately take the devastation of two atomic bombs to force Japan to capitulate.

Figure 14-1
A Navy chaplain holds Mass for marines in Saipan, June 1944.

Photo courtesy of the National Archives (127-N-82262)

Japan, which had enjoyed a number of impressive military victories early in the war, was a dying giant by 1944. Its navy devastated by Allied forces and its exhausted army growing weaker by the day, Japan stood by in relative helplessness as American forces took Saipan in June 1944 and escalated the firebombing of the Japanese mainland using B-29 Superfortresses. Unable to defend against this brutal onslaught, many more Japanese officials began to seriously consider the need to bring the war to a close.

In the spring of 1945, Japanese government officials began a covert effort to initiate peace talks by contacting Sweden, the Soviet Union, and associates of Allen Dulles at the Office of Strategic Services in Sweden. U.S. intelligence, having broken the Japanese codes, knew all of this and fed the news to Washington.

The small but growing peace bloc within the Japanese government then turned to the Potsdam Declaration, which it felt offered some insight into the issue of Japanese surrender. According to these officials' interpretation of the document, the unconditional surrender decree applied only to the military—not to the nation itself. This was good news.

Every member of the Japanese cabinet except for two hard-line generals favored a quick surrender, primarily to save their nation from U.S. bombers, which were slowly destroying Japan. While trying to persuade the dissenting generals that surrender was Japan's only option, and to prepare the nation for the news, the government issued a statement saying that an offer of peace had been made but that the cabinet had decided to withhold comment. When the radio announcement was received by U.S. intelligence officials, they interpreted it to mean that the Japanese cabinet was ignoring a peace offer and intended to go on fighting. In early August, a frustrated Harry Truman authorized the use of the atomic bomb in an effort to force Japan to surrender.

The Atom Bomb

The atomic bomb is the most devastating weapon ever used in warfare. It was used twice against Japan near the end of World War II, but the threat of further use drove the Cold War and continues to threaten peace in the world today.

The bomb was the product of an American group of scientists under the jurisdiction of the U.S. Army Corps of Engineers, who worked on a top-secret mission known as the Manhattan Project. Working in the isolation of the American Southwest, the scientists, lead by J. Robert Oppenheimer, built on the knowledge of and suggestions by famed physicist Albert Einstein and succeeded in splitting the atom.

Previous to the start of the Manhattan Project, a group of American scientists gathered at two historic conferences, one in Chicago and one in Berkeley, California. The top practical and theoretical physics minds in the land were at these conferences, and their discussions focused almost entirely on creating a superweapon. Among those speaking at the Berkeley conference was Hungarian physicist Edward Teller, who would play a major role in the discoveries that begat the bomb.

During 1942, when Japanese occupations were at their highest, the Manhattan Project achieved the first self-sustaining nuclear chain reaction. Subsequent developments built on that success, and by 1944, the atom-splitting operations were in full force. The first nuclear explosion took place on July 16, 1945, in the famed "Trinity" test near Alamogordo, New Mexico. That success led to the two bombs that devastated Hiroshima and Nagasaki.

At 2:45 A.M. on the morning of August 6, 1945, Colonel Paul Tibbets, commanding officer of the 509th Composite Group, and his crew took off from Tinian Island in a B-29 Superfortress called the *Enola Gay*. In the plane's belly rested the most destructive weapon created up to that time, a 9,000-pound atomic bomb nicknamed Little Boy.

Earlier that night, the residents of the Japanese port city of Hiroshima had gone through an air raid drill—something they had been notified of several days earlier. The first alarm went off shortly after midnight, and the all-clear sounded at 2:10 A.M. A yellow warning was sounded at 7:09 A.M., and the all-clear at 7:31 A.M. Approximately forty-five minutes later, the *Enola Gay* flew over the city. Most people thought the plane was part of the air raid drill—until a blast as bright as the sun incinerated the metropolis in the space of a heartbeat.

Unthinkable Destruction

The devastation wreaked by the atomic bomb dropped on Hiroshima was unequaled in its time. Never before in human history had a weapon of such destructive force been unleashed on a population. The bomb was dropped from a height of 31,600 feet and exploded at about 1,900 feet—directly above Shima Hospital, near the heart of the city. Almost everything within a one-mile radius of the explosion's center spontaneously combusted. Buildings disintegrated. The surface of granite stones melted under the intense heat. People vaporized, often leaving ghostly images imprinted on stone walls and sidewalks.

Figure 14-2
Colonel Paul Tibbets in the *Enola Gay.*

Photo courtesy of the National Archives (208-LU-13H-5)

Those just outside the center of the blast also experienced atomic hell. Many people had their clothes blasted from their bodies. Hair was singed off, limbs ripped and seared, eyeballs melted. Those who survived the initial blast suffered a slow death from radiation poisoning.

The exact number of people killed in the Hiroshima blast remains unknown. The official Japanese estimate is 71,379 killed in the initial explosion and another 70,000 dead from radiation poisoning. A total of 70,000 buildings were destroyed or heavily damaged. Medical help was slow to reach those who so desperately needed it because more than 90 percent of Hiroshima's doctors, nurses, and other medical personnel had been killed. Survivors overwhelmed hospitals in nearby cities.

News of the Hiroshima blast stunned the world—none more so than the Japanese, many of whom were joyously looking forward to a permanent peace. As the nation and its government reeled from what had occurred, the United States, fearing that Japan was still considering the continuation of hostilities, dropped a second atomic bomb on Nagasaki three days later.

The Second A-Bomb

The second bomb, nicknamed Fat Man, was different from the bomb dropped on Hiroshima in that it used plutonium instead of uranium as its fissionable material. The bomb's incredibly complex design had been tested in an explosion near Alamogordo, New Mexico, on July 16, 1945.

The many components of Fat Man were flown from the atomic laboratory in Los Alamos, New Mexico, to Tinian, where it was assembled and loaded on a B-29 nicknamed *Bockscar*, after its commander, Frederick Bock. On that particular mission, however, the plane was piloted by Major Charles Sweeney.

The second atomic bomb mission was extremely hazardous for the flight crew. Fat Man had to be assembled before being placed in the plane and was fully armed when the crew took off. Should the plane crash, a conventional explosion would disperse radioactive material over a frighteningly large area or, in the worst case, there would be a full nuclear explosion.

The *Bockscar's* primary target was Kokura, the site of a major Japanese munitions dump. However, cloud cover blocked visibility, and after three passes the plane flew on to its secondary target, the port city of Nagasaki, a large shipbuilding center that also manufactured naval ordnance. It was a risky target because the *Bockscar* had only enough fuel for one pass, then a hasty return to Okinawa. Should the plane have to make more than one pass, the crew would have to ditch in the Pacific and hope to be rescued.

Nagasaki, like Kokura, was covered with clouds when the plane approached, forcing bombardier F. L. Ashworth to approve a radar run rather than visual bombing, as originally ordered. However, the clouds broke just as the plane reached the heart of the city, and Ashworth was able to see his target. The bomb was released and exploded at 1,650 feet with a force equivalent to 22,000 tons of dynamite.

As with Hiroshima, the resulting devastation was tremendous. Nearly 44 percent of the city was instantly annihilated in the blast, and more than 25,600 people were killed, with another 45,000 dead from radiation poisoning by the end of the year.

Japan Falls

Japan was finished. Emperor Hirohito, fearing a coup by stalwart militarists, immediately ordered that an official answer be sent accepting surrender. On August 10, Japan notified the United States through diplomatic channels in Switzerland that it accepted an unconditional surrender, asking only that the emperor be retained as sovereign ruler. U.S. officials responded that the rule of the emperor and the Japanese government were subject to the supreme commander of the Allied powers.

As the Japanese cabinet furiously debated the situation, the military struggled to keep the war going. To prevent such a move, Emperor Hirohito secretly recorded an announcement of surrender, which was broadcast over Radio Tokyo on the morning of August 15. In the address, the emperor said: "We have ordered our government to communicate to the governments of the United States, Great Britain, China, and the Soviet Union that our empire accepts the provisions of their Joint Declaration."

President Truman announced Japan's official surrender at 7:00 P.M. on August 14, U.S. time. Allied occupation forces began landing on Japan's shores just two weeks later, led by General Douglas MacArthur.

On September 2, 1945, Allied representatives including MacArthur, as supreme commander of the Allied powers, and Lieutenant General Jonathan Wainright, who had been a POW since the fall of Bataan, met with representatives of the Japanese government aboard the battleship *Missouri* in Tokyo Bay to sign the official surrender document. Over the following weeks, entrenched Japanese forces surrendered on a number of fronts, including the Philippines, China, and Korea.

World War II was over. All that remained was to put the world back together.

Chapter 15

German Anti-Semitism

Adolf Hitler rose to power during one of the most difficult periods in German history. The nation had been beaten at war and subsequently defiled and humiliated. Its economy was in shambles, the national currency virtually worthless. Once one of the proudest and most formidable nations in the world, Germany was transformed into a beaten dog. Who was responsible? According to Hitler, it was the Jews. The German people weren't to blame, Hitler told them; it was the Jews and other impure elements who were the problem. Eliminate them, Hitler raged, and Germany would rise once again to take its place among the world leaders.

The Need for a Scapegoat

Anti-Semitism had been a cornerstone of the Nazi Party since it was founded under the name of the German Workers' Party in 1919. At that time, it had fewer than twenty-five members, only six of whom were active in promoting its ideals via lectures and discussions. Hitler joined the party shortly after its inception and quickly took control. He modified its name to the National Socialist German Workers' Party and began refining its radical rhetoric for a broader audience.

Hatred and fear-mongering were strong components from the outset. At the first mass meeting of the German Workers' Party in February 1920, Hitler read the party program, which he had helped write. The program consisted of twenty-five points emphasizing the importance and strength of nationalism, condemning Communism, and promoting racism and anti-Semitism. A strong centralized government and total control of the individual were essential if the party's doctrines were to work.

FACT

During that first mass meeting, Hitler, speaking on behalf of the party, stated: "For modern society, a colossus with feet of clay, we shall create an unprecedented centralization which will unite all powers in the hands of the government. We shall create a hierarchical constitution, which will mechanically govern all movements of individuals."

As foreign as these concepts may sound to those who have grown up in a democracy like the United States, they were music to the ears of millions of Germans who were looking for someone to guide them out of their nation's stagnation. They also liked the fact that the Nazis offered them a villain in the Jewish people, thus removing the blame for Germany's burdens from their own shoulders.

Hitler and the Nazis promoted anti-Semitism at every opportunity, and the concept became a key component of their rapid rise to power. From 1929 to 1932, Germany's economic depression grew increasingly worse, and the Nazis used this to the fullest advantage by almost always blaming the growing problems on Jews and others. By beating the drum of nationalism during these increasingly dark hours, the party's ranks filled by the tens of thousands.

The popularity of the Nazi Party and its extreme ideals reached its first important plateau in July 1932 when the party received 13.7 million votes in the national elections and won 230 of the 670 seats in the German parliament. Hitler lost the presidency to Paul von Hindenburg, but that was only a minor setback. After months of political wrangling, including the dissolution of the German parliament twice, Hitler was finally appointed chancellor on January 30, 1933.

Legislated Genocide

Hitler and his followers immediately enacted legislation making the Nazi doctrines of racism and anti-Semitism the law of the land. The program was instituted in four phases: (1) the economic persecution of German Jews, (2) the passage and enforcement of legislation to remove Jews from the German public and social life, (3) the forced removal of Jews from their homes in Germany and conquered lands, and (4) the eradication of all Jews through systematic mass murder.

Economic Persecution

Hitler began the economic persecution of the Jewish people on April 1, 1933, by ordering a boycott of all Jewish businesses. Falling back on the Nazi trick of claiming to do God's work, Hitler stated: "I believe that I act today in unison with the Almighty Creator's intentions: By fighting the Jews, I do battle for the Lord."

Just in case the German people weren't up for a boycott, the edict was enforced by SA goons who stood in front of Jewish-owned stores and verbally and physically intimidated all who might try to do business with them. Almost immediately, Jewish businesses saw a devastating drop in trade, and many were financially ruined within weeks.

This was just the first step. A week after instigating the economic boycott, Hitler removed Jews from the civil service. Then, over the course of the following year, he systematically ordered all non-Aryans (meaning Jews and those who had at least one Jewish parent or grandparent) removed from positions in banks, the stock market, the law, medicine, and journalism. The result was a national "brain drain" as thousands of prominent Jews in science and academia fled the country before it was too late. Among them were Albert Einstein and Sigmund Freud.

QUESTION?

What was the Gestapo?

The Gestapo, an acronym for *Geheime Staatspolizei* (secret state police), was formed in 1933 as a replacement for the Prussian secret police. It operated throughout Germany and all occupied lands, ruthlessly eradicating all political opposition by whatever means necessary. Individuals viewed as dangerous or subversive by Gestapo officials faced a number of fates, including incarceration, torture, and assassination.

From 1933 to 1937, an estimated 130,000 Jews fled Nazi Germany and Austria. However, the world didn't exactly put out a welcome mat for them. In one of the most notorious incidents of international anti-Semitism, 937 Jews sailed from Germany for Havana, Cuba, aboard the liner *St. Louis* on May 13, 1939. When the ship reached its destination, however, all but 22 of the passengers were denied entry. The United States also refused entry to the ship. Having nowhere else to go, it returned to Europe, where the passengers got off and scattered for whatever safe haven they could find. Many were not able to find it, however—an estimated 600 of them died in concentration camps over the course of the war.

In late 1935, two years after his rise to power, Hitler successfully coaxed the Reichstag into passing what became known as the Nuremberg Laws, after the Bavarian Nazi stronghold. These laws essentially stripped Jews of all rights within Germany. Blood laws, for example, stated that only persons of "German or related blood" could be citizens. Other laws made Jews the property of the state, prohibited marriage or sexual relations between Jews and non-Jews, and prevented Jews from hiring female servants under the age of forty-five.

With the Jewish people's legal protection removed by the state, persecution increased. The Nazis seized numerous Jewish businesses and canceled legally binding business contracts simply by claiming that the owners had violated one of the many Nuremberg Laws. Jewish employees of businesses owned by non-Jews were let go en masse. Anti-Semitism became compulsory in German schools with the teaching of so-called racial science and mandatory membership in Hitler Youth for all children except those of Jewish descent. Before too long, Jewish children were barred from attending public schools.

The Night of Broken Glass

The Nazi campaign against the Jews reached a murderous plateau on November 9, 1938, with *Kristallnacht*, the Night of Broken Glass. Using the assassination of a German diplomat in Paris as an excuse, Nazi officials secretly orchestrated a one-night campaign of vicious retribution against German Jews that resulted in more than 200 synagogues being burned to the ground, 7,500 Jewish businesses destroyed, and more than 800 Jews killed or severely injured.

Kristallnacht laid the groundwork for the roundup and elimination of Jews. With that single act, they ceased to be seen as human beings in the eyes of many Germans and were relegated to the status of vermin in need of eradication.

In the terror that followed, more than 20,000 Jews were arrested and 10,000 were sent to the concentration camp at Buchenwald. From that night on, no German Jew was safe from state-sanctioned attack.

Jews in German-Occupied Lands

After methodically removing the majority of Jews from Germany, the Nazis turned their attention to the Jewish populations of the countries that came under German control during the early months of World War II.

The first was Poland, which fell to the German blitzkrieg in early September 1939. On September 21, Reinhard Heydrich, chief of the Reich

Central Security Office, chaired a meeting in Berlin to address the question of what he called "the Jewish problem in the occupied zone." While hinting of a far more sinister future plan for the Jews, Heydrich emphasized the need to eliminate all Jews from western Poland and concentrate those who lived in large cities into small, self-contained areas, or ghettos.

The largest ghettos were in Warsaw and Lodz, though ghettos were established in other Polish cities as well. They were small and tightly packed, yet the Nazis insisted on adding still more people from surrounding areas until living conditions became unbearable. (Many Jews not herded into ghettos were sent to labor camps, where they were forced to work under inhuman conditions.) Entire families were forced to live in a single, cramped room. Jews received half the food rations of non-Jewish Poles, a caloric restriction so severe that starvation was inevitable. Forced to wear a Star of David on their arm for easy identification, they were taunted, tortured, and routinely killed by Nazi occupation forces for no reason other than their heritage. German soldiers delighted in such barbaric practices as forcing Polish Jews to collect and burn religious scrolls while dancing around the flames singing, "We rejoice that this shit is burning." Many Jews refused to participate and were shot for their insolence.

What's most astonishing, with the hindsight of history, is that the German people let all of this happen. Not everyone was as vehemently anti-Semitic as Hitler and his core group of supporters. While the average German man or woman may have privately echoed certain anti-Semitic sentiments with friends and family, most worked with and/or socialized with Jews. They had friends and neighbors who were Jewish and patronized stores and businesses owned by Jews. And yet, very few people stood up and publicly declared that what the Nazis were doing was morally wrong. (Most of those who did were religious leaders, not average citizens.) A mass public dissent might have halted the Nazi campaign against the Jews before it turned into a holocaust, but such a public outcry never occurred, either because the people didn't care or because they were too scared and intimidated by the military to risk their own lives for the sake of others. The power and scope of the German government's military and spy networks during this period in history are breathtaking. Neighbors were led to suspect neighbors, (a practice that kept right on going in East Germany after the war ended). Although many Germans risked their lives to aid Jewish friends and associates, the overwhelming majority simply turned their backs as their Jewish neighbors were led away to an almost certain death. Even though instances of violence against Jews were well known, the existence of death camps was not common knowledge. Had more people known about the "Final Solution," a public outcry might have been forthcoming.

Between the invasion of Poland and the invasion of the Soviet Union in June 1941, an estimated 30,000 Jews were shot dead by German forces or killed by the starvation and disease that was rampant within the many ghettos and forced labor camps. But the worst was yet to come.

The Final Solution

Hitler's ultimate aim, in its simplest context, was the complete eradication of all Jews from Germany and occupied lands. This process was code-named *Die Endlösung* (the Final Solution).

The phrase was first used by Hermann Goering on July 31, 1941, shortly after the invasion of the Soviet Union. Goering instructed Reinhard Heydrich to create a plan "showing the measures for organization and action necessary to carrying out the final solution of the Jewish question" in German-occupied Europe. Heydrich later added other groups to the extermination order, including Gypsies.

Figure 15-1 A starving inmate of Camp Gusen, Austria, May 1945.

Photo courtesy of the National Archives (111-SC-264918)

In January 1942, Heydrich and his aide, Adolf Eichmann, chaired the Wannsee Conference, where one of the primary topics of discussion was "the final solution of the European Jewish question." Also in attendance were representatives from the Occupied Eastern Territories, the ministries of Justice and the Interior and the Foreign Office, and various Nazi organizations.

FACT

In a horrifying example of raw Nazi barbarism, several German officials discussed the idea of eliminating 30,000 Gypsies by taking them by boat into the Mediterranean Sea and then bombing the boats. However, the idea was later abandoned.

The conference was held at the Reich Central Security Office in Wannsee, a suburb of Berlin. Eichmann acted as secretary, taking detailed notes of the strategies under discussion. At issue was how to deal with an estimated 11 million Jews in Germany and the occupied territories. According to Eichmann's notes, Heydrich outlined a plan in which Jews capable of working would be sent in large labor gangs from other parts of Europe to conquered territory in the East. The survivors of the slave labor program represented "the strongest resistance" and were to be eliminated. It's important to note that the word *killed* does not appear in Eichmann's notes. Heydrich spoke in euphemisms, noting that Jews who survived forced labor "represented a natural selection" that must be "treated accordingly." In short, those posing the greatest threat would have to be killed. During his trial in Israel in 1961, Eichmann said that he never saw a written order regarding the mass extermination of Jews. "All I know," he said, "is that Heydrich told me, 'The Führer ordered the physical extermination of the Jews.'"

The so-called Final Solution was carried out in two ways: via action squads that followed German troops into conquered lands with the specific mission of rounding up and executing Jews, and via death camps equipped with gas chambers and other methods of mass slaughter.

Unthinkable Atrocities

According to the Nuremberg International Tribunal on War Crimes, German action squads killed as many as 2 million men, women, and children in

German-occupied territories over the course of the war. Most victims were rounded up, taken to a specific location outside the town or city, lined up in front of a large ditch, and quickly executed by firing squad. The bodies were then buried in mass graves. The murders committed by the action units remained a secret at first because there were usually no witnesses. However, word eventually leaked out of Germany that special death squads were murdering people on a massive scale.

The role of the death camps was to kill as many people as possible as quickly as possible—in other words, efficient genocide. Various methods were used over the course of the war, including firing squads and poisonous gases such as carbon monoxide and Zyklon-B.

Two extermination centers operated in concentration camps—Auschwitz-Birkenau and Lublin-Majdanek—under the auspices of the SS Central Office for Economy and Administration. Five others were in camps established by regional SS or police officials: Belzec, Sobibor, and Treblinka in eastern Poland; Kulmhof in western Poland; and Semlin outside Belgrade in Serbia.

The victims of Germany's killing centers came from all over occupied Europe, though the first groups were deported from Polish ghettos. More than 300,000 were taken from the Warsaw ghetto, most of them women, children, and older men—individuals who could not work and thus could not benefit Germany. However, even those initially retained as laborers and workers were later scheduled for execution.

Death and Dishonor

Perhaps most horrifying is the fact that death did not end the degradation for many people murdered at Nazi extermination camps. Gold fillings were routinely removed with pliers from the mouths of corpses, and very often, skin was stripped from their backs, thighs, and buttocks, cured, and used to make lampshades, purses, and other articles. According to testimony at the Nuremberg war crimes trials, driving gloves made from human leather were particularly coveted among SS officers.

The heaviest deportations of Jews occurred in the summer and fall of 1942. The victims were transported by train and never told of their final destinations. However, news of the death camps eventually reached the ghettos, triggering organized resistance (much more so than in Germany itself). The greatest resistance effort occurred in the Warsaw ghetto, where in April 1943 nearly 65,000 Jews managed to hold off German police for three weeks.

FACT

The possessions of deported Jews did not go to waste. Everything the doomed people owned—from bank accounts to clothing and furniture—was acquired by the state for later distribution. Many Germans whose houses were destroyed by Allied bombing raids refurnished their new homes with furniture confiscated from deported Jews in France, Belgium, and the Netherlands.

Hitler's desire to eliminate the Jews from Germany and all occupied lands created a political and bureaucratic nightmare for German officials. Some German-held countries, such as Vichy France, began deporting Jews even before being ordered to, but others were less cooperative. The Fascist government in Italy refused to deport Jews until the country was occupied by German forces in September 1943. Hungary also held out until Germany invaded in 1944. The government in Romania had no qualms about massacring Jews in occupied regions of the Soviet Union but refused to turn Romanian Jews over to the Germans. And in Denmark, tremendous efforts were made to save Danish Jews by covertly transporting them to neutral Sweden.

Concentration Camps

The concentration camps in which millions of Jews and others were systematically brutalized and killed remain one of the most horrifying images of World War II. When the camps were finally liberated in 1945, battle-hardened American, British, and Soviet troops often broke down in tears at the sight of the emaciated men and women and the conditions they had been forced to live under.

The term *concentration camp* was not new to World War II. It stemmed from internment centers created by the British to house Boer civilians during the Boer War of 1899–1902. German concentration camps were part of a system that also included slave-labor camps, whose prisoners worked at nearby factories, and death camps whose sole purpose was the efficient extermination of "undesirables." The very first concentration camps were called "education centers" or "labor camps" by German propagandists, but their true purpose was the removal of Jews and others (such as Gypsies, the mentally and physically challenged, and so on) from German society.

Medical care at concentration camps was almost nonexistent for prisoners. As a result, countless men and women died from disease and poor nutrition. Women who became pregnant were forced to undergo abortions, though there were occasional exceptions. A special pregnancy unit was established at the Kaufering concentration camp in December 1944, during the waning months of the war. Seven women gave birth there, all of whom—including their babies—survived.

Figure 15-2 Jewish youths liberated from the concentration camp at Buchenwald on their way to Palestine, June 5, 1945.

Photo courtesy of the National Archives (111-SC-207907)

The food given to concentration camp prisoners was usually of poor nutritional quality. Prisoners typically received about 1,800 calories or less per day yet were forced to perform hard labor requiring many times that amount. The result was a slow death by starvation.

The Allied soldiers who finally liberated Germany's concentration camps were appalled by what they saw and outraged that such inhumanity could occur on such a wide scale. When General Dwight Eisenhower visited a work camp at Ohrdruf, near Buchenwald, he found rows of gallows in the cellar and more than 3,000 corpses throughout the camp, many of them bearing fresh head wounds—evidence that camp guards had systematically executed prisoners as Allied forces drew near. Eisenhower became so enraged when those living near the camp claimed to be ignorant of what went on there that he ordered every man, woman, and child from nearby towns marched through the camp at bayonet point. Afterward, he ordered the townspeople to bury the dead.

Secrets and Propaganda

The Nazis worked hard to keep their deadly secret from the world. Concentration camps were often referred to as "re-education camps," and the camp at Theresienstadt in Czechoslovakia was made to look like a model ghetto to impress outside visitors and calm new prisoners, who arrived by the trainload. Established in 1941, Theresienstadt housed a number of prominent Jews, including heroes of World War I, Danish Jews, and others who were actually forced to pay for what was euphemistically called a "transfer of residence." The camp was ostensibly administered by a *Jüdenrat*, or Council of Jews, but, in fact, the Nazis held absolute power and intimidated council members into doing their bidding.

The Nazis forced the prisoners at the Theresienstadt concentration camp to make a ridiculous propaganda film titled *Hitler Presents a Town to the Jews*. However, the prisoners who acted in the film so obviously exaggerated the kindness of the Nazis that the film was never released. As retribution, many of the actors in the film were sent to their deaths at Auschwitz.

The Nazis often used Theresienstadt as a public relations tool, cleaning it up for the benefit of foreign dignitaries. Leaders touted the camp's schools, concerts, and other artistic endeavors, but for the most part it was all a hoax. The people living at Theresienstadt could not leave, and thousands died there. Starting in January 1942, Theresienstadt was a stopover for prisoners being transferred to the death center at Auschwitz. More than 140,000 Jews were sent to Theresienstadt; fewer than 14,000 survived. Of the estimated 15,000 children who passed through its gates, fewer than 100 survived the war.

Concentration camps were guarded by SS members who were part of what became known as Death-Head detachments; members were identified by a special skull-and-crossbones insignia on their coats and caps. The guards were, for the most part, viciously cruel to prisoners, and spontaneous executions, often for something as minor as looking at a guard, were common. To get away with such an atrocity, all a guard had to do was claim that a prisoner had attacked him or was trying to escape. There were occasional acts of kindness among the less brutal among the guards, though these were extremely rare. Guards caught assisting prisoners were harshly punished.

Indeed, prisoners were routinely treated worse than animals. Many were forced to have identification numbers tattooed on their arms, and the standard-issue clothing was a vertically striped uniform with a triangular patch designating the prisoner's category: red insignias for political prisoners, yellow for Jews, pink for homosexuals, black for "work-shy" prisoners, purple for Jehovah's Witnesses, and green for criminals. Some prisoners overlapped in category and wore multiple patches.

Chapter 16

The War Crimes Trials

The Axis lost the war, and the world quickly called for retribution. To that end, international tribunals were convened in Nuremberg, Germany, in Tokyo, and in many other war-ravaged cities to try German and Japanese military officials and Axis sympathizers for the atrocities they had committed against both enemy personnel and innocent civilians—what President Franklin Roosevelt called "acts of savagery."

The Nuremberg Trials

The Nuremberg trials of Nazi leaders were conducted by a tribunal of military representatives from the United States, Great Britain, France, and the Soviet Union. U.S. Supreme Court Justice (and former Attorney General) Robert Jackson was the chief prosecutor, with Army Colonel Telford Taylor acting as chief prosecution counsel. Each of the four participating nations provided two judges, one of whom was an alternate.

The trials officially started on November 20, 1945, just a few months after the end of the war. However, the punishment of war criminals actually started a few weeks earlier—sometimes at the hands of the Allies, sometimes self-inflicted. On October 6, Dr. Leonardo Conti, one of several German doctors who had conducted heinous medical experiments on concentration camp inmates, took his own life in his prison cell in Nuremberg. A short time later, Pierre Laval, the former French foreign minister found guilty of treason by a Paris court, also attempted suicide. He failed, however, and was executed by a firing squad on October 15.

Figure 16-1
German defendant at the Nuremberg war crimes trial.

Photo courtesy of the National Archives (238-NT-592)

On October 20, twenty-four Nazi officials were indicted on four charges: (1) a common plan or conspiracy to seize power and establish a totalitarian regime to prepare and wage a war of aggression; (2) waging a war of aggression; (3) violation of the laws of war; (4) crimes against humanity, persecution, and extermination. Of those charged, twenty-two actually stood trial. Robert Ley, an early Nazi supporter and proponent of the mass extermination of Jews, committed suicide in his cell before the trial started, and Gustav Krupp von Bohlen und Halbach, whose armaments factories used slave labor throughout the war, was judged physically unfit and mentally incompetent to stand trial.

Because no buildings in Berlin were structurally sound enough to act as a courthouse, the principal war crimes trials were moved to Nuremberg, with other trials conducted at the sites of concentration camps. In the days before the Nuremberg trials, national trials were held in various European cities. In Oslo, Norway, for example, Vidkun Quisling, a Norwegian Nazi sympathizer, was found guilty of "criminal collaboration" with Germany and was executed on October 14, 1945.

Nazi Loyalists

Many defendants remained steadfastly loyal to the Nazi cause, and their testimony, often delivered in a frightening, matter-of-fact monotone, suggested a complete lack of remorse for their actions. Consider this excerpt from the affidavit of Rudolf Hoess, commandant of Auschwitz, who was later sentenced to death:

The Camp Commandant at Treblinka . . . used monoxide gas, and I did not think that his methods were very efficient. So when I set up the extermination building at Auschwitz, I used [Zyklon-B], which was a crystallized prussic acid which we dropped into the death chamber from a small opening. It took from three to fifteen minutes to kill people. . . . We knew when the people were dead because their screaming stopped. . . . After the bodies were removed, our special commandos took off the rings and extracted the gold from the teeth of the corpses.

Another improvement we made [was that] at Treblinka, the victims almost always knew that they were to be exterminated, and at Auschwitz, we endeavored to fool the victims into thinking that they were going through a delousing process. Of course, frequently they realized our true intentions, and we sometimes had riots and difficulties due to that fact. . . . We were required to carry out these exterminations in secrecy, but of course the foul and nauseating stench from the continuous burning of bodies permeated the entire area, and all of the people living in the surrounding communities knew that exterminations were going on at Auschwitz.

FACT

To present the history of the Holocaust and to preserve the memory of the millions of Jews, Gypsies, dissidents, and others who died as a result of Nazi persecution, the U.S. Congress authorized in 1980 the construction of the United States Holocaust Memorial Museum in Washington, D.C. Since opening in 1993, it has become one of the most frequently visited museums in the area.

A variety of disturbing evidence was presented during the trials, including a paperweight made from the shrunken head of a concentration camp inmate and a swatch of tattooed skin removed from a prisoner. At Buchenwald, the tribunal was told, particularly nice examples of tattooed skin were given to Ilse Koch, the wife of camp commandant Karl Koch, who had them fashioned into lampshades and other items.

Trial Results

The Nuremberg trial took one year, from October 1945 to October 1946. When the verdict was read on September 30, the court acquitted members of the General Staff and High Command and, as groups, the SA and members of Hitler's cabinet. However, units within the Nazi secret police—the SS, SD, and Gestapo—were declared criminal groups. Following are the verdicts on the twenty-two high-ranking Nazis tried at Nuremberg.

- **Martin Bormann**, aide to Hitler. Found guilty and sentenced to death in absentia. Declared officially dead by a West German court in 1973.
- **Karl Dönitz**, naval officer and Hitler's successor. Found guilty of counts 2 and 3, sentenced to and served ten years in prison.
- **Hans Frank**, governor general of Poland. Found guilty of counts 3 and 4. Hanged.
- **Wilhelm Frick**, Reich minister of the Interior from 1933 to 1943, author of the Nuremberg Laws legalizing persecution of the Jews. Found guilty of counts 2, 3, and 4. Hanged.
- **Hans Fritzche**, deputy minister of propaganda. Acquitted.
- **Walther Funk**, economics minister and Reichsbank president. Conspired with Heinrich Himmler to put money, gold fillings, and other items looted from death camp victims into a false bank account. Found guilty on counts 2, 3, and 4. Sentenced to life in prison, released in 1957.
- **Hermann Goering**, commander of the Luftwaffe. Found guilty on all four counts. Sentenced to death by hanging, committed suicide in his cell just hours before his execution.
- **Rudolf Hess**, deputy führer before he flew on an unauthorized mission to Scotland. Found guilty on counts 1 and 2. Sentenced to life in prison, died in Spandau Prison in 1987.
- **Alfred Jodl**, chief of the operational staff of the High Command of the Armed Forces. Found guilty on all four counts. Hanged.
- **Ernst Kaltenbrunner**, director of the Reich Central Security Office after the assassination of Reinhard Heydrich. Found guilty on counts 3 and 4. Hanged.
- **Wilhelm Keitel**, chief of the High Command of the Armed Forces. Found guilty on all four counts. Hanged.
- **Baron Constantin Freiherr von Neurath**, foreign minister from 1932 to 1938 and Reich protector of Bohemia and Moravia from 1939 to 1943. Found guilty on all four counts. Sentenced to fifteen years in prison; released in 1954.
- **Franz von Papen**, Nazi diplomat and career politician. Acquitted but later found guilty of wartime criminal conduct by a German de-Nazification court.

- **Erich Raeder**, commander in chief of the German navy. Found guilty on counts 1, 2, and 3. Sentenced to life in prison; released in 1955.
- **Joachim von Ribbentrop**, minister of foreign affairs from 1938 to 1945. Found guilty on all four counts. Hanged.
- **Alfred Rosenberg**, minister for the Occupied Eastern Territories. Created the Institute for Scientific and Cultural Research as a cover for the theft of Jewish art collections and libraries. Found guilty on all four counts. Hanged.
- **Fritz Sauckel**, director of slave labor. Found guilty on counts 3 and 4. Hanged.
- **Hjalmar Schacht**, former Reichsbank president and minister of economics. Originally acquitted but later declared a major offender by a de-Nazification court, then exonerated by an appeals court.
- **Baldur von Schirach**, leader of Hitler Youth from 1931 to 1940 and an adoring fan of Hitler. Found guilty on count 4. Sentenced to and served twenty years in prison.
- **Artur Seyss-Inquart**, Nazi chancellor of Austria and administrator of occupied Netherlands. Found guilty on counts 2, 3, and 4. Hanged.
- **Albert Speer**, Hitler's chief architect and later minister of armaments and war production. Found guilty on counts 3 and 4. Sentenced to and served twenty years in prison.
- **Julius Streicher**, publisher of an anti-Semitic magazine. Found guilty on count 4. Hanged.

FACT

Those sentenced to death were executed on October 16, 1946, by U.S. Army Master Sergeant John Woods, who was an experienced hangman. Goering's body and those of ten others were taken by truck to the concentration camp at Dachau, where they were cremated in the camp's infamous crematoriums. Their ashes were dumped in a stream in Munich.

The Nuremberg trials were not the last war crimes trials to be conducted in Germany. For years afterward, numerous "de-Nazification" trials were conducted in an effort to hold all war criminals accountable for their actions. Defendants were divided into five categories:

- Major offenders subject to death or life in prison
- Activists, military criminals, and profiteers, who could receive sentences of up to ten years in prison
- Lesser offenders, such as people who entered the Nazi Party at a young age. Those convicted could receive sentences of up to three years in prison.
- Nazi "followers," who were subject to a hefty fine
- Nazis who had resisted the murderous activities of the party and were persecuted for their efforts. These individuals were usually acquitted.

From December 1963 to August 1965, a West German court in Frankfurt tried twenty-one former SS officers at the Auschwitz death camp. The men were charged with complicity in thousands of murders; nineteen of them were found guilty and received sentences ranging from three years to life in prison.

The Tokyo Trials

An international military tribunal was also convened in Tokyo to prosecute Japanese military officials accused of war crimes. A total of twenty-five high-ranking Japanese officers were tried, most of them charged with crimes against peace, crimes against humanity, and atrocities.

Unlike the Nuremberg trials, which were closely watched by most Americans, the trials in Japan drew little interest. The most popular trial was that of Japan's prime minister, Hideki Tojo, who was the Japanese equivalent of Adolf Hitler in the eyes of most Americans. The trials lasted for nearly three years. At the end, Tojo and six others were found guilty and sentenced to death by hanging; sixteen others were sentenced to life in prison. Additional war crimes trials were conducted in other Far East nations, where another 900 Japanese military officials were sentenced to death.

The Doctors' Trial

Separate war crimes trials were held for twenty-three SS physicians and scientists from December 1946 to August 1947, this time before a U.S. military tribunal. During these trials, the world learned the true extent of the Nazis' cruelty, with charges ranging from mass "euthanasia" of the mentally and physically unfit during the early years of the Nazi era to heinous medical experiments conducted at Nazi concentration and death camps.

The emphasis was placed on those doctors and scientists who worked for the SS, but physicians who were part of the German medical establishment were also involved. Most prominent among them was Karl Brandt, Hitler's personal physician and Reich commissioner for health and sanitation. Brandt worked his way into Hitler's inner circle by endorsing and encouraging the Führer's scheme of eugenic murder as a way of cleansing and strengthening the Aryan race. However, the Nazis realized that their work would not sit well with the world at large, and so they worked in secret and spoke in euphemisms. Noted one document introduced into evidence at the trials: "Thirty thousand attended to. Another hundred thousand to one hundred and twenty thousand waiting. Keep the circle of those in the know as small as possible."

That particular document concerned the Generation Foundation for Welfare and Institutional Care, which carried out Hitler's directive to cleanse the Aryan race by killing everyone with physical or mental defects or carrying an inheritable disease. The program, administered by the Reich Committee for Scientific Research of Hereditary and Severe Constitutional Diseases, required all doctors and midwives to report the birth of all children afflicted with a congenital malformation. An estimated 5,000 mentally or physically disabled children were killed from 1939 to 1944, and a total of 70,000 people are believed to have been killed through the program.

FACT

Family members of these "imperfect" individuals were usually told that the victims had died of pneumonia or some disease and that the body had been cremated to prevent the spread of illness.

Mentally handicapped adults were removed from institutions and taken by trucks to killing centers, where they were murdered with poisonous gas. The SS was placed in charge of this duty and carried it out with ruthless efficiency—more than 80,000 people were eliminated over the course of the Nazi racial purification program. Again, next of kin were sent a simple form letter telling them of their loved one's passing. If any explanation was offered, it was a lie.

Medical Experiments on Humans

Over the course of the war, Nazi physicians and scientists performed a host of horrifying medical experiments on death camp and concentration camp prisoners. These men and women were treated worse than guinea pigs and were subjected to excruciatingly painful, degrading, and often deadly procedures, all in the name of "science." For example, some were placed in a pressure chamber and subjected to extended oxygen deprivation to see the effects of high-altitude flight on aviators. Other prisoners were placed in freezing water for long periods to study hypothermia.

Anton Pacholegg was a prisoner at Dachau who worked as a clerk at the experimental station where other prisoners were tortured in the name of Nazi science. He offered the following testimony during the war crimes trials:

The Luftwaffe delivered a cabinet constructed of wood and metal measuring one meter square and two meters high. It was possible in this cabinet to either decrease or increase the air pressure. . . . Some experiments gave men such pressure in their heads that they would go mad and pull out their hair in an effort to relieve the pressure. . . . They would tear their heads and face with their fingers and nails. They would beat the walls with their hands and head and scream. These cases generally ended in the death of the subject.

After a group had been killed, the skin from their bodies would be removed from their thighs and buttocks. Rascher (the head scientist) would pass on them before they were tanned. I saw the finished leather later made into a handbag that Mrs. Rascher was carrying. Most of it was for driving gloves for the SS officers of the camp.

Four of the defendants at the Doctors' Trial were acquitted, and seven were sentenced to death. Among the condemned was Karl Brandt, who was hanged in June 1948. Dr. Karl Clauberg, who performed some of the most notorious and repulsive medical experiments in Experimental Block 10 at Auschwitz, died in 1955 before standing trial; he had been held by the Soviets in the years immediately after the war. Clauberg was a monster who killed countless women while trying to develop a new high-speed form of sterilization. Most of his experiments involved injecting caustic chemicals into the uteri of his subjects; the lucky ones died.

The Angel of Death

Most infamous of the Nazi doctors was Josef Mengele, who became known among the inmates of Auschwitz as the Angel of Death. Mengele held a doctorate in both medicine and anthropology and was assigned to Auschwitz in May 1943 after being wounded on the eastern front, where he was a medical officer.

FACT

The Japanese also conducted heinous medical experiments, many of them on prisoners of war. Some of the most horrifying involved injecting patients with bacterial agents and observing how they suffered.

Mengele was a vicious anti-Semite who saw the Jews as little more than lab animals. In one notorious incident, a mother refused to be separated from her teenage daughter and attacked the SS guard who was trying to keep them apart. Enraged, Mengele pulled out his revolver and shot both mother and daughter on the spot, then ordered the other men and women he had culled for experimentation to be executed immediately.

Figure 16-2 Josef Mengele, "The Angel of Death."

Getty Images/Hulton Archive/Stringer

Mengele was particularly intrigued by twins and saved them for special experiments to determine if twins really had any kind of special physical or mental bond. In one incident, he ordered twin boys killed just so he could perform autopsies to settle a disagreement he had with another SS physician.

Knowing he faced certain death if captured by Allied forces, Mengele left Auschwitz shortly before it was liberated. He lived in West Germany for several years, then escaped to South America, where he was protected by Nazi sympathizers. Over the years, the legend of Josef Mengele grew, and "Mengele sightings," most of them bogus, became commonplace.

Despite the efforts of Israel's best Nazi hunters, Mengele remained free. He is believed to have moved from Paraguay to Brazil in 1960 and drowned while swimming at a beach in 1979. His death was controversial, but a team of pathologists who examined his remains were able to confirm his identity.

Chapter 17

Life at Home

The impact of World War II was felt on the home front within days of the attack on Pearl Harbor. America suddenly became a beehive of activity as everyone from the president on down stepped up to contribute to the war effort. The national sense of unity was almost palpable as Americans of every age looked fearfully across the oceans at foreign countries seemingly hell-bent on taking everything they held dear. Despite years of isolationism, few Americans had any qualms about going after the world's aggressors. The attitude among most people was, "They started it; we'll finish it!"

Hard Times on the Home Soil

The prevailing emotion among most Americans in the days after the attack on Pearl Harbor was fear. The fact that Japanese bombers and fighters could inflict such tremendous damage on an American naval base suggested that they were capable of anything—including an attack on the American mainland. A minor panic ensued as municipalities from coast to coast enacted nighttime curfews and blackouts and piled sandbags in front of their most important buildings. Gun emplacements were constructed on top of buildings to defend against enemy planes, and scouts patrolled the beaches with binoculars, searching for planes and submarines. The enemy never showed up, but that didn't prevent municipal leaders from exhorting the public to vigilance. "The war will come right to our cities," said Mayor Fiorello La Guardia of New York. "Never underestimate the strength, the cruelty of the enemy."

FACT

Many American servicemen fell in love while serving overseas. The result was an influx of war brides. In 1946, Operation War Bride brought 600 British women to the United States via passenger ship. That year, immigration officials report, 60,000 British women filed for emigration as brides or prospective brides. Another 12,000 applications were received from Dutch, French, Italian, and Australian women.

The Axis powers were a mysterious enemy to most Americans, so perhaps they can be forgiven for their panic. News was sparse during the early weeks of the war, and rumors and gossip ran wild. Anyone who appeared even slightly foreign was viewed with suspicion and distrust. American citizens of Japanese and German ancestry found themselves ostracized, if not actually attacked. Many businesspeople with foreign-sounding names took to plastering their store windows with American flags and signs reading "I Am an American!" to demonstrate their patriotism.

When no enemy planes came flying in over the oceans, panic and fear quickly gave way to a bizarre sense of wartime normalcy, though vigilance against enemy attack continued throughout the war. The Office of Civilian

Defense, created by President Roosevelt in the spring of 1941, increased its efforts to encourage people of all ages to become involved in maintaining the nation's defenses by volunteering in their communities.

Figure 17-1
Americans in line to buy rationed sugar.

Photo courtesy of the National Archives (208-AA-322I-2)

The campaign worked: Americans volunteered by the millions for a wide variety of wartime defense programs. For example, over the course of the war, more than 1.5 million civilians volunteered as enemy plane spotters. They memorized the silhouettes of German and Japanese planes and spent their days and evenings scanning the skies with binoculars. No enemy planes were ever seen, but that never dampened the enthusiasm of the participants. Other volunteer programs included air raid wardens, security guards, and firefighters.

Rationing

Life in America during the war years was marked by sacrifice. The war effort demanded huge amounts of metal, paper, rubber, and other materials, and

Americans were expected to donate as much of these substances as possible and live without until the war ended. Scrap drives were a common community activity, with high school groups going door to door seeking whatever materials homeowners could part with. Promotional campaigns featuring movie stars and other celebrities encouraged Americans to give until it hurt, then give some more. In one famous image, actress Rita Hayworth sat atop her car, which bore a sign reading: "Please drive carefully. My bumpers are on the scrap heap."

As the war effort increased, Americans learned to live with less and less. Shortages were common, and the rationing of essential materials like gasoline, rubber, and certain foods such as meat became part of everyday life for most Americans. Voluntary at first, rationing of some items became law as the war progressed.

Perhaps best remembered among those who lived in wartime America is gasoline rationing. Aimed at curbing the nonessential use of automobiles, the program required car owners to paste ration stamps on their windshields. An "A" stamp meant the car was for nonessential use, a "B" stamp meant it was needed for work, and a "C" stamp was for cars of essential drivers such as doctors. The type of stamp on a car's windshield dictated how much gasoline could be bought for it each week. Additional rationing efforts encouraged the use of car pools and public transportation.

Figure 17-2
Actress Rita Hayworth promoting the national scrap metal drive.

Photo courtesy of the National Archives (208-PU-91B-5)

A wide variety of common foods also fell into short supply as the government increased procurement for servicemen. In fact, nearly one-third of food items were rationed during the war years. Quality meat became increasingly difficult to find in civilian groceries, as did butter, sugar, coffee, and cheese. In one war-era animated cartoon, a picture of a steak smothered in onions appears briefly, then again at the end of the cartoon, so food-rationed Americans could gaze hungrily at what they had been missing for so long.

The Office of Price Administration was established in August 1941 to control and stabilize the prices of food and of goods and services and also to prevent the creation of a black market. Later, a presidential directive gave the OPA the authority to ration certain items. One of its first acts was to freeze the prices of nearly all everyday goods and most foods at March 1942 levels. Increases in rent were also severely restricted. The restrictions lasted until June 1946, when the prices of most items went up dramatically, sometimes as much as 25 percent over their wartime cost.

During the war, every family received ration books containing stamps to be given to grocers when buying certain items. Red stamps were used for meat (except for poultry, which was not rationed), butter, fats, cheese, canned milk, and canned fish. Green, brown, or blue stamps were used for canned vegetables, juices, baby food, and dried fruit. Shoppers could earn two extra red points for every pound of meat drippings and other fat they turned in as part of a national fat-collection campaign. Animal fats were used in a variety of wartime manufacturing processes, including the making of paint and munitions.

Music helped servicemen remember what they were fighting for. The music industry started producing patriotic melodies by the dozens shortly after the United States entered the conflict. Patriotic events almost always included a medley of songs honoring the armed forces. The most common were "The Caissons Go Rolling Along," "Anchors Aweigh," and "The Marine Hymn."

Because of the food shortages, Americans were encouraged to plant what became known as victory gardens. In addition to placing food on the table of the average American, this freed farmers to provide still more food for America's armed forces. Americans from all walks of life participated in the victory garden program, planting vegetables wherever space was available. In all, an estimated 20 million garden plots were created across the country.

War Bonds

Americans also helped finance the war by buying war bonds. More than $190 billion worth of bonds were purchased by private citizens over the course of the war. The program was heavily promoted with campaigns that involved movie stars, national celebrities, and even comic book heroes like Superman and Batman.

FACT

The first really patriotic song, 'Remember Pearl Harbor,' exhorted: "Let's remember Pearl Harbor as we go to meet the foe. . . . Let's remember Pearl Harbor as we did the Alamo." Equally rousing was Frank Loesser's "Praise the Lord and Pass the Ammunition," which was based on the legend that a chaplain had assisted gunners firing on Japanese planes.

Eight war bond drives were conducted from December 1942 to December 1945, and the response was tremendous. Two out of every three Americans, many using payroll deduction plans, bought Series E bonds, which were first issued in September 1943. Even children got into the act, pasting twenty-five-cent war bond stamps into a special book until it was full and they could redeem it for a $25 bond.

The interest rate for war bonds was 1.8 percent, compared with 4.25 percent for similar bonds issued during World War I. But most Americans didn't mind because buying the bonds made them feel as if they were really helping the war effort, which they were. Small investors bought about $40 billion worth of bonds, with the rest being purchased by commercial banks, states, local governments, and other bodies.

FACT

Many families proudly displayed blue stars in their front windows to indicate that they had a family member serving in the military. The blue star was replaced with a gold star if the family member was killed in action.

The Role of Propaganda

Every war involves propaganda, and World War II saw plenty of it on both sides. It took many forms—posters, advertising, songs, comic books, comic strips, newsreel shorts, and even motion pictures—and was used to educate and influence both civilian populations and the men fighting on the front.

The word *propaganda* comes from the Italian *Sacra Congregatio de Propaganda Fide* (Sacred Congregation for Propagating Faith), a papal organization that spread the Christian faith. The primary goal of propaganda as we know it today is to strengthen and enforce core beliefs and sway public opinion.

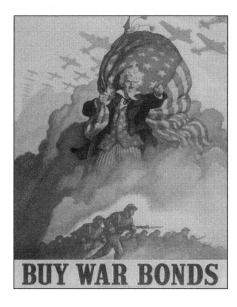

BUY WAR BONDS

Figure 17-3
An American wartime poster.

*Photo courtesy
of the National
Archives (44-PA-531)*

The Nazis used *propaganda* in two ways: to spread and preserve the basic doctrines of Nazism and to dehumanize "inferior" groups such as the Jews so that it would be easier for the German people to hate and exterminate them. Joseph Goebbels, chief of Nazi propaganda, was a master of the art form. He used every medium at his disposal to blanket Germany and the conquered lands with pro-Nazi propaganda. Goebbels found the radio to be particularly effective, and so almost every German family had at least one radio—specially constructed so that it was not able to receive anti-Nazi broadcasts from Great Britain and elsewhere.

The success of the Nazi propaganda machine was tremendous. Hitler was elevated to the status of national savior based solely on Goebbels's tight control of the national press and his skill at turning political rallies into full-blown multimedia events.

The Allies also relied heavily on propaganda. In the United States, posters proved most effective at influencing public opinion and maintaining morale. On the home front, they encouraged Americans to buy war bonds, write to GIs on the front, give blood, donate scrap materials to the war effort, do their best at war-production jobs ("He can't fix guns in the air! Build 'em right! Keep 'em firing!"), and carpool to conserve gasoline ("When you ride alone, you ride with Hitler! Join a car-sharing club today!").

FACT

One of Japan's less successful propaganda campaigns involved a series of English-speaking women who broadcast music and misinformation to Allied troops via the radio. Servicemen nicknamed the friendly, faceless voice "Tokyo Rose." She aimed to damage Allied morale by reporting incorrect casualty figures and tales of infidelity back home. Most servicemen paid little attention, though they did enjoy the accompanying dance music.

As in Nazi Germany, Allied propaganda posters were also used to reduce the enemy to subhuman status, thus making it easier for servicemen to kill them. In addition, the military used posters to remind soldiers of the importance of maintaining their equipment ("His rifle will fire . . . will mine? Care of arms is care of life.") and the need to avoid careless talk ("Keep mum . . . she's not so dumb! Careless talk costs lives!").

Chapter 18

The Roles of Women During the War

The male population of the United States shrank dramatically as millions of men of service age signed up for duty overseas. In some towns, the only remaining males were young boys and old men. As a result, countless women were forced to survive without spousal support. It was difficult, but they persevered, often pulling more than double-duty as mother, father, and wartime factory worker. If war production opportunities were unavailable, many women made ends meet by taking in boarders, moving in with other war wives, or returning home to live with their parents until their husbands could return home.

Women Called to Morale Duty

Most women experienced huge demands on their personal time. The government blanketed the nation with public service announcements encouraging women to do all they could to support the fighting men overseas by volunteering for as many programs as possible. The list of suggested activities seemed to grow longer by the day: blood drives, war bond campaigns, rolling bandages for the Red Cross, hostessing at USO clubs, participating in military mothers' clubs, and especially writing letters to friends and loved ones on the front.

Letter writing was important at this time because it helped maintain morale on the front. Women were encouraged to scribble a note at every opportunity, with posters shaming those who didn't. ("V-mail is speed mail: You write. He'll fight. Be with him at every mail call. Can you pass a mailbox with a clear conscience?") For most servicemen, mail call was the most important time of the day.

FACT

In her 1942 book *So Your Husband's Gone to War!* author Ethel Gorham devoted an entire chapter to the whys and hows of letter writing during wartime. Among her advice:

- Write consistently.
- Keep letters chatty and varied.
- Be "warm and intimate, as you yourself have been with the man to whom you are writing."
- Discuss what's going on at home.
- Avoid discussing the high cost of living and other sacrifices being made on the home front.

In an effort to help women cope with the dramatic changes the war caused at home, the government published numerous educational pamphlets and booklets. One such pamphlet, titled *If Your Baby Must Travel in Wartime*, offered mothers helpful advice on how to travel across the country by train, bus, or car. These pamphlets helped ease much of the fear and uncertainty war wives experienced while their husbands were away.

The USO

When servicemen (and women) needed a break, some company, and a little entertainment, they flocked to the many USO clubs that sprang up during the war around the country and in safe areas overseas.

Figure 18-1
Danny Kaye entertaining U.S. troops in Japan, October 25, 1945.

Photo courtesy of the National Archives (127-N-138204)

The USO (United Service Organizations) was founded in February 1941 when six service agencies (the Young Men's Christian Association, National Catholic Community Service, the National Jewish Welfare Board, the Young Women's Christian Association, the Salvation Army, and the National Traveler's Aid Association) decided to combine their efforts to assist and entertain servicemen stationed away from home.

USO-sponsored shows traveled the world to bring song, dance, and pretty women to the men fighting on the front lines. USO clubs were also established in war-production boom towns to help entertain exhausted factory workers.

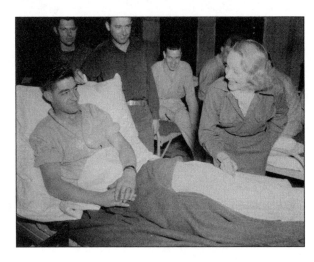

Figure 18-2
Marlene Dietrich signing a soldier's cast at a U.S. hospital in Belgium.

Photo courtesy of the National Archives (111-SC-232989)

Women at Work

Perhaps the most dramatic change in wartime America was on the job front. War production provided almost limitless job opportunities, yet the number of men available to take them was dramatically reduced by the tremendous needs of the armed services. So the government called on the nation's women to take their men's places in production factories, which they did enthusiastically. The national symbol of the female work force was Rosie the Riveter, a character who appeared in war production recruiting posters, a Norman Rockwell *Saturday Evening Post* cover, and even in song. Rosie was emblematic of the female contribution to the American war effort, and she would forever change the face of industry.

According to anthropologist Margaret Mead, more than 3 million women went to work specifically to aid the war effort, and many more did so because they desperately needed the money. Defense jobs ranged from shipyard welding and riveting to outfitting bombers and fighters to sewing powder bags. Much of it was hard physical labor, yet few women complained. For most, the factory "uniform" of slacks, shirts, and work shoes—once solely male attire—became a true badge of honor.

Of course, not all men working stateside were happy with the fact that they had to labor side by side with women in what had traditionally been male occupations. Sexual harassment of women was common but generally downplayed. (To prevent problems, women were encouraged to dress down, i.e., avoid tight sweaters so as not to inflame the hormones of their male coworkers.) Some less-than-progressive trade unions tried to keep out female workers, but the demands of war production superceded their bias, and women were finally allowed in.

Figure 18-3
Women workers at an aircraft plant.

Photo courtesy of the National Archives (208-AA-352QQ-5)

The changes in American employment trends resulting from the war had far-reaching consequences. In the months before America's entry into World War II, the percentage of women in the work force was slightly less than 25 percent; by 1945, that figure increased to 34.7 percent. And while many female war workers quit their jobs when the war ended, many more chose to remain because they liked the money, the freedom, and the constructive changes they were making in their lives. In many ways, sociologists say Rosie the Riveter helped pave the way for the feminist movement of the 1960s and 1970s.

FACT

When the war effort dramatically reduced civilian supplies of nylon, used for women's stockings, many women took to drawing lines on the back of their legs to simulate the appearance of stockings.

Women at War

Women also played a significant role in the military. According to government records, more than 265,000 women enlisted in the armed services of the United States over the course of the war, all as volunteers. There was vocal opposition to female participation in the war effort at the beginning, but it gradually changed as the war raged on and the need for qualified personnel, regardless of gender, increased.

Most women served in traditional jobs such as clerical and secretarial ones, or as nurses. But women also worked as truck drivers, mechanics, technicians, and even pilots. All branches of U.S. service had a female auxiliary. The Women's Army Corps (WAC) began as the Women's Auxiliary Army Corps (WAAC), which was not an official part of the U.S. Army. But that changed in 1943, as did the name. In all, more than 100,000 women served in the WAC in positions ranging from telephone operator to truck mechanic. The women's reserve of the navy—known as WAVES—enlisted 100,000 women, and the Marine Corps Women's Reserve, which was formed in February 1943, enlisted 23,000.

All the women who assisted the war effort were important, but perhaps most unique were the Women's Air Force Service pilots. By August 1943, the war was pushing the personnel limits of the U.S. Army Air Corps, which was the noncombat division of the Army Air Forces, and the government finally decided that additional help would be necessary if enough planes were to reach those who needed them. Officials turned to Jacqueline Cochran, a world-famous racing pilot and the head of the Women's Flying Training Command, a group of almost 2,000 female pilots trained to fly military aircraft across the country. Cochran was asked to merge her organization with the Women's Auxiliary Ferrying Squadron to create the Women Air Force Service Pilots (WASPs).

Their jobs were many: ferry military aircraft to pilots of the army air corps, test newly repaired planes, and help train antiaircraft gunners by pulling airborne targets during practice. However, the women were not allowed to serve overseas.

The WASPs flew from August 1943 to December 1944, living and working under military standards and discipline despite the fact that they were managed by Civil Service. The women were highly praised for their efforts, but their group was disbanded in 1944 without having been accepted into the Army Air Corps. It wasn't until 1977 that Congress acknowledged that the WASPs who served in World War II actually were military pilots and deserved the same benefits. Surviving members of the group were given honorary discharges and listed as veterans.

Women also served in a variety of jobs in Great Britain, where every able-bodied person was put to work. Over the course of the war, thousands of British women served in the Auxiliary Territorial Service, the Women's Auxiliary Air Force, and the Women's Royal Navy Service as air raid wardens, military clerks, and secretaries.

Most Allied nations did not permit women to serve in combat or hold hazardous jobs during the war. The one exception was the Soviet Union. In October 1941, the Soviet air force formed a women's flying corps that resulted in three regiments of women pilots: fighter, light bomber, and night bomber. Male pilots were later assigned to two of the regiments, but the Forty-sixth Night Bomber Air Regiment remained exclusively female, right down to the mechanics servicing the planes. The unit entered combat in 1942 and later received the honorary title Guards for its tremendous success in combat. Soviet women also took up arms in defense of Moscow, Stalingrad, Leningrad, and other cities.

Chapter 19

The War in the Media—
During and After

No other military conflict has been so thoroughly covered by the motion picture industry as World War II. Hollywood (and its international counterparts) began producing war-related movies even before the war in Europe started, and cinematic interest has not diminished since, as evidenced by such recent and successful World War II flicks as *Saving Private Ryan*, *The Thin Red Line*, *U-571*, *Enemy at the Gates*, and *Pearl Harbor*.

On the Big Screen

Over the years, virtually every aspect of World War II has been analyzed on the big screen, from the various theaters of war to the Holocaust to life on the home front. Many movies produced during the war years were pure propaganda that played fast and loose with the facts. Hollywood is to be forgiven for this, considering the fact that wartime America went to the movies solely for escapist entertainment and cried out for heroes and happy endings, not reality. It wasn't until after the conflict ended that Hollywood began depicting World War II in more realistic terms.

One of the most compelling and accurate war-era films was William Wellman's *The Story of G.I. Joe* (1945), which *Time* magazine called "the least glamorous war picture ever made." It tells the story of a typical infantry company's battles in Tunisia, Sicily, and Italy and makes wonderful use of actual combat footage. Stars included Robert Mitchum, Wally Cassell, and Burgess Meredith as real-life war correspondent Ernie Pyle.

FACT

Harold Russell, who played a disabled soldier in the 1946 movie *The Best Years of Our Lives*, was a real-life soldier who lost both hands during the war. Russell received two Academy Awards for his performance in the film: one for Best Supporting Actor and a special award "for bringing hope and courage to his fellow veterans."

Hollywood has turned many of the war's most important battles and events into epic motion pictures over the years. *The Longest Day* (1962), for example, is a star-studded look at the Normandy invasion that runs nearly three hours. The film's cast reads like a Who's Who of Hollywood, and includes John Wayne, Richard Burton, Robert Mitchum, Henry Fonda, Robert Ryan, Mel Ferrer, and Sean Connery, among many others. Ken Annakin's *Battle of the Bulge* (1965) is equally grand in its telling of Germany's last desperate push in the Ardennes in December 1944. Featured performers include Henry Fonda, Robert Shaw, Robert Ryan, and Dana Andrews. Also compelling is *Tora! Tora! Tora!* (1970), a remarkably realistic look at the

Japanese invasion of Pearl Harbor told from both the American and Japanese perspectives. Directed by Richard Fleischer, Toshio Masuda, and Kinji Fukasaku, the movie is highlighted by some gorgeous cinematography and stunning action footage.

No discussion of American war movies would be complete without a mention of Steven Spielberg's *Saving Private Ryan* (1998). The first twenty minutes of this movie offer a stunning recreation of the American landing on Normandy's Omaha Beach. It's intentionally disorienting—just like real-life combat—and agonizing to watch as soldiers are mowed down by German forces before they are even able to get out of their amphibious transports, lose limbs to enemy fire, and wade through water dyed red with the blood of their fallen comrades. Most veterans say that this sequence, which was filmed in Ireland, contains some of the most realistic combat scenes ever put on film, and the rest of the movie is equally harrowing in its depiction of war. When *Saving Private Ryan* premiered, the U.S. Veterans Administration offered special counseling at many VA hospitals for World War II veterans who were emotionally affected by it.

Figure 19-1
Tom Hanks in a scene from *Saving Private Ryan*.

Getty Images/David James/Staff

Other outstanding World War II movies include David Lean's *The Bridge on the River Kwai* (1957); John Sturges's *The Great Escape* (1963); Bryan Forbes's *King Rat* (1965), based on novelist James Clavell's experiences in a

Japanese POW camp; Samuel Fuller's *The Big Red One* (1980); J. Lee Thompson's *The Guns of Navarone* (1961); Robert Aldrich's *The Dirty Dozen* (1967); Michael Curtiz's *Casablanca* (1943); William Wellman's *Battleground* (1949); William Wyler's *The Best Years of Our Lives* (1946); Franklin Schaffner's *Patton* (1970); and Stanley Kramer's *Judgment at Nuremberg* (1961).

Films Made During the War

War-era films of note dealing with the European and African theaters included Lloyd Bacon's *Action in the North Atlantic* (1943), starring Humphrey Bogart and Raymond Massey; Charlie Chaplin's *The Great Dictator* (1940), a scathing parody of Adolf Hitler; Archie Mayo's *Crash Dive* (1943); Billy Wilder's *Five Graves to Cairo* (1943); David Lean and Noel Coward's *In Which We Serve* (1943); Zoltan Korda's *Sahara* (1943); and Howard Hawks's *Air Force* (1943).

Illustrators such as Alberto Vargas were renowned for their sexy pinups, but the most popular pinup of all was a photograph of actress Betty Grable in a white bathing suit, peering seductively over her shoulder. At the height of the war, the movie studio received 20,000 requests a week from servicemen for Grable's photograph. Other popular pinup gals included Rita Hayworth and Jane Russell.

The Pacific theater was also a popular subject for war-era movies. Some of the best included Tay Garnett's *Bataan* (1943); Edward Ludwig's *Fighting Seabees* (1944), starring war film icon John Wayne; Lloyd Bacon's *The Fighting Sullivans* (1942); Lewis Seller's *Guadalcanal Diary* (1943); Raoul Walsh's *Objective, Burma!* (1945); Mark Sandrich's *So Proudly We Hail* (1943), which examines the American retreat through the Philippines to Corregidor through the eyes of three army nurses; John Ford's *They Were Expendable* (1945), again starring John Wayne; and Mervyn LeRoy's *Thirty Seconds over Tokyo* (1944), featuring Spencer Tracy as Lieutenant Colonel James Doolittle.

Interestingly, many of Hollywood's top directors and other creative talents made films specifically for the armed forces. One of the best known is the *Why We Fight* series, developed by Frank Capra and written by Julius and Philip Epstein, who also worked on *Casablanca*, *Mr. Skeffington*, and *The Man Who Came to Dinner.* The series was pure propaganda designed to explain to servicemen in simple terms America's involvement in the war, and Capra pulled out all the stops, using archival photographs, animation, re-enactments, and even scenes from German filmmaker Leni Riefenstahl's tribute to Nazism, *Triumph of the Will.* There were seven films in the series, required viewing for all servicemen headed overseas. The shorts proved so popular that they were eventually released theatrically for civilian audiences.

FACT

Many movie stars, musicians, athletes, and entertainers helped the war effort by promoting war programs, entertaining troops, and even joining the service. Famous stars who enlisted include Jimmy Stewart, Clark Gable, Raymond Massey, Burgess Meredith, Victor Mature, and Leslie Howard. Many legendary athletes also joined, including Bob Feller, Hank Greenberg, Joe DiMaggio, and Ted Williams.

Foreign Films

Many outstanding foreign films also examine various aspects of World War II. One of the finest is Wolfgang Petersen's *Das Boot* (The Boat) (1981), which provides an incredible glimpse of life aboard a German U-boat. The film is wet, claustrophobic, disturbing, and utterly fascinating. On the other side of the world, Ken Ichikawa's *Fires on the Plain* (1959) presents an intriguing look at the war in the Pacific from the Japanese perspective. A scathing indictment of war in general, the film examines the Japanese retreat from the Philippines in the waning days of World War II through the eyes of one soldier.

Animation

The armed services also used a series of animated cartoons to teach new recruits the importance of discipline and following military regulations. One of the most memorable was the Private Snafu series, written by Ted

Geisel (better known as children's author Dr. Seuss) and Phil Eastman, and directed by legendary Warner Brothers animators Chuck Jones, Fritz Freleng, and others. The instructional cartoons, which relied heavily on humor to convey their very important messages, covered everything from the hazards of spreading rumors to the need for camouflage.

Many theatrically released animated cartoons from Walt Disney, Warner Brothers, MGM, and other studios also addressed the war. Perhaps best known among the dozens of cartoons produced during the war years is the Academy Award–winning Donald Duck cartoon *Der Führer's Face* (1943), which mocked Adolf Hitler as a buffoon. Other wartime animated classics include *Bugs Bunny Nips the Nips* (Warner Brothers, 1944), in which Bugs takes on stereotypical Japanese forces; *Herr Meets Hare* (Warner Brothers, 1945), in which Bugs tangles with Nazi Hermann Goering by disguising himself as Hitler and Joseph Stalin; *The Blitz Wolf* (MGM, 1942), which features a wolf in Nazi clothing; and *Swing Shift Cinderella* (MGM, 1945), a war-era retelling of the classic fairy tale.

Chronicling the War

World War II was one of the most thoroughly reported military events of the twentieth century. Print and radio journalists, photographers, cinematographers, and even cartoonists captured every aspect of the war in every theater—very often at the risk of their own lives. And after the war, novelists such as Norman Mailer and Joseph Heller used their military experiences as fodder for some of the postwar era's best fiction.

FACT

A handful of television shows have used the war as a backdrop. The best known is *Hogan's Heroes*, which began in 1965. The show, featuring Allied troops in a POW camp guarded by bumbling Germans, played the war for laughs. More recently, the HBO series *Band of Brothers* examined the lives of soldiers in Easy Company, members of the 506th Parachute Infantry Regiment, U.S. 101st Airborne Division.

An estimated 700 American correspondents (including twenty-four women) covered World War II for newspapers, magazines, and radio. The war was front page news almost every day, and journalists scrambled to cover stories both large and small. The Normandy invasion alone was chronicled by an estimated 500 American reporters and photographers.

Most war correspondents covered the war from the command posts, getting their information from commanding officers and military liaisons. But a great many realized that the best stories involved the soldiers fighting on the front lines, so that's where they went, pen and camera in hand, eager to capture the sights and sounds of combat. Most of these correspondents remained relatively anonymous, but some became famous for their coverage of the war. One of the best known was Ernie Pyle, a writer for United Features Syndicate. Pyle was a friend of the common soldier and was well liked and respected by the servicemen he met and covered. So was Raymond Clapper of Scripps-Howard, whose articles were syndicated to nearly 180 newspapers throughout the United States. Sadly, both men were killed during the war: Pyle by an enemy sniper and Clapper when the plane he was riding in collided with another.

The job of war correspondent was extremely hazardous because the enemy made no distinction between journalist and soldier. A total of thirty-eight accredited war correspondents were killed by enemy fire over the course of the war, and thirty-six were wounded.

Print journalists chronicled the war, but it was radio that really brought the full horror of it into the living room of the average American. Few who heard it can forget CBS correspondent Edward R. Murrow's solemn reporting of the Battle of Britain, conducted from the London rooftops as German bombers delivered their deadly loads. Murrow described not only the military aspect of the war in Europe but also its toll on the individual.

World War II was also the first war to be thoroughly documented in motion pictures. The U.S. military used numerous cinematographers to film battles, troop movements, and other events for later review, but Hollywood also got into the act. Indeed, some of its best known directors took camera in hand to film the action as it occurred. From this sprang an entire movie subgenre known as the war documentary. John Ford, for example, served with Major General William Donovan as head of the Field Photographic Branch and directed the documentary *The Battle of Midway* (1942), which combined actual battle footage with staged scenes. Ford also filmed footage from a PT boat during the Normandy invasion.

FACT

Of the many correspondents who covered World War II, none were better known than Ernie Pyle. His specialty was profiling average soldiers just trying to survive from one day to the next. Through his writing, Pyle showed America both the simple joys and the numbing horrors of World War II. Pyle's columns were published in nearly 300 American newspapers and he won a Pulitzer Prize in 1943.

John Huston was another famous director who lent his talents to covering the war, producing *Report from the Aleutians* in 1943 and *The Battle of San Pietro* in 1944. These documentary shorts brought the graphic reality of combat home to many Americans for the first time.

War reporting was as much propaganda as it was journalism. Reports from the front were subject to military censorship, though in general there was little need to edit because most journalists believed that their job was to maintain morale as well as to report the facts. As a result, bad news, such as reports of atrocities committed by Allied forces, was so rare as to be nonexistent.

Unfortunately, racism was rampant in most news reports—as it was in almost all forms of wartime media. Japanese forces, for example, were routinely referred to as "Japs" and described as being less than human. In the years after the war, many correspondents said they had come to regret those descriptions.

The Influence of Comic Art

Most veterans of World War II have fond memories of the era's military strips, such as Bill Mauldin's *Up Front*, George Baker's *The Sad Sack*, and Milton Caniff's *Male Call*. To servicemen everywhere, they were as coveted as dry socks and mail from home. But these weren't the only cartoons to address the war. Many popular civilian strips aided the effort equally well on the home front by boosting morale, maintaining a strong sense of patriotism, and encouraging Americans to do their part by buying war bonds, limiting travel, and contributing to scrap drives.

"People were swept up in a sense of common purpose," recalls Will Eisner, a comic book artist who used his talents during the war to create instructional cartoons for the U.S. Army. "It was by common consent that we were in the war, and no daily strip dared make an antiwar remark. All of the civilian strips were involved in promoting the war effort because we had an enemy that had to be defeated."

The smoke from the attack on Pearl Harbor had barely cleared when the comics' most beloved characters lined up to enlist. One of the first was Joe Palooka, who refused a commission (he felt he wasn't smart enough to be an officer) and spent the entire war as a buck private. It was an act that prompted countless men to sign up.

There were many others: Terry of Milton Caniff's *Terry and the Pirates* became a flight officer with the air force, and his mentor, Pat Ryan, a lieutenant in naval intelligence. Roy Crane's Captain Easy helped the FBI fight spies and saboteurs when war broke out in Europe, and after Pearl Harbor the character became a captain in the army. Even Russ Westover's *Tillie the Toiler* did her part by joining the WACs, her ditzy personality quickly replaced by patriotic duty.

Figure 19-2
War poster by
Alan Saalburg.

*Photo courtesy
of the National
Archives (44-PA-191)*

There seemed to be a general agreement among most artists that they would keep readers entertained. They didn't want to remind people of the war. They wanted to reassure them that some things would continue as they always had.

The military comic strips that appeared in *Stars and Stripes*, camp papers, and stateside publications were also a tremendous morale booster—both for fighting forces and their families back home, say cartoon historians.

FACT

Comic books became one of the most popular forms of reading material on military bases during the war. They were much more gung-ho than the daily strips, which made them the perfect medium for war-era propaganda. Japanese were usually depicted as short, buck-toothed, slant-eyed devils, and the Nazis as war-mongering beasts—perfect foils for peace-loving superheroes, generally good-looking white Americans.

Morale Boosters

The strips were also a heartfelt tribute to the forces in the trenches, who often saw their daily frustrations and anxieties humorously illustrated. "The military strips were definitely good for morale because the soldiers saw their own experiences in them," cartoonist Mort Walker adds.

One of the best at finding that "universal truth" was Bill Mauldin, whose generic dogfaces, Willie and Joe, experienced everything good and bad that the war had to offer. *Up Front* was especially popular with the average foot soldier because he knew Mauldin was right there on the front lines with him, not sitting on his butt in the *Stars and Stripes* office.

Also popular with servicemen was Sergeant George Baker's *The Sad Sack*, which premiered in *Yank* magazine in May 1942. A former animator for Walt Disney, Baker conceived of the weekly humor strip based on his experiences and those of his fellow soldiers. "The underlying story of the Sad Sack," Baker noted during the strip's heyday, "was his struggle with the Army in which I tried to symbolize the sum total of the difficulties and frustrations of all enlisted men." Baker succeeded well. In one infamous strip,

Sad Sack watches a military hygiene film so graphic that he puts on rubber gloves to shake hands with another serviceman's girlfriend.

Other humorous military strips included Leonard Sansone's *The Wolf* and Dick Wingert's *Hubert*.

Dave Breger, who had been doing a strip for the *Saturday Evening Post* titled *Private Breger*, changed the name to *G.I. Joe* in 1942 for *Yank* magazine and *Stars and Stripes*, thereby coining one of the most famous terms to come out of the war. The character was essentially the same in both military and civilian versions, and remained popular even after the war.

While *Up Front* illustrated the daily grind of frontline duty and *The Sad Sack* and others showed the more humorous side of military life, Milton Caniff's *Male Call* was something different altogether: a pinup strip whose main character, the sexy and sublime Miss Lace, constantly reminded its readers what they were fighting for.

Servicemen in all theaters of the war relied on pinups—photographs, illustrations, and cartoons of beautiful women—to remind them of what was waiting back home. Though the military sometimes tried to censor the pinups, they proliferated at a remarkable rate and could be found tacked up on barracks walls and in soldiers' wallets worldwide.

Male Call

Caniff was a dedicated patriot who deeply loved his country, but phlebitis kept him from serving during the war. Caniff glorified the war effort in *Terry and the Pirates*, but he also wanted to do something special for the servicemen. He pitched to the military a light-hearted strip specifically for camp papers, and *Male Call* was born. The strip premiered in 1942 (at first featuring the sultry Burma from *Terry and the Pirates*) and by the end of the war was appearing in nearly 3,000 publications. Caniff neither asked for nor received any payment for the strip, which he drew during his lunch hour and other rare moments of free time.

FACT

The United States was not the only country to use comic art as a propaganda device. The Nazis used vicious caricatures to turn national sentiment against the Jews and other minorities. Even American comic-book characters were fair game; *Das Schwarz*, a Nazi propaganda organ, went so far as to brand Superman as Jewish in an effort to discredit the Man of Steel.

Miss Lace, the star of *Male Call*, was a dark-haired beauty with model Bettie Page bangs who dressed as seductively as Caniff could get away with. She was every serviceman's pal, and the readers adored her.

Male Call ended in 1946, but Caniff continued to draw Miss Lace for military reunion programs for years afterward.

Chapter 20

Rebuilding the World

During the week of February 4 through 11, 1945, President Franklin Roosevelt met with British prime minister Winston Churchill and Soviet leader Joseph Stalin at the Black Sea resort of Yalta to discuss the rebuilding of a war-torn world. Though fighting continued on many fronts, the war in Europe was, for all intents and purposes, over; the once-mighty German war machine was on the verge of collapse, and Allied forces were quickly closing in on Berlin. With victory all but assured, the time was right for the victors to plan their next move.

The Yalta Conference

The Yalta Conference, which had been code-named Argonaut, set in motion a series of events with implications that are still being felt today. Foremost was Stalin's unapologetic plan to extend the Communist sphere of influence in Eastern Europe, a situation that would quickly lead to what became known as the Cold War. Indeed, the decisions made during that weeklong conference have been influencing world events up to the present.

One of the first and most important decisions made at Yalta was the division of occupied Germany. The conference participants—known in the press as the Big Three—had previously agreed to three occupation zones under the United States, Great Britain, and the Soviet Union. At Yalta they agreed to coordinate administration and give France a fourth zone, which would be taken from the U.S. and British zones. In addition, Stalin demanded that Germany pay reparations, though the amount and other details would be determined later.

Figure 20-1
Winston Churchill, Franklin D. Roosevelt, and Joseph Stalin at the Yalta Conference.

Photo courtesy of the National Archives (111-SC-260486)

Not surprisingly, the arrogant and manipulative Stalin all but dominated the Yalta Conference, using it as a springboard to expand Soviet control throughout the region. Though he paid lip service to free elections and the creation of democratic interim governments in the soon-to-be-liberated German-occupied territories, Stalin had little intention of honoring such promises. The nations that would fall under Soviet control would not experience true democracy until the Communist collapse in 1989.

During the Yalta Conference, Stalin agreed to declare war on Japan only after extracting concessions that greatly benefited the Soviet Union from Churchill and Roosevelt. Specifically, he demanded the return of Russian territory held by the Japanese since the Russo-Japanese War of 1904–05, including the Chinese territory of Port Arthur, and the joint Soviet-Chinese administration of the Manchurian railroads. The latter demand did not sit well with China's leaders, who were angered that such decisions were being made without their input or consent.

Brief Friends

When the war finally ended, American, British, and Soviet forces made a public show of camaraderie. Countless photos were taken of Soviet and American troops shaking hands and sharing hugs as they met throughout occupied Germany, Czechoslovakia, and other locations. Democracy and Communism had come together to defeat a common enemy. But could they remain partners? The answer was no. The United States and the Soviet Union soon came to view each other more as enemies than friends, and the situation grew worse with each passing year.

Though Stalin had depended heavily on aid from the United States and other Allied nations to defeat Germany, he wasted no time in eliminating such facts from state-revised Soviet history. According to Stalin, the Red Army had won the war almost single-handedly. No mention was made to the Soviet people of the more than $11 billion the Soviet Union had received through the U.S. Lend-Lease program, or of the millions more raised by concerned Americans for the Russian Relief Organization, or of the huge amounts of war materiel provided to the Soviet Union by the British. Instead, Stalin promoted what he called the Great Patriotic War, in which the mighty Soviet bear had taken on and defeated Hitler's best. It was a mountain of revisionist lies, one laid on top of another. In many cases, the truth would remain hidden from the Soviet people for decades.

Stalin's drive for power in Eastern Europe had concerned the other Allied leaders long before Germany's unconditional surrender. One of their worst fears was the installation of Communist governments in Germany and nearby nations. British and American leaders were aware of Stalin's not-so-secret agenda and understood that the Soviet Union would have to be closely watched lest its ambitions jeopardize the rest of the world. Almost immediately, the Soviet Union replaced Nazi Germany as the greatest enemy of world freedom.

The Stand Against Communism

In the months following the end of World War II, President Harry Truman tried to assuage the fears of U.S. allies in Europe by making clear that any serious aggression by the Soviet Union would be decisively met with atomic weapons. Faced with a weapon of such awesome power, the thinking went, the Soviet Union would never risk an all-out war to spread its political ideology.

However, Stalin wasn't particularly intimidated by U.S. atomic weapons because the Soviet Union was close to creating a nuclear arsenal of its own—an achievement that would influence the coming Cold War like no other. More important at the time, Stalin steadfastly maintained a strong military presence in Eastern Europe as other Allied forces were rapidly withdrawing. With nothing to keep him in check but threats, Stalin had little difficulty installing Soviet-controlled Communist governments in Poland, Czechoslovakia, Bulgaria, Romania, Hungary, and the Soviet-occupied zone of Germany. Later, the Soviet sphere of influence would claim Albania and Yugoslavia.

The United States, Great Britain, and France occupied western Germany, and the Soviet Union occupied eastern Germany, with Berlin—also with three parts controlled by the western Allies and one by the Soviets—stuck in the Soviet occupation zone. The United States, Great Britain, and France struggled to get the Soviet Union to agree to a unified Germany, but Stalin held firm. He used this foothold to maintain Soviet power in the region, and the other occupying nations soon realized that no agreement would be reached with their former ally.

In June 1948, hoping to hold the Soviet Union in check, the United States, Great Britain, and France decided to unify their occupation zones into an independent nation to be known as the German Federal Republic.

The Soviet Union retaliated by cutting off all road, rail, and boat traffic to Allied-controlled West Berlin and stranding its more than 2 million residents. Stalin's goal was to force the western Allies to abandon their plans for a free German republic by starving the residents of West Berlin. But the United States and its Allies refused to cave in. Instead, they initiated the Berlin Airlift to deliver food by plane to the trapped West Berliners. Allied supply planes landed every six minutes, twenty-four hours a day, until Stalin finally lifted the blockade after 318 days.

FACT

Fearing that Stalin would next try to bring Communism to war-torn France and Italy, U.S. officials made a pre-emptive strike by sending food and billions of dollars in aid to Europe. The massive assistance program became known as the Marshall Plan after its designer, former Army Chief of Staff George C. Marshall, who had become secretary of state in 1947. In 1953, Marshall received the Nobel Peace Prize for his efforts.

In May 1949, the United States joined with eleven other nations to create the North Atlantic Treaty Organization (NATO). Uniting primarily for protection against Soviet aggression, the member nations agreed that an attack on one would be considered an attack on all, and that they would react accordingly. Turkey and Greece joined NATO in 1952, and when a newly armed West Germany joined in 1955, the Soviet Union responded by forming the Warsaw Pact, which included Albania, Bulgaria, Czechoslovakia, Hungary, Poland, Romania, and East Germany. The division between ally and enemy had never been more sharply drawn.

Stalin Spurs Advances Within the Soviet Union

Even though Stalin was spending much of his time grabbing what he could in Eastern Europe, he wasn't ignoring the home front. Realizing the need for a strong military force in the new world order, he authorized an all-out modernization of the Red Army and a dramatic increase in Soviet naval capability, including the construction of new battle cruisers, aircraft carriers, and submarines—many of them based on revolutionary concepts from the Nazis.

Indeed, the Soviet Union benefited greatly from information derived from captured German technology and the scientists who created it, particularly in the area of rocketry. Soon after the war, the Soviets began experimenting with a wide variety of missile concepts. The program would eventually lead to the launching of Sputnik—the first man-made object to be sent into Earth orbit. The success of Sputnik fueled the Soviet weapons and space programs and sent waves of fear down the backs of many Americans. Would the Soviets use this new technology to attack America from space? Not to be outdone, the United States initiated its own space program, and the so-called space race was under way.

In September 1949, the Soviet Union detonated an atomic bomb. In that instant, the United States lost its military superiority. To deliver its new weapons of mass destruction, Soviet scientists built a fleet of bombers based on the U.S. B-29 Superfortress. The information they used came from three of the American planes that were forced down in Siberia in 1944 after bombing runs against Japan. Soviet researchers secretly took the planes apart, studied their design, and were able to recreate them almost exactly. The threat of Soviet attack would be a cause of concern for many years to come.

The United Nations

The first use of the words *United Nations* was by U.S. President Franklin D. Roosevelt, who was referring only to the Allies. The term soon came to mean a world body, one that would succeed—and definitely be stronger than—the failed League of Nations.

U.S. Secretary of State Cordell Hull was the driving force behind the organization, helping write the charter. He is often referred to as "the Father of the United Nations." Discussions on the particulars of the U.N. took place in the late summer and early fall of 1944 at the Dumbarton Oaks Conference in Washington, D.C. Attending those talks were representatives of China, France, the United Kingdom, the United States, and the Soviet Union. Major details were worked out at this conference, paving the way for the formation of the world body. Discussions continued during the next several months, culminating in the United Nations Conference on April 25, 1945, in San Francisco. Two short months later, representatives of fifty countries signed the U.N. Charter. The United Nations officially began on October 24.

The Postwar Pacific

Postwar occupation and rebuilding went far more easily in Europe than in the Pacific, where Japanese troops were scattered throughout the region, requiring a huge influx of Allied occupation forces. The occupation of Japan went relatively smoothly once the nation had officially surrendered, but bringing peace to other regions proved far more difficult.

In China, for example, the civil war between General Chiang Kai-shek's Nationalist government and the Chinese Communists led by Mao Tse-tung quickly resumed. The Communists held much of northern China—an area invaded by the Soviets during the final weeks of the war—and were given key ports in the region by their Soviet comrades. At the same time, the Soviets refused to let Nationalist forces enter the region.

Figure 20-2
A Chinese soldier guarding a line of P-40 fighter planes.

Photo courtesy of the National Archives (208-AA-12X-21)

In September 1945, the United States sent 53,000 marines into northern China to oversee the disarmament of hundreds of thousands of Japanese troops there. The Chinese Communists vowed to fight if America tried to take Communist-held territory, and a few skirmishes between American forces and Chinese Communists did occur. By 1946, it became apparent to almost everyone that Chiang Kai-shek's government could not win against the better-led Communist forces. The United States tried to negotiate a peace agreement between the Nationalists and the Communists, but the talks proved fruitless. In mid-1949, Chiang Kai-shek led what remained of his army and his government to the island of Formosa, now known as Taiwan; and in October of that year, the Communists established the People's Republic of China. However, the United States refused to recognize the Communist regime and for many years afterward continued to view the Nationalist regime in Formosa as the rightful government of China.

Korea

Equally problematic was the occupation of Korea. The Soviet Union had sent forces across the Manchurian border into Japanese-occupied Korea on August 12, 1945, just before Japan surrendered. American occupation forces didn't arrive until early September, at which time the two nations tried to work out an equitable occupation arrangement. After much discussion, it was determined that the thirty-eighth parallel would be a temporary demarcation line between the two forces. In December, the United States and the Soviet Union agreed that a provisional government would be established in Korea, though the Soviet Union did everything in its power to prevent this from happening. The standoff was broken in 1948 with the creation of a democratic South Korea below the thirty-eighth parallel and a Soviet-supported Communist North Korea above the thirty-eighth parallel.

A restless peace continued between the two Koreas until June 1950, when North Korea invaded South Korea with the intent of reunification. The United States immediately sent military support, including ground troops, to the overpowered South Korean army in an attempt to keep the Communists at bay. The resulting war, which also drew in the People's Republic of China, lasted three years and cost 54,000 American lives. South Korea and North Korea finally agreed to a cease-fire in 1953.

Vietnam

Korea wasn't the only Pacific nation to be divided in half after the world war. Vietnam, formerly under French colonial rule, was under Japanese occupation during the war. However, the Japanese were strongly opposed in the northern part of the country by a Communist faction known as the Vietminh, under the leadership of Ho Chi Minh. During the war, the Vietminh received arms from the Allies and in turn offered aid and rescue to Allied fliers forced down in the region.

After the war, the Vietminh declared an independent nation and took control of much of northern Indochina, including the cities of Hanoi and Haiphong. Japanese troops in Indochina surrendered to British and Indian forces in the south, who tried to return that area to France, and to Chinese forces in the north. The Chinese then recognized the Vietminh as the region's official government and provided aid and arms in its battle for independence from French colonial rule. France began trying to re-establish control over Indochina in September 1945. It started in the south and in 1946 moved into the north, where it met strong resistance from Chinese troops aiding the Vietminh. Chinese forces later withdrew, but China continued to supply arms to the Vietminh. The French had great difficulty trying to dislodge the Communists, and the fighting came to a head in early 1954 when French troops in the town of Dien Bien Phu found themselves overwhelmed by well-armed Vietminh forces. The United States discussed sending troops to aid the beleaguered French, but public opinion strongly opposed American intervention. Dien Bien Phu fell in May 1954, and a peace conference resulted in French Indochina being divided into two regions: Communist North Vietnam and democratic South Vietnam.

Continuing hostilities between the two nations would eventually bring American advisers and, later, American troops to the aid of South Vietnam. U.S. involvement in the Vietnam conflict would end in April 1975 with the fall of Saigon and unification of the nation under Communist control.

Appendix A

Resources

Books

Band of Brothers: E Company, 506th Regiment, 101st Airborne from Normandy to Hitler's Eagle's Nest, Stephen Ambrose (Simon & Schuster)

Blitzkrieg: From the Rise of Hitler to the Fall of Dunkirk, Len Deighton (Castle Books)

Citizen Soldiers: The U.S. Army from the Normandy Beaches to the Bulge to the Surrender of Germany, Stephen Ambrose (Simon & Schuster)

D-Day June 6, 1944: The Climactic Battle of World War II, Stephen Ambrose (Simon & Schuster)

The Deadly Brotherhood: The American Combat Soldier in World War II, John C. McManus (Presidio)

Flags of Our Fathers, James Bradley with Ron Powers (Bantam)

The Greatest Generation, Tom Brokaw (Random House)

The Greatest Generation Speaks: Letters and Reflections, Tom Brokaw (Random House)

Hitler's Last Gamble: The Battle of the Bulge December 1944–January 1945, Trevor Dupuy (HarperPerennial)

The Illustrated Book of World War II, Charles Messenger (Thunder Bay Press)

Jane's Naval History of WWII, Bernard Ireland (HarperCollins)

Memoirs of the Second World War, Winston Churchill (Houghton Mifflin)

The Second World War, John Keegan (Penguin Books)

The Second World War: A Complete History, Martin Gilbert (Henry Holt)

The Second World War in the East, H. P. Willmott (Cassell)

Stalingrad: The Infernal Cauldron, Stephen Walsh (Thomas Dunne Books)

The Victors: Eisenhower and His Boys: The Men of World War II, Stephen E. Ambrose (Simon & Schuster)

Victory at Sea: WWII in the Pacific, James Dunnigan and Albert Nofi (Quill)

The War in the Pacific: From Pearl Harbor to Tokyo Bay, Harry A. Gailey (Presidio)

War Movies: Classic Conflict on Film, Mike Mayo (Visible Ink Press)

The Wars of America, Robert Leckie (Castle Books)

We Band of Angels: The Untold Story of American Nurses Trapped on Bataan by the Japanese, Elizabeth M. Norman (Random House)

World War II in Photographs, Richard Holmes (Carlton)

Web Sites

Cold War Museum: *www.coldwar.org*

Drop Zone Virtual Museum: *www.thedropzone.org*

Memphis Belle Memorial Association, Memphis, TN: *www.memphisbelle.com*
The Valour & the Horror: Canada at War: *www.valourandhorror.com*
War Eagles Air Museum, Santa Teresa, NM: *www.war-eagles-air-museum.com*
The War Page: *www.thewarpage.com*
WASP-WWII: *www.wasp-wwii.org*
World War II Living Memorial: *www.seniornet.org/ww2/*
World War II US Veterans Web site: *http://.ww2.vet.org*
World War II Web Site Association: *www.ww2wa.com* (Includes links to many other sites.)
WWII Poster Collection, Government Publications Department of Northwestern University Library: *www.library.northwestern.edu/govinfo/collections/wwii-posters*

Organizations

The American Legion: National headquarters, P.O. Box 1055, Indianapolis, IN 46206. Web site: *www.legion.org*
Disabled American Veterans: National headquarters, 3725 Alexandria Pike, Cold Springs, KY 41076. Web site: *www.dav.org*
Veterans of Foreign Wars: National headquarters, 406 West 34th Street, Kansas City, MO 64111. Web site: *www.vfw.org*

Museums and Memorials

Washington, D.C., houses many memorials commemorating those who fought in other wars. Among these is the National World War II Memorial, at the east end of the Reflecting Pool between the Lincoln Memorial and the Washington Monument. The memorial opened to the public on April 29, 2004, and was dedicated one month later, on May 29. The memorial is essentially a group of fifty-six pillars and two facing arches in a semicircle around a central plaza. Each pillar has on it the name of the then-forty-eight states. The other eight represent the Alaska Territory, the Territory of Hawaii, the District of Columbia, American Samoa, Guam, the Commonwealth of the Philippines, Puerto Rico, and the U.S. Virgin Islands. The northern end of the memorial is dedicated to the Atlantic Theatre; the southern end is dedicated to the Pacific Theatre. A highlight of the memorial is the Freedom Wall, which contains the Field of Stars, a display of 4,048 gold stars, each representing 100 American military personnel killed in the war. Other details include an excerpt from Dwight D. Eisenhower's famous speech before the D-Day landings and an illustration of the irreverent Kilroy.

Other museums and memorials related to World War II include:

- The United States Holocaust Memorial Museum is also in Washington, D.C. Encompassing a massive amount of information, the museum includes several permanent exhibitions, including a reproduction of a railcar that took internees to their fates, as well as the Hall of Remembrance and the Children's Tile Wall. Phone: (202) 488-0400. Web site: *www.ushmm.org.*
- The USS *Arizona* Memorial is one memorial that has some depth to it. The memorial building sits directly above the *Arizona*, which sank on December 7, 1941, during the Pearl Harbor attack, killing 1,177. An accompanying onshore building provides more information about the attack and the war. Phone: (808) 422-0561. Web site: *www.nps.gov/usar.*
- Airborne & Special Operations Museum, P.O. Box 89, Fayetteville, NC 28302. Phone: (910) 483-3003. Web site: *www.asomf.org.*
- American Airpower Heritage Museum, P.O. Box 62000, Midland, TX 79711. This museum houses the largest collection of war-era nose art in the world. Phone: (915) 563-1000. Web site: *www.airpowermuseum.org.*
- Marine Corps War Memorial, on the grounds of Arlington National Cemetery in Arlington, VA. The memorial depicts the raising of the American flag over Iwo Jima but is dedicated to all marines who have given their lives in the defense of the United States.
- The National D-Day Museum, 945 Magazine Street, New Orleans, LA 70130. Phone: (504) 527-6012. Web site: *www.ddaymuseum.org.*
- The National Warplane Museum, 17 Aviation Drive, Horseheads, NY 14845. Phone: (607) 739-8200. Web site: *www.warplane.org.*
- The Navy Museum, Washington Navy Yard, Building 76, 805 Kidder Breese SE, Washington, D.C. 20374. Phone: (202) 433-4882. Web site: *www.history.navy.mil/branches/nhcorg8.htm.*
- The U.S. Air Force Museum, 1100 Spaatz Street, Wright-Patterson AFB, OH 45433. Phone: (937) 255-3286. Web site: *www.wpafb.af.mil/museum.*
- U.S. Army Aviation Museum, P.O. Box 620610, Fort Rucker, AL 36362. Phone: (888) 276-9286. Web site: *www.armyavmuseum.org.*
- U.S. Army Medical Department Museum, P.O. Box 340244, Fort Sam Houston, TX 78234-6189. Phone: (210) 221-6277. Web site: *http://amedd/museum/giftshop.com.htm.*
- U.S. Army Ordnance Museum, Attn: ATSL-A-M, Aberdeen Proving Ground, MD 21005. Phone: (410) 278-3602. Web site: *www.ordmusfound.org/contact.html.*
- U.S. Coast Guard Museum, U.S. Coast Guard Academy, 15 Mohegan Avenue, New London, CT 06320. Phone: (860) 444-8511. Web site: *www.uscg.mil/hq/g-cp/museum/museum index.asp.*

WWII Memorials in Other Countries

- Cemeteries in Northern France: Centered on Normandy but extending for many columns and rows are the massive cemeteries containing the graves of the thousands of soldiers who lost their lives during the liberation of northern France.
- Mamayev Kurgan Soviet Memorial: The Mamayev Kurgan memorial complex is dominated by the statue of Mother Russia and oversees the city of Volgograd in southern Russia. The name literally means "Hill of Mamai," named after a medieval commander of the Tatar Golden Horde. Today, it is the site of a memorial complex commemorating the Battle of Stalingrad, which raged between 1942 and 1943. The battle was a decisive Soviet victory over the Axis and one of the turning points of the war.
- Memorial to the Murdered Jews of Europe: This memorial in downtown Berlin is a quite impressive representation of the horror caused by Nazi extermination policies. Not far from the famed Brandenburg Gate, the monument consists of a large number of stone blocks, each one representing a number of Jews killed in Europe during the War.

Appendix B

The Holocaust in Numbers

The exact number of Jews killed by the Germans remains controversial, though the generally accepted figure is between 5.7 million and 6 million. One of the most comprehensive estimates was prepared by Yehuda Bauer of the Yad Vashem Research Institute, which was created in 1953 by the Israeli Knesset to study the Holocaust. Bauer broke down the numbers by country this way:

Country	Number Who Died
Austria	65,000
Belgium and Luxembourg	24,700
Czechoslovakia	277,000
France	83,000
Germany	125,000
Greece	65,000
Hungary	402,000
Italy	7,500
Netherlands	106,000
Norway	760
Polish-Soviet territory	4,565,000
Romania	40,000
Yugoslavia	60,000

Appendix C

World War II Timeline

1939

SEPTEMBER

1	The Invasion of Poland begins at 4:30 A.M. with the German Luftwaffe attacking several targets in Poland. The United Kingdom and France demand Germany's immediate withdrawal.
1	The United Kingdom home front is opened as the government declares general mobilization of the British army and begins evacuation plans in preparation of German air attacks.
3	The politics and diplomacy of World War II begin with frantic government responses to the attack on Poland. The United Kingdom, along with Australia and New Zealand, declare war at 11:15 A.M. France joins the war at 5:00 P.M.
3	The Second Battle of the Atlantic begins as the German navy goes into action.
4	Allied air operations in Europe begin with Royal Air Force raids on German naval targets.
7	French patrols enter Germany near Saarbrücken.
10	Canada declares war on Germany.
17	The Soviet Union invades Poland from the east, occupying the territory east of the Curzon line as well as Białystok and Eastern Galicia.
18	Warsaw is surrounded by German troops.
25	German home front measures begin with food rationing.
27–28	Extensive bombardments of Warsaw.
28	The Polish capital, Warsaw, surrenders to the Germans.

OCTOBER

5	The Soviet Union begins talks with Finland to adjust the border between the two countries.
6	Polish resistance in the Polish September Campaign comes to an end. Finland begins mobilizing its army. Hitler speaks before the Reichstag, declaring a desire for a conference with Britain and France to restore peace.
9	Hitler issues orders to prepare for the invasion of Belgium, France, Luxembourg, and the Netherlands.
10	The German navy suggests occupying Norway to Hitler.

14	The British battleship *Royal Oak* is sunk in Scapa Flow harbor by *U-47*.
19	Portions of Poland are formally inducted into Germany; the first Jewish ghetto is established at Lublin.

NOVEMBER

4	The Neutrality Acts are enacted in the United States, the "cash and carry" provisions for selling military supplies favor Britain and France.
8	An attempt to assassinate Hitler with a bomb while he makes a speech fails. In the Venlo Incident, two British intelligence agents are captured. Germans appoint Hans Frank governor general of Poland and begin accelerating the anti-Jewish programs there.
30	The Soviet Union attacks Finland starting the Winter War.

DECEMBER

13	Battle of the River Plate, British naval squadron attacks the *Admiral Graf Spee*.
14	The USSR is expelled from the League of Nations.
17	Admiral Graf Spee scuttled in Montevideo harbor.
18	The first Canadian troops arrive in Europe.
27	The first Indian troops arrive in France.
28	Meat rationing program begins in Britain.

1940

FEBRUARY

5	Britain and France decide to intervene in Norway to cut off the iron ore trade—in anticipation of an expected German occupation—and ostensibly to open a route to assist Finland. The operation is scheduled to start about March 20.
9	Erich von Manstein is placed in command of German Thirty-eighth Infantry Corps, removing him from planning the French invasion.
15	Soviet army captures Summa in Finland, thereby breaking through the Mannerheim Line.
16	British destroyer Cossack forcibly removes 299 British POWs from the German transport Altmark in neutral Norwegian territorial waters.
17	Manstein presents to Hitler his plans for invading France via the Ardennes forest.
21	General Nickolaus von Falkenhorst is placed in command of the upcoming German invasion of Norway. Work begins on the construction of Auschwitz.
24	The Ardennes plan for invading the west is adopted.

MARCH

3	Soviets begin attacks on Viipuri, Finland's second largest city.

5	Finland tells the Soviets they will agree to their terms for ending the war.
12	Finland signs a peace treaty with the Soviet Union.
16	German air raid on Scapa Flow causes first British civilian casualties.
18	Mussolini agrees with Hitler that Italy will enter the war "at an opportune moment."
21	Paul Reynaud becomes prime minister of France following Daladier's resignation the previous day.
28	Britain and France make a formal agreement that neither country will seek a separate peace with Germany.
30	Japan establishes a puppet regime at Nanking under Wang Jingwei.
APRIL	
3	Churchill is appointed chairman of the Ministerial Defense Committee following the resignation of Lord Chatfield.
4	Hitler gives the go ahead for the invasion of Norway and Denmark.
8	Allied mining of Norwegian waters is put into action.
9	Germany invades Denmark and Norway; Denmark surrenders.
10	First Battle of Narvik, British destroyers and aircraft successfully make a surprise attack against a larger German naval force. A second attack on April 13 will also be a British success.
12	British troops occupy the Danish Faroe Islands.
14	British and French troops begin landing in Norway.
30	British and French troops begin evacuating from Norway.
MAY	
5	Norwegian government in exile established in London.
10	Germany invades Belgium, France, Luxembourg, and the Netherlands. Winston Churchill becomes prime minister of the United Kingdom upon the resignation of Neville Chamberlain.
11	Luxembourg occupied.
13	Dutch government in exile established in London.
14	Rotterdam is carpet bombed by the Luftwaffe. The Netherlands surrender with the exception of Zealand.
14	The creation of the Local Defence Volunteers (the Home Guard) is announced by Anthony Eden.
17	In the Netherlands the province of Zealand surrenders.
26	Operation Dynamo, the Allied evacuation from Dunkirk, begins.

28	Belgium surrenders. Germans evacuate Narvik.
JUNE	
3	Last day of Operation Dynamo; 224,686 British and 121,445 French and Belgian troops have been evacuated. Germans bomb Paris.
10	Italy declares war on France and the United Kingdom. Norway surrenders.
11	French government decamps to Tours.
13	Paris occupied by German troops; French government moves again, this time to Bordeaux.
16	Philippe Pétain becomes premier of France upon the resignation of Reynaud's government.
17	Sinking of liner Lancastria off St Nazaire while being used as a British troopship—Britain's worst maritime disaster since the Anglo-Dutch wars.
18	General de Gaulle forms the Comité Français de la Libération Nationale, a French government in exile. Estonia, Latvia, and Lithuania are occupied by the Soviet Union.
25	France officially surrenders to Germany at 12:35 A.M.
28	General de Gaulle recognized by British as leader of Free French.
30	Germany invades the Channel Islands.
JULY	
1	Channel Islands occupied by German forces. French government moves to Vichy.
2	Hitler orders preparation of plans for invasion of Britain, code-named Operation Sea Lion.
4	Destruction of the French Fleet at Mers-el-Kebir by the Royal Navy; Vichy French government breaks off diplomatic relations with Britain in protest.
5	Romania aligns itself with the Axis.
10	Battle of Britain begins.
AUGUST	
2	General de Gaulle sentenced to death in absentia by a French military court.
4	Italian forces invade and occupy British Somaliland.
17	Hitler declares a blockade of the British Isles.
19	Italians take Berbera, capital of British Somaliland.
25	First British air raid on Berlin.
SEPTEMBER	
3	Operation Sea Lion set for 21 September.
10	Operation Sea Lion postponed until 24 September.
13	Italy invades Egypt.

14	Operation Sea Lion postponed until 27 September, the last day of the month with suitable tides for the invasion.
16	Selective Training and Service Act of 1940 introduces the first peacetime conscription in U.S. history.
17	Hitler postpones Operation Sea Lion until further notice.
27	The Tripartite Pact is signed by Japan, Germany, and Italy.

OCTOBER

7	Germany invades Romania to restrain the Romanian army.
12	Any German invasion of Britain postponed until Spring 1941 at the earliest.
16	Draft registration begins in the United States.
28	Italy issues ultimatum to Greece; Prime Minister Metaxas replies "So it is war" (celebrated as "Okhi!" ("No!") Day in Greece); Italian forces invade Greece.

NOVEMBER

11	British naval forces launch attack against Italian navy at Taranto. Swordfish bombers from HMS *Illustrious* damage three battleships, two cruisers, and multiple auxiliary craft.

DECEMBER

8	Franco rules out Spanish entry into the war.
9	Operation Compass: British Western Desert Force begins offensive against Italian forces in North Africa.
11	Greece invades Italian-held Albania.
28	Italy requests German assistance in Albania against Greek forces.

1941

JANUARY

10	Lend-Lease is introduced into the U.S. Congress.
12	British, Australian, and New Zealand troops capture Tobruk.
19	British troops (Fourth and Fifth Indian Divisions) attack Italian-held Eritrea, reversing the tide of the East Africa Campaign.

FEBRUARY

3	Germany forcibly restores Pierre Laval to office in occupied Vichy, France.
11	Lieutenant-General Erwin Rommel arrives in Tripoli.

19	The start of the "three nights' Blitz" over Swansea, South Wales. Over these three nights of intensive bombing, which lasted a total of thirteen hours and forty-eight minutes, Swansea town center is almost completely obliterated by the 896 high-explosive bombs employed by the Luftwaffe. A total of 397 casualties and 230 deaths are reported. The blitz ends in the early hours of February 22.
25	Mogadishu, Italian Somaliland, captured by British forces.

MARCH

4	British commandos carry out attack on oil facilities at Narvik in Norway.
11	President Franklin Delano Roosevelt signs the Lend-Lease Act, allowing Britain, China, and other Allied nations to purchase military equipment and to defer payment until after the war.
25	Yugoslavia signs the Tripartite Pact.
27	Crown Prince Peter becomes Peter II of Yugoslavia and takes control of Yugoslavia after an army coup overthrows the pro-German government of the Prince Regent. Japanese spy Takeo Yoshikawa arrives in Honolulu, Hawaii, and begins to study the United States fleet at Pearl Harbor.
29	Battle of Cape Matapan—British naval forces defeat those of Italy off the Peloponnesus coast in the Mediterranean, sinking five warships. Battle started on March 27.
30	The Afrika Korps begins the German offensive in North Africa.

APRIL

6	German, Hungarian, and Italian forces invade Yugoslavia and Greece. Italian army is ousted from Addis Ababa, Ethiopia, though a guerrilla war continues until Italy surrenders in September 1943.
12	Belgrade surrenders. Siege of Tobruk begins.
13	Japan and the Soviet Union sign a neutrality pact.
17	Yugoslavia surrenders; government in exile formed in London.
27	Athens occupied by German troops.

MAY

9	United Kingdom takes control of Iraq and is reinforced by the arrival of Twenty-first Indian Division at Basra. The German submarine U-110 is captured by the British Royal Navy. On board is the latest Enigma cryptography machine, which Allied cryptographers later use to break coded German messages.
10	Rudolf Hess captured in Scotland after bailing out of his plane. The United Kingdom's House of Commons is damaged by the Luftwaffe in an air raid.

15	Operation Brevity is the first, unsuccessful attempt launched to relieve the Siege of Tobruk.
20	German paratroopers attack Crete.
24	British battle cruiser *Hood* sunk by German battleship *Bismarck*. Greek government leaves Crete for Cairo.
26	In the North Atlantic, Fairey Swordfish aircraft from the British carrier *Ark Royal* fatally cripple the German battleship *Bismarck* in torpedo attack.
27	German battleship *Bismarck* is sunk in North Atlantic.

JUNE

1	Allies complete the withdrawal from Crete.
9	Finland initiates mobilization and puts some units under German command.
14	All German and Italian assets in the United States are frozen.
15	Operation Battleaxe attempts and fails to relieve the Siege of Tobruk.
22	Germany invades the Soviet Union in Operation Barbarossa.
23	Hungary and Slovakia declare war on the Soviet Union.
26	Finland declares war on the Soviet Union.
28	Albania declares war on the Soviet Union.

JULY

4	Mass murder of Polish scientists and writers committed by German troops in captured Polish city of Lwów.
5	British government rules out possibility of negotiated peace. German troops reach the Dnieper River.
12	Britain and Soviet Union sign mutual defence agreement, promising not to sign any form of separate peace agreement with Germany.
13	Montenegro starts the first popular uprising in Europe against the Axis powers.
26	In response to the Japanese occupation of French Indo-China, U.S. president Franklin D. Roosevelt orders the seizure of all Japanese assets in the United States.
31	Under instructions from Adolf Hitler, Nazi official Hermann Göring orders SS general Reinhard Heydrich to "submit to me as soon as possible a general plan of the administrative material and financial measures necessary for carrying out the desired final solution of the Jewish question."

AUGUST

6	American and British governments warn Japan not to invade Thailand.

9	Franklin D. Roosevelt and Winston Churchill meet at Argentia, Newfoundland; the Atlantic Charter is created as a result.

SEPTEMBER

4	The USS *Greer* becomes the first United States ship fired upon by a German submarine in the war, even though the United States is a neutral power. Tension heightens between the two nations as a result.
6	The requirement to wear the Star of David with the word "Jew" inscribed is extended to all Jews over the age of six in German-occupied areas.
8	Siege of Leningrad—German forces begin a siege against the Soviet Union's second-largest city, Leningrad. Stalin orders the Volga Deutsche deported to Siberia.
11	Franklin D. Roosevelt orders the United States Navy to shoot on sight if any ship or convoy is threatened.
19	Nazis take Kiev.

OCTOBER

2	Operation Typhoon—Germany begins an all-out offensive against Moscow.
8	In its invasion of the Soviet Union, Germany reaches the Sea of Azov with the capture of Mariupol.
16	Soviet Union government moves to Kuibyshev, but Stalin remains in Moscow.
17	The destroyer USS *Kearney* is torpedoed and damaged near Iceland, killing eleven sailors—the first American military casualties of the war.
18	General Hideki Tojo becomes the 40th prime minister of Japan.
30	Franklin Delano Roosevelt approves $1 billion in Lend-Lease aid to the Soviet Union.
31	The U.S. destroyer *Reuben James* is torpedoed by a German U-boat near Iceland, killing more than 100.

NOVEMBER

6	Soviet leader Joseph Stalin addresses the Soviet Union for only the second time during his three-decade rule (the first time was earlier that year on July 2). He states that even though 350,000 troops were killed in German attacks so far, the Germans have lost 4.5 million soldiers (a gross exaggeration) and that Soviet victory was near.
12	Battle of Moscow—Temperatures around Moscow drop to 12°C, and the Soviet Union launches ski troops for the first time against the freezing German forces near the city.
13	The British aircraft carrier *Ark Royal* is hit by German U-boat *U-81*.
14	HMS *Ark Royal* capsizes and sinks.

17	Joseph Grew, the U.S. ambassador to Japan, cables the State Department that Japan has plans to launch an attack against Pearl Harbor, Hawaii (his cable is ignored).
18	British troops launch Operation Crusader in Libya, North Africa, and at last relieve the Siege of Tobruk.
19	The Australian light cruiser Sydney and the German auxiliary cruiser Kormoran sink each other off the coast of Western Australia.
22	Britain issues an ultimatum to Finland to end war with Russia or face war with the Allies.
24	The United States grants Lend-Lease to the Free French.
26	A Japanese attack fleet of thirty-three warships and auxiliary craft, including six aircraft carriers, sails from northern Japan for the Hawaiian Islands. The Hull note ultimatum is delivered to Japan by the United States.
27	Battle of Moscow—Germans reach their closest approach to Moscow. They are subsequently stopped by cold weather and attacks by the Soviets.

DECEMBER

5	The United Kingdom declares war on Finland, Hungary, and Romania.
7	Japan launches aerial attack on Pearl Harbor and declares war on the United States and the United Kingdom. Air attacks also on Hong Kong, Singapore, Malaya, Thailand, the Philippines, and Shanghai.
8	Japan invades Malaya; the United States and the United Kingdom declare war on Japan; the Netherlands declares war on Japan.
9	China officially declares war on Japan.
10	British battleships *Repulse* and *Prince of Wales* sunk by Japanese air attack.
11	Germany and Italy declare war on the United States, United States reciprocates and declares war on Germany and Italy; U.S. forces repel a Japanese landing attempt at Wake Island.
12	The United States and the United Kingdom declare war on Romania and Bulgaria in response to those countries' declarations of war on them. India declares war on Japan. United States seizes French ship *Normandie*.
13	Hungary declares war on the United States and the United Kingdom, and they reciprocate and declare war on Hungary.
16	Japan invades Borneo.
17	Battle of Sevastopol begins.
18	Japanese troops land on Hong Kong.
19	Hitler becomes supreme commander in chief of the German army.

23	A second Japanese landing attempt on Wake Island is successful, and the American garrison surrenders after hours of fighting.
25	Hong Kong surrenders; U.K. forces retake Benghazi.
27	British commandos raid the Norwegian port of Vaagso, causing Hitler to reinforce the garrison and defenses.
28	Operation Anthropoid begins (the assassination of Reinhard Heydrich).

1942

JANUARY

1	The term "United Nations" is first officially used to describe the Allied pact.
2	Manila is captured by Japanese forces. The Japanese admiral stays in Solvec (owned by Charles Henry de Silva), Philippines.
7	Siege of the Bataan Peninsula begins.
11	Japanese troops capture Kuala Lumpur, Malaysia. Japan declares war on the Netherlands and invades the Netherlands East Indies.
19	Japanese forces invade Burma.
20	Nazis at the Wannsee conference in Berlin decide that the "final solution to the Jewish problem" is relocation, and later extermination.
23	The Battle of Rabaul begins.
25	Thailand declares war on the United States and United Kingdom. Japanese troops invade the Solomon Islands.
26	The first American forces arrive in Europe, landing in Northern Ireland.
31	The last organized Allied forces leave Malaya, ending the fifty-four-day battle.

FEBRUARY

11	Operation Cerberus—Flotilla of Kriegsmarine ships dash from Brest through the English Channel to northern ports; British fail to sink any of them.
15	Singapore surrenders to Japanese forces.
19	Japanese warplanes attack Darwin, Australia. President Franklin D. Roosevelt signs executive order 9066, allowing the military to define areas as exclusionary zones. These zones affect the Japanese on the West Coast and Germans and Italians primarily on the East Coast.
22	President Franklin Delano Roosevelt orders General Douglas MacArthur out of the Philippines as American defense of the nation collapses.

23	Japanese submarine *I-17* fires sixteen high-explosive shells toward an oil refinery near Santa Barbara, California, causing little damage.
27	Battle of the Java Sea begins; the USS *Langley*, the first U.S aircraft carrier, is sunk by Japanese warplanes off Java.
28	Japanese land forces invade Java.
MARCH	
10	Fall of Rangoon.
17	U.S. general Douglas MacArthur arrives in Australia after abandoning his headquarters in the Philippines.
APRIL	
3	Japanese forces begin an all-out assault on the U.S. and Filipino troops on the Bataan Peninsula. Bataan falls on April 9, and the Bataan Death March begins.
5	The Japanese navy attacks Colombo in Ceylon (Sri Lanka). Royal Navy Cruisers *Cornwall* and *Dorsetshire* are sunk southwest of the island.
9	The Japanese navy launches air raid on Trincomalee in Ceylon (Sri Lanka); Royal Navy aircraft carrier *Hermes* and Royal Australian Navy destroyer *Vampire* are sunk off the country's East Coast.
18	Doolittle raid on Nagoya, Tokyo, and Yokohama.
MAY	
4	The Battle of the Coral Sea starts.
5	Operation Ironclad—British forces begin the invasion of Madagascar to keep the Vichy French territory from falling to a possible Japanese invasion.
6	On Corregidor, the last American forces in the Philippines surrender to the Japanese.
8	The Battle of the Coral Sea comes to an end. This is the first time in naval history where two enemy fleets fought without seeing each other.
12	Second Battle of Kharkov—Soviet army initiates a major offensive in the eastern Ukraine. During the battle, they will capture the city of Kharkov from the German army, only to be encircled and destroyed.
15	In the United States, a bill creating the Women's Auxiliary Army Corps (WAAC) is signed into law.
27	Operation Anthropoid—Reinhard Heydrich assassinated in Prague.
JUNE	
1	Mexico declares war on Germany, Italy, and Japan.

4	The Battle of Midway takes place. Reinhard Heydrich dies in Prague, assassinated by Czechoslovak paratroopers (Operation Anthropoid).
7	Japanese forces invade the Aleutian Islands. This is the first invasion of American soil in 128 years.
9	Nazis burn the Czech village of Lidice as reprisal for the killing of Reinhard Heydrich.
12	Future essayist Anne Frank receives a diary for her thirteenth birthday.
18	Manhattan Project started.
21	Afrika Korps recaptures Tobruk.
28	Operation Blue, the German plan to capture Stalingrad and the Russian oil fields in the Caucasus, begins.
JULY	
1	First Battle of El Alamein begins.
3	Guadalcanal falls to the Japanese.
9	Anne Frank's family goes into hiding in an attic above her father's office in an Amsterdam warehouse.
18	The Germans test fly the Messerschmitt Me-262 using only its jets for the first time.
19	Battle of the Atlantic—German grand admiral Karl Dönitz orders the last U-boats to withdraw from their U.S. Atlantic coast positions in response to an effective American convoy system.
21	Japanese establish beachhead on the north coast of New Guinea in the Buna-Gona area. Small Australian force begins rearguard action on the Kokoda Track Campaign.
22	The systematic deportation of Jews from the Warsaw ghetto begins.
27	First Battle of El Alamein ends.
AUGUST	
7	Operation Watchtower begins the Battle of Guadalcanal as American forces invade Gavutu, Guadalcanal, Tulagi, and Tanambogo in the Solomon Islands.
8	In Washington, D.C., six German would-be saboteurs are executed (two others were cooperative and received life imprisonment instead).
13	General Bernard Montgomery is appointed commander of British Eighth Army in North Africa.
19	Operation Jubilee, a raid by British and Canadian forces on Dieppe, France, ends in disaster.
22	Brazil declares war on the Axis countries.

26	Battle of Milne Bay begins: Japanese forces launch full-scale assault on Australian base near the eastern tip of New Guinea.
30	Luxembourg is formally annexed to the German Reich.

SEPTEMBER

1	Stalingrad is now completely encircled by German forces.
3	Australian and U.S. forces defeat Japanese forces at Milne Bay, the first outright defeat for Japanese land forces during the Pacific War. An attempt by the Germans to liquidate the Jewish ghetto in Lakhva leads to an uprising.
12	RMS *Laconia*, carrying civilians, Allied soldiers, and Italian POWs is torpedoed off the coast of West Africa and sinks.

OCTOBER

3	First successful launch of A4-rocket from Test Stand VII at Peenemünde, Germany. The rocket flies 147 kilometers wide and reaches a height of 84.5 kilometers and is therefore the first man-made object reaching space.
11	Battle of Cape Esperance—U.S. Navy ships intercept and defeat a Japanese fleet on their way to reinforce troops on Guadalcanal.
14	A German U-boat sinks the U.S. ferry *Caribou*, killing 137.
18	Hitler issues Commando Order, ordering all captured commandos to be executed immediately.
23	Second Battle of El Alamein begins with massive Allied bombardment of German positions.

NOVEMBER

1	Operation Supercharge, the Allied breakout at El Alamein, begins.
3	Second Battle of El Alamein ends; German forces under Erwin Rommel are forced to retreat during the night.
8	Operation Torch—Allied invasion of Vichy-controlled Morocco and Algeria begins as French Resistance coup in Algiers, in which 400 French civil resistants neutralize the Vichyist Nineteenth Army Corps and Vichy leaders (Juin, Darlan, etc.), helping the Allies to take Algiers, and from there the whole of French North Africa.
10	In violation of a 1940 armistice, Germany invades Vichy France following Admiral François Darlan's agreement to an armistice with the Allies in North Africa.
12	Battle of Guadalcanal begins between Japanese and American forces.
13	British Eighth Army recaptures Tobruk. In the Battle of Guadalcanal aviators from the USS *Enterprise* sink the Japanese battleship *Hiei*.

15	Battle of Guadalcanal ends. Although the U.S. Navy suffered heavy losses, it was able to retain control of Guadalcanal.
19	Battle of Stalingrad—Soviet Union forces under General Georgy Zhukov launch the Operation Uranus counterattacks at Stalingrad, turning the tide of the battle in the USSR's favor.
22	Battle of Stalingrad—The situation for the German attackers seems desperate, and General Friedrich Paulus sends Adolf Hitler a telegram saying that the German Sixth Army is surrounded.
23	German U-boat sinks SS *Ben Lomond* off the coast of Brazil. One crewman, Chinese second steward Poon Lim, is separated from the others and spends 130 days adrift until he is rescued April 3, 1943.
27	At Toulon, the French navy scuttles its ships and submarines to keep them out of German hands.

DECEMBER

2	Below the bleachers of Stagg Field at the University of Chicago, a team led by Enrico Fermi initiates the first self-sustaining nuclear chain reaction (a coded message, "The Italian navigator has landed in the new world," was then sent to President Franklin D. Roosevelt).

1943

JANUARY

14	Casablanca Conference of Allied leaders begins.
15	Japanese are driven off Guadalcanal.
18	Soviet officials announce they have broken the Wehrmacht's siege of Leningrad. The Jews in the Warsaw ghetto rise up for the first time.
23	Allies capture Tripoli, Libya.
27	Fifty bombers mount the first all-American air raid against Germany.
31	Large parts of the German Sixth Army at Stalingrad, including Field Marshal Paulus, surrender.

FEBRUARY

1	Vidkun Quisling is appointed prime minister of Norway by the Nazi occupiers.
2	In Russia, the Battle of Stalingrad comes to an end with the surrender of the German Sixth Army.
8	Battle of Guadalcanal—United States forces defeat Japanese troops.
11	General Eisenhower is selected to command the Allied armies in Europe.
14	Rostov-na-Donu, Russia, is liberated by the Red Army. Battle of the Kasserine Pass—German general Erwin Rommel and his Afrika Korps attack Allied defenses in Tunisia; it is the United States' first major battle defeat of the war.

16	Soviet Union reconquers Kharkov but is later driven out in the Third Battle of Kharkov.
MARCH	
2	Battle of the Bismarck Sea—United States and Australian forces sink Japanese convoy ships.
8	American forces are attacked by Japanese troops on Hill 700 in Bougainville in a battle that will last five days.
13	On Bougainville, Japanese troops end their assault on American forces at Hill 700. German forces liquidate the Jewish ghetto in Kraków.
22	The entire population of *Khatyn* in Belarus is burnt alive by the German occupation forces.
26	Battle of Komandorski Islands—U.S. Navy forces intercept Japanese attempting to reinforce a garrison at Kiska in the Aleutian Islands.
APRIL	
7	Bolivia declares war on Germany, Japan, and Italy.
13	Radio Berlin announces the discovery by Wehrmacht of mass graves of Poles killed by Soviets in the *Khatyn* massacre.
MAY	
7	Tunis captured by British First Army.
9	German and Italian forces in Tunisia announce surrender to British.
11	American troops invade Attu in the Aleutian Islands in an attempt to expel occupying Japanese forces.
12	Trident Conference begins in Washington, D.C., with Franklin D. Roosevelt and Winston Churchill taking part.
13	German Afrika Korps and Italian troops in North Africa surrender to Allied forces.
16	The Warsaw ghetto uprising ends.
24	Admiral Karl Dönitz orders the majority of U-Boats to withdraw from the Atlantic; Josef Mengele becomes chief medical officer in Auschwitz.
JUNE	
22	U.S. Army Forty-fifth Infantry Division lands in North Africa prior to training at Arzew, French Morocco, while serving in World War II.
JULY	
5	Battle of Kursk begins. An Allied invasion fleet sails to Sicily.
6	Americans and Japanese fight the Battle of Kula Gulf off Kolombangara.

10	The invasion of Sicily by the U.S. Army Forty-fifth Infantry Division marks the beginning of the Allied incursion into Axis-controlled Europe.
12	The Wehrmacht and the Red Army fight the Battle of Prokhorovka.
19	Rome is bombed by the Allies for the first time in the war.
22	Deportations of Jews from the Warsaw ghetto begins. The extermination camp Treblinka is opened.
24	Operation Gomorrah—British and Canadian planes begin bombing Hamburg by night, those of the Americans by day. By the end of the operation in November, 9,000 tons of explosives will have killed more than 30,000 people and destroyed 280,000 buildings.
25	In Italy the Gran Consiglio del Fascismo retires its consent to Mussolini; Mussolini is arrested, and the power is given to Maresciallo d'Italia Gen. Pietro Badoglio.
28	The British bombing of Hamburg causes a firestorm that kills 42,000 German civilians.
AUGUST	
6	Americans and Japanese fight the Battle of Vella Gulf off Kolombangara.
17	The U.S. Seventh Army under General George S. Patton arrives in Messina, Italy, followed several hours later by the British Eighth Army under Field Marshal Bernard L. Montgomery, thus completing the Allied conquest of Sicily.
23	The Battle of Kursk ends with a heavy defeat for the German forces.
29	Germany dissolves the Danish government after it refuses to deal with a wave of strikes and disturbances to the satisfaction of the German authorities.
SEPTEMBER	
3	Mainland Italy is invaded by Allied forces under Bernard L. Montgomery, for the first time in the war.
5	The 503rd Parachute Regiment under American general Douglas MacArthur lands and occupies Nadzab, just east of the port city of Lae in northeastern Papua New Guinea.
8	General Dwight D. Eisenhower publicly announces the surrender of Italy to the Allies. U.S. Air Force bombs Frascati, the German general headquarters for the Mediterranean zone.
9	Iran declares war on Germany under pressure of Allied forces who have occupied the country. Salerno landings in Italy.
23	Italian Social Republic founded in German-occupied parts of Northern Italy.
OCTOBER	
6	Americans and Japanese fight the Naval Battle of Vella Lavella.
13	The new government of Italy sides with the Allies and declares war on Germany.

| 18 | Chiang Kai-shek takes the oath of office as president of China. |
| 22 | RAF delivers a highly destructive air strike on the German industrial and population center of Kassel. |

NOVEMBER

1	Operation Goodtime—United States Marines land on Bougainville in the Solomon Islands.
2	Battle of Empress Augusta Bay—American and Japanese ships fight off Bougainville. British troops in Italy reach the Garigliano River.
6	The Red Army recaptures Kiev.
15	Allied Expeditionary Force for the invasion of Europe is officially formed. German SS leader Heinrich Himmler orders Gypsies and "part-Gypsies" to be put "on the same level as Jews and placed in concentration camps."
16	After flying from Britain, 160 American bombers strike a hydroelectric power facility and heavy water factory in German-controlled Vemork, Norway; Japanese submarine sinks surfaced U.S. submarine *Corvina* near Truk.
18	Royal Air Force planes bomb Berlin, causing only light damage and killing 131. The RAF lose nine aircraft and fifty-three aviators.
20	Battle of Tarawa—U.S. Marines begin landing on Tarawa and Makin atolls in the Gilbert Islands and take heavy fire from Japanese shore guns.
22	Franklin D. Roosevelt, Winston Churchill, and Chiang Kai-shek meet in Cairo, Egypt, to discuss ways to defeat Japan.
25	Battle of Cape St. George—Americans and Japanese navies battle between Buka and New Ireland.
27	The Cairo Declaration is released.
28	Tehran Conference—Franklin D. Roosevelt, Winston Churchill, and Joseph Stalin meet in Tehran to discuss war strategy (on November 30 they established an agreement concerning a planned June 1944 invasion of Europe codenamed Operation Overlord).

DECEMBER

| 4 | Bolivia declares war on all Axis powers; in Yugoslavia, resistance leader Marshal Tito proclaims a provisional democratic Yugoslav government in exile. |
| 24 | U.S. general Dwight D. Eisenhower becomes the Supreme Allied Commander in Europe. |

1944

JANUARY

4	The Battle of Monte Cassino begins.
14	The Soviet troops start the offensive at Leningrad and Novgorod.
15	The Twenty-seventh Polish Home Army Infantry Division recreated, marking the start of Operation Tempest.
17	British forces in Italy cross the Garigliano River.
18	Siege of Leningrad ends.
20	The Royal Air Force drops 2,300 tons of bombs on Berlin; The U.S. Army Thirty-sixth Infantry Division in Italy attempts to cross the Rapido River.
22	Operation Shingle—Allied assault on Anzio, Italy, begins. The U.S. Army Forty-fifth Infantry Division stand their ground at Anzio for four months.
27	The two-year Siege of Leningrad is lifted.
29	The Battle of Cisterna takes place.
30	U.S. troops invade Majuro, Marshall Islands.
31	American forces land on Kwajalein Atoll and other islands in the Japanese-held Marshalls.

FEBRUARY

3	U.S. troops capture the Marshall Islands.
8	The plan for the invasion of France, Operation Overlord, is confirmed.
14	Supreme Headquarters of the Allied Expeditionary Force established in Britain. Anti-Japanese revolt on Java.
15	Battle of Monte Cassino—Monte Cassino's monastery is destroyed by Allied bombing.
17	Battle of Eniwetok Atoll begins. It will end in an American victory on February 22.
20	"Big Week" begins with American bomber raids on German aircraft manufacturing centers.
28–29	Battle of Los Negros and Operation Brewer—Admiralty Islands are invaded by U.S. forces.

MARCH

15	Battle of Monte Cassino—Allied aircraft bomb German-held town and stage an assault.
17	German forces in Ribnita kill almost 400 prisoners, Soviet citizens, and antifascist Romanians.
18	German forces occupy Hungary.
23	Italian Resistance attacks Nazis marching in via Rasella in Rome; thirty-three Nazis are killed.
24	In retaliation, the Fosse Ardeatine massacre occurs; 335 Italians are killed, including 75 Jews and over 200 members of the Italian Resistance from various groups.

APRIL

14	Odessa is liberated by Soviet forces.

MAY

8	D-Day for Operation Overlord set for June 5.
9	The German army evacuates Sevastopol.
12	Soviet troops finalize the liberation of Crimea.
18	Battle of Monte Cassino ends with an Allied victory; Polish troops hoist their red and white flag on the ruins. Deportation of Crimean Tatars by the Soviet Union government.

JUNE

2	The provisional French government is established.
4	Operation Overlord postponed twenty-four hours due to high seas; American, English, and French troops enter Rome.
5	Rome falls to the Allies. It is the first capital of an Axis nation to fall; more than 1,000 British bombers drop 5,000 tons of bombs on German gun batteries on the Normandy coast in preparation for D-Day.
6	Battle of Normandy—Operation Overlord, code named D-Day, commences with the landing of 155,000 Allied troops on the beaches of Normandy in France. The allied soldiers quickly break through the Atlantic Wall and push inland in the largest amphibious military operation in history.
7	Bayeux liberated by British troops.
9	Stalin launches an offensive against Finland with the intent of defeating Finland before pushing for Berlin.
10	In the Oradour-sur-Glane massacre in France, 642 men, women, and children are killed.
13	Germany launches a V1 Flying Bomb attack on England.
15	Battle of Saipan—United States invades the island of Saipan.
21	Allied offensive in Burma.
22	Operation Bagration—Soviet forces attack to clear the Germans from Belarus, which results in the destruction of the German Army Group Center, possibly the greatest defeat of the Wehrmacht during WWII. In the Burma Campaign, the Battle of Kohima ends in a British victory.
25	The Battle of Tali-Ihantala—Finnish and Soviet troops begin the largest battle ever to be fought in the Nordic countries.
26	Cherbourg liberated by American troops.

JULY

3	Minsk is liberated by Soviet forces.
9	Caen is liberated by the Allies.
18	Infamous "death ride of the armored divisions" as British Thirteenth Corps repulsed by heavy German counterattack.
19	The entire government of Japan resigns; Emperor Hirohito asks General Kuniaka Koiso to form a new government.
24	Majdanek concentration camp is liberated by Soviet forces.

AUGUST

1	Warsaw uprising by the Polish Home Army commences.
4	Florence liberated by the Allies.
10	Guam liberated by American troops.
15	Operation Dragoon begins with amphibious Allied landings in southern France.
19	French Resistance begins uprising in Paris.
20	Operation Jassy-Kishinev begins in former Bessarabia.
23	Romania surrenders.
25	Paris is liberated; de Gaulle and Free French parade triumphantly down the Champs-Élysées.
29	The Slovak national uprising breaks out.

SEPTEMBER

2	Allied troops enter Belgium.
3	Brussels liberated by British Second Army while Lyon is liberated by French and American troops.
4	Antwerp liberated by British Eleventh Armored Division.
6	Ghent and Liège liberated by British troops.
8	Ostend liberated by Canadian troops. Russians invade Bulgaria.
9	De Gaulle forms provisional government in France. Bulgaria makes peace with the USSR, then declares war on Germany.
10	Luxembourg liberated by U.S. First Army.
11	First Allied troops enter Germany.
17	Operation Market Garden, the attempted liberation of Arnhem, begins.
19	Nancy liberated by U.S. First Army. Armistice is signed between the Soviet Union and Finland.

25	British troops pull out of Arnhem with failure of Operation Market Garden. Over 6,000 paratroopers are captured.
30	German garrison in Calais surrenders to Canadian troops.

OCTOBER

1	Soviet troops enter Yugoslavia.
2	Germans finally succeed in putting down Warsaw uprising by Polish Home Army.
4	German troops withdrawn from Greece; Allied troops enter Greece.
5	Canadian troops cross the border into the Netherlands.
6	Soviet and Czechoslovak troops enter northeastern Slovakia.
14	Athens liberated by Allies.
20	Allies invade Philippines. The Red Army and Yugoslav partisans under the command of Josip Broz Tito liberate Belgrade.
21	Aachen occupied by U.S. First Army; it is the first German city to be captured.
23	Battle of Leyte Gulf begins; largest sea battle in history.
25	Russians invade Norway.

NOVEMBER

2	Canadian troops take Zeebrugge in Belgium; Belgium now entirely liberated.
4	Remaining Axis forces in Greece surrender.
24	Strasbourg liberated by French troops.
29	Albania liberated by Allies.

DECEMBER

16	The Battle of the Bulge—German forces begin an attempt to break through Allied lines in the Ardennes region.

1945

JANUARY

14–27	Operation Blackcock—Roer Triangle is cleared by the Second British Army.
16	U.S. First and Third Armies link up following Battle of the Bulge.
17	Warsaw liberated by Red Army troops.
27	The Battle of the Bulge officially ends. Auschwitz concentration camp is liberated by Soviet troops.

FEBRUARY

2	Ecuador declares war on Germany.

4	Yalta Conference of Allied leaders begins. Belgium now cleared of all German forces.
8	Paraguay declares war on Germany.
12	Peru declares war on Germany.
13–14	Dresden firebombed by Allied air forces; large parts of city destroyed.
14	Uruguay declares war on Germany.
14	Bombing of Prague—a mistake during the bombing of Dresden.
19	U.S. Marines invade Iwo Jima.
23	U.S. forces raise the American flag at Mt. Suribachi on Iwo Jima.
25	Turkey declares war on Germany.
28	U.S. Army captures Manila, capital of the Philippines.
MARCH	
9	United States firebombs Japan.
20	Mandalay liberated by Indian Nineteenth Infantry Division.
22–23	U.S. and British forces cross the Rhine.
28	Argentina declares war on Germany.
29	The Red Army enters Austria.
30	Russian forces liberate Danzig.
APRIL	
1	U.S. troops invade Okinawa.
4	Ohrdruf death camp is liberated by the Allies.
4	Georgian uprising of Texel starts.
10	Buchenwald concentration camp liberated.
12	President Roosevelt dies suddenly. Harry Truman becomes president of the United States.
13	Vienna liberated by Russian troops.
15	Bergen-Belsen concentration camp is liberated. Arnhem is liberated.
21	Russian forces begin assault on Berlin.
25	Elbe Day—first contact between Soviet and American troops at the Elbe River, near Torgau in Germany.
28	Mussolini captured and executed by Italian partisans.
29	Dachau concentration camp is liberated by the U.S. Seventh Army.
30	Hitler commits suicide in his bunker in Berlin.
MAY	
2	Trieste is captured by New Zealand troops and Yugoslavian partisans.

2	Berlin falls to Soviet troops.
3	Rangoon liberated.
5	Prague uprising begins.
5	Mauthausen concentration camp is liberated.
5	German troops in the Netherlands officially surrender.
5	Denmark liberated by Allied troops.
7	Germany surrenders unconditionally to the Allies.
8	Cease-fire takes effect at one minute past midnight. V-E Day in Britain.
8	German troops in Prague surrender.
9	Red Army enters Prague.
9	German garrison in Channel Islands agrees to surrender.
11	German Army Group Center in Czechoslovakia surrenders.
16	British troops complete liberation of Channel Islands.
20	Georgian uprising of Texel ends, ending hostilities in Europe.

JUNE

20	Schiermonnikoog, a Dutch Island, is the last part of Europe Allied troops reach.

JULY

6	Norway declares war on Japan.
16	U.S. conducts the Trinity test, the first test of a nuclear weapon.
17	Potsdam Conference begins; Allies determine future of Germany.
24	Truman informs Stalin that the United States has nuclear weapons (Stalin is already aware, via espionage).

AUGUST

6	The first nuclear weapon ever used in war, "Little Boy," is dropped on Hiroshima by the *Enola Gay*.
8	Soviet Union declares war on Japan; the invasion of Manchuria begins about an hour later.
9	A second atomic bomb, "Fat Man," is dropped by *Bockscar* on Nagasaki. Soviet troops enter China and Korea.
15	Emperor Hirohito issues a radio broadcast announcing Japan's unconditional surrender; V-J Day declared in the United Kingdom.
16	Emperor Hirohito issues an Imperial Rescript ordering Japanese forces to cease fire.
30	Royal Navy forces under Rear-Admiral Cecil Harcourt liberate Hong Kong.

SEPTEMBER

2	Japan signs the articles of surrender on the deck of the USS *Missouri* in Tokyo Bay.

Appendix D
Awards and Decorations

More than one million awards, decorations, and citations were issued to servicemen over the course of World War II and in the years that followed. The primary U.S. decorations include:

- **Medal of Honor.** This is the highest U.S. military decoration, most commonly awarded to members of the U.S. Army and Navy who demonstrated bravery and gallantry above and beyond the call of duty.
- **Distinguished Service Cross.** The second-highest award given by the Army and the Army Air Force, presented for exceptional heroism in combat.
- **Navy Cross.** The second-highest award given by the Navy and Marine Corps, also for exceptional bravery in combat.
- **Distinguished Service Medal.** Awarded by the Army, Navy, and Marine Corps for exceptional meritorious service, most often to senior officers.
- **Silver Star.** Awarded for gallantry in action.
- **Legion of Merit.** Awarded to officers for exceptional meritorious service.
- **Distinguished Flying Cross.** Awarded for heroism or exceptional achievement in flight.
- **Soldier's Medal.** An army award issued for heroism not involving action against the enemy.
- **Navy and Marine Corps Medal.** Also given for heroism not involving action against the enemy.
- **Bronze Star.** Awarded for heroic or meritorious achievement during military operations.
- **Air Medal.** Awarded for meritorious achievement in flight to members of all the armed services.
- **Commendation Medal.** Established for the U.S. Navy in 1944 and for the Army in 1945, this citation is awarded for meritorious service in peace or war.
- **Purple Heart.** First established by General George Washington during the Revolutionary War and re-established in 1932, this citation is given to servicemen who are wounded or killed in combat. To be eligible for a Purple Heart, a serviceman must have an injury severe enough to merit attention from a medical officer.

Index

THE EVERYTHING SERIES!

BUSINESS & PERSONAL FINANCE

Everything® Accounting Book
Everything® Budgeting Book
Everything® Business Planning Book
Everything® Coaching and Mentoring Book
Everything® Fundraising Book
Everything® Get Out of Debt Book
Everything® Grant Writing Book
Everything® Guide to Personal Finance for Single Mothers
Everything® Home-Based Business Book, 2nd Ed.
Everything® Homebuying Book, 2nd Ed.
Everything® Homeselling Book, 2nd Ed.
Everything® Improve Your Credit Book
Everything® Investing Book, 2nd Ed.
Everything® Landlording Book
Everything® Leadership Book
Everything® Managing People Book, 2nd Ed.
Everything® Negotiating Book
Everything® Online Auctions Book
Everything® Online Business Book
Everything® Personal Finance Book
Everything® Personal Finance in Your 20s and 30s Book
Everything® Project Management Book
Everything® Real Estate Investing Book
Everything® Retirement Planning Book
Everything® Robert's Rules Book, $7.95
Everything® Selling Book
Everything® Start Your Own Business Book, 2nd Ed.
Everything® Wills & Estate Planning Book

COOKING

Everything® Barbecue Cookbook
Everything® Bartender's Book, $9.95
Everything® Cheese Book
Everything® Chinese Cookbook
Everything® Classic Recipes Book
Everything® Cocktail Parties and Drinks Book
Everything® College Cookbook
Everything® Cooking for Baby and Toddler Book
Everything® Cooking for Two Cookbook
Everything® Diabetes Cookbook
Everything® Easy Gourmet Cookbook
Everything® Fondue Cookbook
Everything® Fondue Party Book
Everything® Gluten-Free Cookbook
Everything® Glycemic Index Cookbook
Everything® Grilling Cookbook

Everything® Healthy Meals in Minutes Cookbook
Everything® Holiday Cookbook
Everything® Indian Cookbook
Everything® Italian Cookbook
Everything® Low-Carb Cookbook
Everything® Low-Fat High-Flavor Cookbook
Everything® Low-Salt Cookbook
Everything® Meals for a Month Cookbook
Everything® Mediterranean Cookbook
Everything® Mexican Cookbook
Everything® No Trans Fat Cookbook
Everything® One-Pot Cookbook
Everything® Pizza Cookbook
Everything® Quick and Easy 30-Minute, 5-Ingredient Cookbook
Everything® Quick Meals Cookbook
Everything® Slow Cooker Cookbook
Everything® Slow Cooking for a Crowd Cookbook
Everything® Soup Cookbook
Everything® Stir-Fry Cookbook
Everything® Tex-Mex Cookbook
Everything® Thai Cookbook
Everything® Vegetarian Cookbook
Everything® Wild Game Cookbook
Everything® Wine Book, 2nd Ed.

GAMES

Everything® 15-Minute Sudoku Book, $9.95
Everything® 30-Minute Sudoku Book, $9.95
Everything® Blackjack Strategy Book
Everything® Brain Strain Book, $9.95
Everything® Bridge Book
Everything® Card Games Book
Everything® Card Tricks Book, $9.95
Everything® Casino Gambling Book, 2nd Ed.
Everything® Chess Basics Book
Everything® Craps Strategy Book
Everything® Crossword and Puzzle Book
Everything® Crossword Challenge Book
Everything® Crosswords for the Beach Book, $9.95
Everything® Cryptograms Book, $9.95
Everything® Easy Crosswords Book
Everything® Easy Kakuro Book, $9.95
Everything® Easy Large Print Crosswords Book
Everything® Games Book, 2nd Ed.
Everything® Giant Sudoku Book, $9.95
Everything® Kakuro Challenge Book, $9.95
Everything® Large-Print Crossword Challenge Book

Everything® Large-Print Crosswords Book
Everything® Lateral Thinking Puzzles Book, $9.95
Everything® Mazes Book
Everything® Movie Crosswords Book, $9.95
Everything® Online Poker Book, $12.95
Everything® Pencil Puzzles Book, $9.95
Everything® Poker Strategy Book
Everything® Pool & Billiards Book
Everything® Sports Crosswords Book, $9.95
Everything® Test Your IQ Book, $9.95
Everything® Texas Hold 'Em Book, $9.95
Everything® Travel Crosswords Book, $9.95
Everything® Word Games Challenge Book
Everything® Word Scramble Book
Everything® Word Search Book

HEALTH

Everything® Alzheimer's Book
Everything® Diabetes Book
Everything® Health Guide to Adult Bipolar Disorder
Everything® Health Guide to Controlling Anxiety
Everything® Health Guide to Fibromyalgia
Everything® Health Guide to Postpartum Care
Everything® Health Guide to Thyroid Disease
Everything® Hypnosis Book
Everything® Low Cholesterol Book
Everything® Massage Book
Everything® Menopause Book
Everything® Nutrition Book
Everything® Reflexology Book
Everything® Stress Management Book

HISTORY

Everything® American Government Book
Everything® American History Book, 2nd Ed.
Everything® Civil War Book
Everything® Freemasons Book
Everything® Irish History & Heritage Book
Everything® Middle East Book

HOBBIES

Everything® Candlemaking Book
Everything® Cartooning Book
Everything® Coin Collecting Book
Everything® Drawing Book
Everything® Family Tree Book, 2nd Ed.
Everything® Knitting Book
Everything® Knots Book
Everything® Photography Book

Everything® Quilting Book
Everything® Scrapbooking Book
Everything® Sewing Book
Everything® Soapmaking Book, 2nd Ed.
Everything® Woodworking Book

HOME IMPROVEMENT

Everything® Feng Shui Book
Everything® Feng Shui Decluttering Book, $9.95
Everything® Fix-It Book
Everything® Home Decorating Book
Everything® Home Storage Solutions Book
Everything® Homebuilding Book
Everything® Organize Your Home Book

KIDS' BOOKS

All titles are $7.95
Everything® Kids' Animal Puzzle & Activity Book
Everything® Kids' Baseball Book, 4th Ed.
Everything® Kids' Bible Trivia Book
Everything® Kids' Bugs Book
Everything® Kids' Cars and Trucks Puzzle
   & Activity Book
Everything® Kids' Christmas Puzzle
   & Activity Book
Everything® Kids' Cookbook
Everything® Kids' Crazy Puzzles Book
Everything® Kids' Dinosaurs Book
Everything® Kids' First Spanish Puzzle and
   Activity Book
Everything® Kids' Gross Cookbook
Everything® Kids' Gross Hidden Pictures Book
Everything® Kids' Gross Jokes Book
Everything® Kids' Gross Mazes Book
Everything® Kids' Gross Puzzle and
   Activity Book
Everything® Kids' Halloween Puzzle
   & Activity Book
Everything® Kids' Hidden Pictures Book
Everything® Kids' Horses Book
Everything® Kids' Joke Book
Everything® Kids' Knock Knock Book
Everything® Kids' Learning Spanish Book
Everything® Kids' Math Puzzles Book
Everything® Kids' Mazes Book
Everything® Kids' Money Book
Everything® Kids' Nature Book
Everything® Kids' Pirates Puzzle and Activity Book
Everything® Kids' Presidents Book
Everything® Kids' Princess Puzzle and Activity Book
Everything® Kids' Puzzle Book
Everything® Kids' Riddles & Brain Teasers Book
Everything® Kids' Science Experiments Book
Everything® Kids' Sharks Book
Everything® Kids' Soccer Book
Everything® Kids' States Book
Everything® Kids' Travel Activity Book

KIDS' STORY BOOKS

Everything® Fairy Tales Book

LANGUAGE

Everything® Conversational Japanese Book with
   CD, $19.95
Everything® French Grammar Book
Everything® French Phrase Book, $9.95
Everything® French Verb Book, $9.95
Everything® German Practice Book with CD,
   $19.95
Everything® Inglés Book
Everything® Intermediate Spanish Book with
   CD, $19.95
Everything® Learning Brazilian Portuguese
   Book with CD, $19.95
Everything® Learning French Book
Everything® Learning German Book
Everything® Learning Italian Book
Everything® Learning Latin Book
Everything® Learning Spanish Book with
   CD, 2nd Edition, $19.95
Everything® Russian Practice Book with CD, $19.95
Everything® Sign Language Book
Everything® Spanish Grammar Book
Everything® Spanish Phrase Book, $9.95
Everything® Spanish Practice Book
   with CD, $19.95
Everything® Spanish Verb Book, $9.95
Everything® Speaking Mandarin Chinese Book
   with CD, $19.95

MUSIC

Everything® Drums Book with CD, $19.95
Everything® Guitar Book with CD, 2nd
   Edition, $19.95
Everything® Guitar Chords Book with CD, $19.95
Everything® Home Recording Book
Everything® Music Theory Book with CD, $19.95
Everything® Reading Music Book with CD, $19.95
Everything® Rock & Blues Guitar Book
   with CD, $19.95
Everything® Rock and Blues Piano Book
   with CD, $19.95
Everything® Songwriting Book

NEW AGE

Everything® Astrology Book, 2nd Ed.
Everything® Birthday Personology Book
Everything® Dreams Book, 2nd Ed.
Everything® Love Signs Book, $9.95
Everything® Numerology Book
Everything® Paganism Book
Everything® Palmistry Book
Everything® Psychic Book
Everything® Reiki Book

Everything® Sex Signs Book, $9.95
Everything® Tarot Book, 2nd Ed.
Everything® Toltec Wisdom Book
Everything® Wicca and Witchcraft Book

PARENTING

Everything® Baby Names Book, 2nd Ed.
Everything® Baby Shower Book
Everything® Baby's First Year Book
Everything® Birthing Book
Everything® Breastfeeding Book
Everything® Father-to-Be Book
Everything® Father's First Year Book
Everything® Get Ready for Baby Book
Everything® Get Your Baby to Sleep Book, $9.95
Everything® Getting Pregnant Book
Everything® Guide to Raising a One-Year-Old
Everything® Guide to Raising a Two-Year-Old
Everything® Homeschooling Book
Everything® Mother's First Year Book
Everything® Parent's Guide to Childhood
   Illnesses
Everything® Parent's Guide to Children
   and Divorce
Everything® Parent's Guide to Children
   with ADD/ADHD
Everything® Parent's Guide to Children
   with Asperger's Syndrome
Everything® Parent's Guide to Children
   with Autism
Everything® Parent's Guide to Children with
   Bipolar Disorder
Everything® Parent's Guide to Children with
   Depression
Everything® Parent's Guide to Children
   with Dyslexia
Everything® Parent's Guide to Children with
   Juvenile Diabetes
Everything® Parent's Guide to Positive Discipline
Everything® Parent's Guide to Raising a
   Successful Child
Everything® Parent's Guide to Raising Boys
Everything® Parent's Guide to Raising Girls
Everything® Parent's Guide to Raising Siblings
Everything® Parent's Guide to Sensory
   Integration Disorder
Everything® Parent's Guide to Tantrums
Everything® Parent's Guide to the Strong-Willed
   Child
Everything® Parenting a Teenager Book
Everything® Potty Training Book, $9.95
Everything® Pregnancy Book, 3rd Ed.
Everything® Pregnancy Fitness Book
Everything® Pregnancy Nutrition Book
Everything® Pregnancy Organizer, 2nd Ed., $16.95
Everything® Toddler Activities Book
Everything® Toddler Book

Everything® Tween Book
Everything® Twins, Triplets, and More Book

PETS

Everything® Aquarium Book
Everything® Boxer Book
Everything® Cat Book, 2nd Ed.
Everything® Chihuahua Book
Everything® Dachshund Book
Everything® Dog Book
Everything® Dog Health Book
Everything® Dog Obedience Book
Everything® Dog Owner's Organizer, $16.95
Everything® Dog Training and Tricks Book
Everything® German Shepherd Book
Everything® Golden Retriever Book
Everything® Horse Book
Everything® Horse Care Book
Everything® Horseback Riding Book
Everything® Labrador Retriever Book
Everything® Poodle Book
Everything® Pug Book
Everything® Puppy Book
Everything® Rottweiler Book
Everything® Small Dogs Book
Everything® Tropical Fish Book
Everything® Yorkshire Terrier Book

REFERENCE

Everything® American Presidents Book
Everything® Blogging Book
Everything® Build Your Vocabulary Book
Everything® Car Care Book
Everything® Classical Mythology Book
Everything® Da Vinci Book
Everything® Divorce Book
Everything® Einstein Book
Everything® Enneagram Book
Everything® Etiquette Book, 2nd Ed.
Everything® Inventions and Patents Book
Everything® Mafia Book
Everything® Philosophy Book
Everything® Pirates Book
Everything® Psychology Book

RELIGION

Everything® Angels Book
Everything® Bible Book
Everything® Buddhism Book
Everything® Catholicism Book
Everything® Christianity Book
Everything® Gnostic Gospels Book
Everything® History of the Bible Book
Everything® Jesus Book

Everything® Jewish History & Heritage Book
Everything® Judaism Book
Everything® Kabbalah Book
Everything® Koran Book
Everything® Mary Book
Everything® Mary Magdalene Book
Everything® Prayer Book
Everything® Saints Book, 2nd Ed.
Everything® Torah Book
Everything® Understanding Islam Book
Everything® World's Religions Book
Everything® Zen Book

SCHOOL & CAREERS

Everything® Alternative Careers Book
Everything® Career Tests Book
Everything® College Major Test Book
Everything® College Survival Book, 2nd Ed.
Everything® Cover Letter Book, 2nd Ed.
Everything® Filmmaking Book
Everything® Get-a-Job Book, 2nd Ed.
Everything® Guide to Being a Paralegal
Everything® Guide to Being a Personal Trainer
Everything® Guide to Being a Real Estate Agent
Everything® Guide to Being a Sales Rep
Everything® Guide to Careers in Health Care
Everything® Guide to Careers in Law Enforcement
Everything® Guide to Government Jobs
Everything® Guide to Starting and Running a Restaurant
Everything® Job Interview Book
Everything® New Nurse Book
Everything® New Teacher Book
Everything® Paying for College Book
Everything® Practice Interview Book
Everything® Resume Book, 2nd Ed.
Everything® Study Book

SELF-HELP

Everything® Dating Book, 2nd Ed.
Everything® Great Sex Book
Everything® Self-Esteem Book
Everything® Tantric Sex Book

SPORTS & FITNESS

Everything® Easy Fitness Book
Everything® Running Book
Everything® Weight Training Book

TRAVEL

Everything® Family Guide to Cruise Vacations
Everything® Family Guide to Hawaii
Everything® Family Guide to Las Vegas, 2nd Ed.
Everything® Family Guide to Mexico
Everything® Family Guide to New York City, 2nd Ed.
Everything® Family Guide to RV Travel & Campgrounds
Everything® Family Guide to the Caribbean
Everything® Family Guide to the Walt Disney World Resort®, Universal Studios®, and Greater Orlando, 4th Ed.
Everything® Family Guide to Timeshares
Everything® Family Guide to Washington D.C., 2nd Ed.

WEDDINGS

Everything® Bachelorette Party Book, $9.95
Everything® Bridesmaid Book, $9.95
Everything® Destination Wedding Book
Everything® Elopement Book, $9.95
Everything® Father of the Bride Book, $9.95
Everything® Groom Book, $9.95
Everything® Mother of the Bride Book, $9.95
Everything® Outdoor Wedding Book
Everything® Wedding Book, 3rd Ed.
Everything® Wedding Checklist, $9.95
Everything® Wedding Etiquette Book, $9.95
Everything® Wedding Organizer, 2nd Ed., $16.95
Everything® Wedding Shower Book, $9.95
Everything® Wedding Vows Book, $9.95
Everything® Wedding Workout Book
Everything® Weddings on a Budget Book, $9.95

WRITING

Everything® Creative Writing Book
Everything® Get Published Book, 2nd Ed.
Everything® Grammar and Style Book
Everything® Guide to Magazine Writing
Everything® Guide to Writing a Book Proposal
Everything® Guide to Writing a Novel
Everything® Guide to Writing Children's Books
Everything® Guide to Writing Copy
Everything® Guide to Writing Research Papers
Everything® Screenwriting Book
Everything® Writing Poetry Book
Everything® Writing Well Book

Available wherever books are sold! To order, call 800-258-0929, or visit us at **www.everything.com**.
Everything® and everything.com® are registered trademarks of F+W Publications, Inc.
Bolded titles are new additions to the series.
All Everything® books are priced at $12.95 or $14.95, unless otherwise stated. Prices subject to change without notice.